Refugees and State Crime

Sydney Institute of Criminology Series No 21

Series Editors: Chris Cunneen, Mark Findlay, Julie Stubbs
University of Sydney Law School

Other titles in the series

Aboriginal Perspectives on Criminal Justice, C Cunneen (out of print)
Doing Less Time: Penal Reform in Crisis, J Chan
Psychiatry in Court, P Shea
The Man in White is Always Right: Cricket and the Law, D Fraser (out of print)
The Prison and the Home, A Aungles
Women, Male Violence and the Law, J Stubbs (ed)
Fault in Homicide, S Yeo
Anatomy of a French Murder Cas, B McKillop
Gender, Race and International Relations, C Cunneen and J Stubbs
Reform in Policing: Lessons from the Whitrod Era, J Bolen
A Culture of Corruption: Changing an Australian Police Service, D Dixon (ed)
Defining Madness P Shea
Developing Cultural Criminology, C Banks (ed)
Indigenous Human Rights, Garkawe, Kelly & Fisher (eds)
When Police Unionise: the politics of law and order in Australia, M Finnane
Regulating Racism: Racial Vilification Laws in Australia, L McNamara
A History of Criminal Law in New South Wales, GD Woods
Bin Laden in the suburbs, Poynting, Noble, Tabar & Collins
Global Issues, woman and justice, Pickering and Lanbert (eds)
Separated, Buti

Refugees and State Crime

Sharon Pickering

THE FEDERATION PRESS
2005

Published in Sydney by:
The Federation Press
PO Box 45, Annandale, NSW, 2038
71 John St, Leichhardt, NSW, 2040
Ph (02) 9552 2200 Fax (02) 9552 1681
E-mail: info@federationpress.com.au
Website: http://www.federationpress.com.au

National Library of Australia
Cataloguing-in-Publication entry

Pickering, Sharon.
Refugees and State Crime.

Bibliography.
Includes index.
ISBN 1 86287 541 3

1. Refugees legal status laws, etc. 2. Refugees –
Government policy. 3. Asylum, right of. I. Title.

341.486

Typeset by The Federation Press, Leichhardt, NSW.
Printed by Ligare Pty Ltd, Riverwood, NSW.

Preface

> The stateless person, without right to residence and without the right
> to work, had of course constantly to transgress the law. He was liable
> to jail sentences without ever committing a crime. More than that, the
> entire hierarchy of values which pertain in civilized countries was
> reversed in his case. Since he was the anomaly for whom the general
> law did not provide it was better for him to become an anomaly for
> which it did provide, that of the criminal.

> H Arendt, *The Origins of Totalitarianism* (1966)

A criminal justice reading of refugee policy has the potential to shed
a different light on the ways ideas broadly understood as 'deviancy'
and 'criminalisation' have been mobilised to usher in a new era in
the treatment of refugees. It will also help redirect our questions to
ideas such as 'humanitarianism', 'transnational crime' and 'state
crime'. It will aid an examination of the ways in which crimes
committed on those who seek asylum (by home or host country) are
diminished or denied and how the act of seeking protection is
routinely represented as criminal: in short how the victims of state
crime are produced as criminals when they seek to do something
about that crime. Why is such a reading important? Because the
criminalisation of refugees and asylum seekers affects the ability of
those who have suffered persecution to gain protection, because the
criminalisation of refugees relies on belittling and marginalising
international law and civil society and because criminalisation is
rooted in racial intolerance and dangerous nationalisms.

Why does it matter that criminal justice rhetoric, principles,
processes and practices have come to define refugee policy? Why
does it matter that the conflation of refugee protection and criminal
justice (largely in terms of criminalisation) is not simply a side issue
for migration policies but is *the* impetus, *the* incentive and *the*
rationale in coming to terms with the condition of the refugee? It is
central because criminalisation as a strategy, as a process and as an
ideology is a most dangerous force in any society. It alienates,
demonises and belittles. It places itself before and above fair and just
systems and in so doing shakes the foundations upon which they
operate. To undermine systems of fairness and justice is to place us
all precariously in relation to the operation of justice.

This book focuses on the responses of Western democracies to
asylum seekers arriving on their shores and at their borders.

Therefore, the analysis is of safe third country practices rather than with the refugee determination processes operated by the United Nations High Commission for Refugees (UNHCR) in countries of first asylum. While examining conceptual issues for Western democracies that are trans-state, I will ground much of my discussion in the Australian context. As Australia hurtles down previously unexplored paths in undermining ideas about asylum and protection it offers a particularly important and complex case study in the ways Western democracies are steeling themselves and their constituents for the radical reformulation of refugee protection. This process is well underway in Australia with the eyes of other nations on the results.

This book begins by mapping the ways refugee deviancy is produced and then turns to examine the potential recognition and censure of state deviancy in relation to the refugee. Chapters 2 and 3 focus on the role of the media and language in the production of refugee criminality. The construction of deviancy in ordinary and everyday media discourse will be examined in Chapter 2, with Chapter 3 focusing on the production of refugee deviancy in moments of crisis. Chapter 4 outlines the rise of deterrence narratives and how they are sustained in the Global North (a term used to denote developed nations). Chapter 5 considers law enforcement responses to forced migration generally and people smuggling specifically. Chapter 6 highlights the way the state is being challenged and censured in relation to what I have called the 'renegade judiciary' and judicial attempts to resist the denigration and abrogation of the rule of law. I will raise questions about the ways judicial censure potentially recasts the treatment of refugees in terms of state deviancy. Chapter 7 concludes by revisiting the notion of sovereignty as it has been played out across the chapters in this collection, arguing for a reconceptualisation that simultaneously helps rework processes of criminalisation and recognition of state crime. I want to critique one of the most systematically repressive areas of government policy and the potential of a state crime reading within these.

The treatment of refugees can help focus on how the state and civil society operate and contribute to the 'discourse on controlling state crime' (Friedrichs 2000, p 53). Criminalising refugees and questioning the criminality of the state is not a rhetorical exercise. The refugee that arrives at the border or on the beaches of the wealthy nation-state is, by legislative mandate, subjected to the popular, material and ideological trappings of criminalisation without any of the safeguards. Criminalisation of the refugee brings the refugee back into the system of states, reaffirming crumbling territorial sovereignty in an age of globalisation by invoking the familiar discourses of crime and punishment. As Arendt noted in the post-war period, core values of civilized states are reversed in the case of the refugee. Therefore our study of the refugee must take account of their 'crime' as well as the criminality and illegality of the state. This book will undertake an examination of how states have criminalised the refugee in the developed North so we can locate the illegality of state practices in relation to the refugee.

Sharon Pickering
Melbourne
February 2005

For Tom

Contents

Abbreviations

AAT	Administrative Appeals Tribunal
ACM	Australasian Correctional Management
AFP	Australian Federal Police
BCM	Brisbane Courier Mail
DIMA	Department of Immigration and Multicultural Affairs
DIMIA	Department of Immigration, Multicultural and Indigenous Affairs
ICCPR	International Covenant on Civil and Political Rights
ICESCR	International Covenant on Economic, Social and Cultural Rights
IDC	Immigration Detention Centre
IDP	Internally Displaced Person
INP	Indonesian National Police
SMH	Sydney Morning Herald
RAN	Royal Australian Navy
RRT	Refugee Review Tribunal
UDHR	Universal Declaration of Human Rights
UNHCR	United Nations High Commission for Refugees

Acknowledgements

Globally, the treatment of refugees and displaced people worsens. This book has been written within an increasingly hostile world and I acknowledge that while I have been writing, thousands have died seeking to gain entry to the Global North. That violence marks this academic venture.

A conversation in a Montreal café with Rachel Paul confirmed my suspicions that there was something to be gained in exploring refugee protection, criminalisation and state crime. I am grateful to her and Likestillings Senternet for bringing me to Norway in 2001 and engaging me in many of the ideas explored in this book.

I would like to thank all of the contributors to the special edition of *Current Issues in Criminal Justice* on criminology and refugee issues. Their work collectively helped propel this book forward. Throughout the book I constantly return to the work of Hannah Arendt and Saskia Sassen and it is only right that from the very start I acknowledge the important role their writings have played in the formation of my ideas.

Chris Cuneen, Julie Stubbs, Leanne Weber, Pete Billings, Richard Devetak and Russell Hogg provided the crucial encouragement that my research material would make a book. They have given generously of their time and support. I was ably assisted by a most dedicated and professional group of researchers in Caroline Lambert, Melissa Philips, Rachel Mosely, Mary O'Kane and Shane Samuelson. This book could not have been completed within its designated timeframe without their exceptional contributions. I am appreciative of Tiffany Bodiam's assistance with the compilation of footnotes and the bibliography. The staff at Charles Sturt University library and the Monash University Library at Clayton, as always, were outstanding. The editorial work of Chris Holt and his team at Federation Press was painstaking.

I am grateful to Charles Sturt University for granting me special study leave to get the writing of this project started and the Law School at the University of Westminster for a collegial and supportive environment in which it could happen.

Marisa Silvestri and Steven Nichols laboured through the early carriage of this book and their love and support was immeasurable and invaluable, as was the care of Frances and Klaus Heidensohn. Penny Green and Christina Curry provided great encouragement and even greater distractions during my time at Westminster and beyond.

I am grateful for discussions with Margaret Piper and Heaven Crawley as well as for the feedback from participants at the International Association of Refugee Law Judges Conference in Wellington New Zealand. Participants at presentations at the University of Westminster, Edgehill College, the Australian and New Zealand Society of Criminology and the Sydney University Institute of Criminology all gave valuable comments on the ideas presented in this book.

Marisa Sivestri, Michael Gard and Shane Samuelson selflessly gave of their time and read over very long drafts. Their comments have greatly improved the clarity of ideas presented in the book. Many of the ideas contained in this book were also discussed at length with my wonderful friends and colleagues Jude McCulloch and Dean Wilson.

My family and friends have patiently listened and talked through the various ideas in this book. Jan, Graham and Fiona continue to support and encourage my work. This book was written in light of the outstanding work of my postgraduate students at Charles Sturt University and Monash University. Their commitment and energy made teaching forced migration delightfully challenging and their work has been an inspiration for my writing.

This book took far longer to complete than expected and Tom Banks patiently listened and challenged as it was finally born. His love and support made it all bearable. So after many long years this book is dedicated to him with all the love and thanks in the world.

Parts of Chapter 2 have been drawn from my article, 'Common sense and original deviancy' published in the *Journal of Refugee Studies*, vol 4 (2001).

Chapter 1

Refugee law and order:
Sovereign crime

This book is about mapping the construction of refugee deviancy and how the ensuing state response can be considered illegitimate and potentially criminal. It moves across three vital contributions to the maintenance of hegemonic relations around the refugee: civil society (using the media as an example); the administration (law enforcement); and domestic and international legal mechanisms (the courts and the international human rights regime). Across these three sectors this book deconstructs the law and order politics that constitute refugee policy in Australia. It will examine the role sovereignty has come to play in law and order politics and will attempt to turn the notion of sovereignty into a foundation for launching an alternative framework to understand refugee policy: state crime.

Law and order and the refugee

The dominant contemporary approach to refugees in the Global North[1] and specifically in Australia, can be located in a kind of law and order politics. In considering refugee policies and the potential for change, this chapter will posit two models that are at odds with each other: law and order and state crime. While I will canvass the alternative model, state crime, later in the chapter, I first want to outline the model I target for ideological and political redundancy: law and order.

Law and order rests on neo-liberal ideas about the respon-sibility of the individual for their situation: the responsibility of the individual to know what is wrong and to refrain from doing it and the responsibility of the state to administer punishment when the

---

1   The Global North commonly refers to developed nations and/or Western nations.

law is contravened. This assumes that the criminal act is committed in a context where the consequences are carefully considered and evaluated. If crime is the choice then punishment must be administered to deter such choices or similar choices by others. Important in maintaining this position is the dismissal of discussions surrounding the failure of the state to provide economic, social and cultural rights and their relationship to the commission of street crimes. Consequently, law and order repudiates structural explanations of street crime.[2] In relation to refugees the following matters have become part of a broader law and order approach: the detention of all asylum seekers who arrive by boat in immigration detention centres for extended and indefinite periods of time, the inadequate provision of legal advice to asylum seekers in immigration detention centres, the denial and repression of cultural practices, policies that interdict boats at sea and return them to Indonesia, the force feeding of hunger strikers in detention centres and the use of chemical restraint and solitary confinement.

Brake and Hale have described the kind of conservative agenda that underpins law and order politics as follows:

> First, social conditions are irrelevant to criminality; it is the individual who is basically evil. Second, punishment and retribution are central. Third, and this follows on from the first two, there is a pessimistic emphasis on crime prevention through greater vigilance and awareness of the individual citizen. There is an essentialist flavour to this which rejects both psychological maladjustment and economic conditions in the aetiology of crime. Criminals are basically evil and the responsibility for this lies with themselves and their families who failed to install basic decency and morality.[3]

In the domestic setting, law and order politics have focused on street crime. It has been the basis upon which saturation policing, the need for policies of deterrence and major prison building programs have been undertaken in the Global North.[4] Particularly since the 1980s, it

---

2   Street crime is a criminological term denoting crimes that have received most coverage in the press and attention of policy makers that occur between ordinary members of society as opposed to crimes of the powerful.

3   Brake, M and Hale, C, (1992), *Public order and Private Lives: The Politics of Law and Order*, London: Routledge, p 8.

4   Downes, D and Morgan, R, (1997), 'Dumping the 'Hostages to Fortune'? The Politics of Law and Order in Post-War Britain', in M Maguire, R Morgan and R Reiner (eds), *The Oxford Handbook of Criminology*, 2nd edn, Oxford: Oxford University Press.

has underpinned the increase in funding for law enforcement activities while in many jurisdictions budgets of other areas of service provision such as health and education have been cut. This has occurred with the promise of reducing crime, an aim that has rarely been met.[5]

Nonetheless, governments of the Global North, particularly Australia, have used law and order politics in the development and implementation of refugee policy. In so doing, they draw on a history of success that such approaches have brought in State elections, particularly in New South Wales, Western Australia and Queensland. In 2001, a federal election year, this framework proved indispensable.

A companion definition for Brake and Hale's articulation of law and order politics with regards to Australian refugee policy could read:

First and foremost, the country conditions of the asylum seeker who arrives by boat in Australia are increasingly irrelevant. It is the individual in relation to their disrespect for the 'rule of law' (that is, Australia's approach to 'unauthorised arrivals') that characterises their deviancy. Second, punishing such 'queue jumping' behaviour is integral in the maintenance of Australia's refugee program. Third, there is an obsession with deterring and preventing people seeking protection in Australia within other countries, on Australia's sea borders and on the shores of the Australian coastline. This approach rejects that there is a range of reasons as to why a person seeks Australia's protection by risking their lives and arriving by boat to seek asylum. It also rejects that because it is largely people from Afghanistan, Iraq and Iran that arrive in such a fashion that policies responding to this kind of arrival are racialised. Asylum seekers are basically disingenuous by not waiting as part of the offshore refugee program and by arrival is essentially a deviant in this process, undermines this process and a person to whom Australia should not feel obliged to protect regardless of international legal obligations.

Law and order politics have been widely critiqued for harbouring deeply racist and sexist approaches to preventing and punishing crime and young black men and single mothers have been key targets in the attempt to 'get tough on crime'.[6] In Australia, Indigenous peoples have borne the brunt of zero tolerance style

---

5   Brake and Hale, op cit.
6   Parenti, C, (1999), *Lockdown America: Police and Prisons in the Age of Crisis*, London: Verso.

policing and other such law and order initiatives.[7] Law and order politics make great gains from the disrespect for the rule of law that some sections of the population show,[8] particularly in those communities where relations with policing have irrevocably broken down. In making political mileage out of such lack of respect, many commentators fail to note the blatant hypocrisy in the ways law and order politics demands the diminution of the rule of law through limiting judicial review.

A range of irrationalities are discernible in the law and order approach to refugee issues. For example, when asylum seekers arrive by boat without 'authorisation' we are routinely reminded that they are showing no respect for Australian law. At the same time, the government seeks to all but completely remove the chance for the judiciary to review decisions that reject asylum claims. Respect for the law is something that is only deemed necessary on the street and on the borders and is considered less weighty from within parliament or in the drafting of policy. On the one hand the asylum seeker who arrives by boat is deviant (in that they 'undermine' the offshore protection process and the territorial sovereignty of the nation-state), while on the other hand the nation-state abrogates the shadow of the rule of law at the international level (most particularly in relation to the Refugee Convention) in order to justify such an approach. In short, the alleged deviancy of the asylum seeker is matched by the deviancy of the nation-state on the international human rights stage.

But this is not the only dilemma in adopting a law and order approach. Law and order politics flourish within the rhetoric of economic rationalism, where state funded services recede.[9] However, the implementation of law and order politics is costly, requiring massive numbers of police, causing backlogs in the courts and a spiralling prison population. Despite such contradictions, law and order approaches are routinely represented as a matter of common sense. In the case of the refugee, this has manifest in rising budgets dedicated to immigration detention centres across Australia and the Pacific as well as the heavy policing of the border by the Australian Navy and 'disruption' activities by the Australian Federal Police in transit countries such as Indonesia. At the heart of a law and order

---

7   See, eg, Cuneen, C, (2001), *Conflict, Politics and Crime: Aboriginal Communities and the Police*, Sydney: Allen and Unwin.
8   Parenti, (1999) op cit.
9   Brake and Hale, 1992.

agenda, be it in relation to crime or refugees, are irreconcilable ir-rationalities. Such contradictions underpin what others have termed a culture of control in relation to criminal justice, a label apt for current refugee policy.[10]

In many ways bipartisan immigration policy mirrors the bipartisan support for law and order criminal justice policies in many jurisdictions. Sharing the same basic principles about the non-structural nature of crime, political parties simply attempt to outbid each other as to who is most serious about law and order: a matter of who will build more prisons, who will restrict the discretion of judges more, who will fund more police and so on. A similar con-sensus underpins responses to refugees. In many places liberals and conservatives have come to agree about the causes of immigration and the best ways to regulate it – with the only remaining question being how strictly immigration should be limited.[11] Bipartisan immi-gration policy has meant there has been very little debate even on the remaining question of how strictly immigration should be limi-ted. Few cracks have appeared in immigration policy even during periods when the treatment of refugees has come to be *the* national issue. During the 2001 Australian federal election campaign the two major parties were all but indistinguishable on refugee policy.[12]

When major parties refuse to debate, or only engage in debate on peripheral issues to immigration, then the space for questioning and the space for civil society to exert itself are often reduced. Bipartisanship has resulted in the broad usage of problematic terms and ideas about refugees that have gone largely unchallenged. In response to the closing down of debate on refugees by bipartisan policies, a range of grassroots organisations have worked to develop alternative approaches with varying levels of success. However, bipartisanship on the major tenets of refugee policy has continued to reinforce problematic discourses on the refugee. For example, both parties have invested in the construction of the 'economic migrant' in the definition and development of refugee policy that has largely gone unnoticed and certainly unchallenged in mainstream political

---

10 Ibid; Christie, N, (1993), *Crime Control As Industry*, London: Routledge; Garland, D, (2001), *Culture of Control: Crime and Social Order in Late Modern Societies*, Oxford: Oxford University Press.
11 Sassen, S, (1998), *Globalization and Its Discontents: Essays on the New Mobility of People and Money*, New York: The New Press, p 32.
12 Rundle, G, (2001), 'The Opportunist: John Howard and the Triumph of Reaction,' 3 *Quarterly Essay* 1; Also see Chapter 4.

discourse.[13] This is despite the fact that being able to define the 'economic migrant' has allowed the government to define the 'refugee' more narrowly and, in so doing, clearly articulate how the government has come to construct the *need* for 'deterrence'. Successive Ministers for Immigration have repeatedly commented that many who purport to be asylum seekers are in fact 'economic migrants', for example:

> People pay smugglers for many reasons, including to seek protection, because of limited opportunity for legitimate migration and to pursue economic opportunity.[14]

If we take the Refugee Convention as our reference point (not an unproblematic reference point) for who is legally defined as a refugee[15] then we must be willing to acknowledge that not all those who seek refugee status will meet the legal conditions to gain refugee status. However, this does not mean that terms such as 'economic migrant' are benign and simply refer to those misguided souls who believe the refugee determination process may be a route to a better life. Rather discourses of 'economic migrants' are used to cast doubt on all refugee applicants. In taking up the rhetoric of 'economic migrant', refugee policy becomes about selection. Refugees 'choose' Australia and out of generosity or compassion, Australia chooses to admit them. It is no longer about rights or justice but about choice and selection. Defining refugees as economic migrants distances them from the orchestrated harms that have affected them and

---

13 In many ways this reminds me of the production of the juvenile delinquent: a young person who has not necessarily broken the law but receives state attention because of their very presence in public space. In turn this becomes the grounds for more repressive policing measures despite the vague form and largely rhetorical purpose of 'juvenile delinquency'.

14 See <www.immi.gov.au/facts/73smuggling.htm> 'People Smuggling' accessed 18 February 2002.

15 The definition of who qualifies as a refugee at international law is found in Art 1A of the Convention Relating to the Status of Refugees: 'Owing to a well-founded fear of being persecuted for reasons of race, religion, nationality, membership of a Particular Social Group or Political Opinion, is outside [her/his] country of origin and is unable or, owing to such fear, is unwilling to avail [her/his self] of the protection of that country; or who, not having nationality and being outside the country of [her/his] former habitual residence as a result of such events, is unable or, owing to such fear, is unwilling to return to it'.

reduces the act of seeking asylum to a single cause: a better life. It also distances refugees from notions of inclusion and citizenship.

Forms of citizenship have been discussed by a range of scholars, mostly in relation to the kind of state being developed or transformed. It has also been talked about in terms of the regulation of society and the development of antagonistic classes of citizens. Exclusive citizenship can also be read as a way that a given society seeks to regulate and enforce values, beliefs and dogma. We can also understand the development of exclusive citizenship in terms of the state and the foreigner. Saskia Sassen has argued that there are 'guests and aliens' within the category of the 'foreign'. Such a separation has been largely a 20th century phenomenon – most notably post World War I when states began to reinforce their borders in relation to massive refugee flows. Exclusive citizenship is also related to the idea of the 'stranger' (which has stemmed from ideas around otherness). For example, Ahmed's recent work on the production of the stranger within multiculturalism argues that the *Western* and the *nation* is constructed, mobilised and legitimated through the fetishisation of the stranger.[16] But we need to question whether the idea of the 'stranger' goes far enough in communicating the nature of current refugee policy, media coverage and public opinion. Does strangeness help us to think about exclusion and criminalisation?

The criminalisation inherent in the law and order approach to contemporary refugee policy should also be considered within broader moves towards the formation of exclusive citizenship.[17] Approaches such as criminalisation (generally) and deterrence (specifically) stand to contribute to rapidly narrowing approaches to citizenship and the rights and obligations of both citizens and states. The criminalisation of refugees is the means by which different categories of not belonging are mass communicated.

Exclusion and criminalisation also incite ideas about the dangerousness of refugees. 'Dangerous offenders' and discourses around 'dangerousness' are rooted in law and order approaches. Therefore, this book will consider if various processes of criminalisation are

---

16 Ahmed, S, (2000), *Strange Encounters: Embodied Others in Post-Coloniality*, London: Routledge.
17 Although, understanding this in terms of exclusive citizenship may be rather misleading – it suggests that there has ordinarily been forms of inclusive citizenship. However, the very notion of citizenship is predicated upon simultaneous inclusion and exclusion

simply another attempt to move refugees closer again to their 'pure' state as the 'ultimate' offender – the embodiment of the most dangerous offender of them all – one that simultaneously goes against their own country and the host country, one that represents all that is evil and beyond human. The criminal refugee is a twisted reflection of the simultaneous inclusion and exclusion of citizenship; doubly excluded from the home and host country. Therefore, criminalisation is simply the resource for us to draw upon as we respond to, invent and respond to again, the refugee as the 'dangerous offender'. The refugee is an easy target for discourses of dangerousness as the violence of the refugee, their dangerousness can be read by their very presence – the act of coming, of arriving.

It now becomes a question of how far law and order policies of policing, deterrence and punishment of refugees will go. Are poster campaigns in refugee-producing countries or interdiction at sea enough? Will more immigration detention centres need to be built? Will refugees never be granted permanent status and instead have to live a life of uncertainty and constant re-application in order to deter others? More importantly, what are the consequences of policing, deterring and punishing asylum seekers? When law and order politics and in turn systematic criminalisation, is turned against those who are already 'outsiders' it is both an instrument of self-definition as well as a method of social, political, racial and cultural exclusion. As such, a law and order approach to refugees can be usefully read within a state crime framework.

Definitions of state crime

State crime is an alternative framework to that of law and order politics for understanding refugee policy. In the first instance, readings of state crime can assist us in better understanding the conditions that refugees flee from, specifically at the hands of their government, as well as the treatment they receive from refugee-receiving countries such as Australia.

Criminal justice, social science and the humanities have traditionally focused on street crime and non-state actors. Studying refugees and asylum seekers requires shifting the focus to the state as criminal (as persecuting agent) or the state as colluding in or tacitly approving of persecution, or the state being unable to protect (or redress) its citizens from persecution carried out by non-state actors. It also requires consideration of refugee-receiving states to be obliged (legally, politically, morally) to offer state protection to ensure that those meeting the legal definition of the refugee are not failed by the administrative legal system of the host country or any criminal practices of that state. Studying refugees through a criminal justice prism also requires that this shift in focus includes moving from a domestic to a transnational field of reference – by definition refugees are a transnational issue and as such the study must be transnational.

In attempting to splice understandings of state crime, persecution and the refugee we must first come to rest on a workable definition of state crime. Such definitions wax and wane in relation to understandings of what constitutes the state and civil society. Additionally and in the same way that there are varying definitions of crime, there are also many and varied definitions of state crime: from legalistic definitions to those drawn loosely from the discourse of human rights. Edwin Sutherland began stretching and challenging traditional definitions of crime in the 1940s when he argued that crime should be understood in relation to moral criteria and concepts of legal sanctions (both civil and criminal) or social injury.[18] The Schwendingers advance a broad definition of state crime within a framework of human rights that includes both first generation (civil and political) rights and second generation (economic, cultural and social) rights.[19] In many ways their definition morphs state crime into the length and breadth of human rights and therefore raises questions of the workability of such a wide reading. Cohen, while sympathetic to the human rights approach made by the Schwendingers, argued that they made no distinction between human rights violations and do not establish the criminality of human rights violations. In short he argues their work, while bringing human rights and criminology together, ends with a moral crusade where the implications of understanding state crime in terms of human rights are not articulated. Instead, while also taking a human rights approach, Cohen argues that state crime should really stick to civil and political (first generation) rights:

> A more restricted and literal use of the concept 'state crime'; however, is both more defensible and useful. If we come from the

---

18 Sutherland, E, (1949), *White Collar Crime*, New York: Holt, Rinehart and Winston.
19 Schwendinger, H and Schwendinger, J, 'Defenders of order or guardians of human rights?', in Taylor, I, Walton, I and Young, J, (eds), *Critical Criminology*. London: Routledge, 1975.

discourse of human rights, this covers what is known in jargon (for once, not euphemistic) as 'gross' violations of human rights … [20]

This of course is a safe and predictable option for criminologists, considering that the most obvious criminal acts on the international stage neatly fall within the remit of torture, disappearances, extra judicial killings and the like. It is an area in which rich and valuable contributions can be made. Unfortunately, such an approach, while acknowledging some critiques of human rights in general, does not adequately address some of the most cogent critiques of civil and political rights; in particular, the critiques of feminist scholars who have argued for broader readings of rights to ensure their applicability to more than the male subject of international law.[21] For example, standard readings of 'gross human rights violations' have largely ignored the experiences of torture suffered by women. Therefore, we need to explore state crime definitions that seek to move beyond a civil and political rights approach to state crime and utilise intersectional analyses of gender, race, ethnicity and class.

Friederichs makes distinctions between state crime, governmental crime, political crime and white collar crime arguing for the adoption of the term governmental crime as a broad all encompassing term for a range of illegal and demonstrably harmful activities carried out from within, or in association with, governmental status.[22] State crime (as a sub-class of governmental crime), according to Friederichs, refers to 'one major class of crimes that can be committed by those acting from within government'.[23] Such an understanding seems to leave little room for the role of non-state actors or the failure of the state to respond to non-state crime and deviance. More recently Green and Ward have argued that to label something a (state) 'crime' the behaviour must be both 'objectively' illegitimate and 'subjectively' deviant whereby the label state crime should apply to 'the area of overlap between two distinct

20 Cohen, S, (1995), 'Human Rights and Crimes of the State: the Culture of Denial', 26 *Australian & New Zealand Journal of Criminology* 97.
21 Charlesworth, H and Chinkin, C, (2000), *The Boundaries of International Law: A Feminist Analysis*, Manchester: Manchester University Press; Cook, R, (ed), (1994), *Human Rights and Women: National and International Perspectives*, Philadelphia: University of Pennyslvania.
22 Friederichs, D,(2001). 'State Crime or Governmental Crime: Making Sense of the Conceptual Confusion', in Ross, J (ed), *Controlling State Crime*. New Brunswick: Transactive.
23 Ibid, p 74.

phenomena: (1) violations of human rights and (2) state organised deviance'. State organisational deviance is considered as behaviour by agents of the state working for organisational goals that if exposed to the community would risk formal or informal censure and sanctions that would impact on their activity: 'Such censure of sanctions may originate "from above" (formal legal or disciplinary powers), "from below" (delegitimation, ie, conduct manifesting a withdrawal or erosion of consent, see Beetham 1991), "from within" (informal norms of the organisational culture), or "from without" (international pressure)'.[24] Included in this definition are both acts and omissions that constitute violations of human rights by both individuals and corporations and acknowledges:

> There is a continuum here between crimes that are plainly instigated and condoned by state agencies (such as the activities of anti-independence militias in East Timor), through the 'capture' of regulatory agencies by the bodies they are supposed to regulate, through negligent policing that reflects institutionalised race, class, or gender bias, to errors of judgment that may be apparent only in hindsight. Such definitional problems should not, however, preclude the recognition of crimes of complicity or omission as an important dimension of state crime.[25]

In such a reading the nature and scope of such rights is debatable. This definition directly addresses the diminution of acts carried out by state actors being read as 'street crime' type offences (which do not mobilise refugee-protection machinery) rather than 'state crime' type offences (which do mobilise refugee-protection machinery) and the role of non-state actors in acts of persecution. Understanding persecution within international human rights for those in refugee-like situations has the potential to make a potent application of Green and Ward's definition. In so doing, this definition becomes simultaneously useful in understanding the actions of the refugee-producing state as acts of persecution as well as the refugee-receiving state.

---

24 Green, P and Ward, T, (2000), 'State Crime, Human Rights and the Limits of Criminology,' 27 *Social Justice* 110.
25 Ibid, p 111.

State crime, refugee policy and the responsibilities of the Global North

How can this same definition of state crime begin to be applied to refugee policies of Western democracies? One way of considering the legitimacy of a state and its actions is to assess the state's actions against international standards of human rights. Another is to ask whether the state's actions are 'deviant'. Green and Ward argue that a state practice is deviant if:

> [I]t is either censured as illegitimate or perceived as likely to be censured by others. Deviance is not an inherent property of the act, but denotes a relationship between the act, the actor and a particular audience.[26]

On this basis, the way in which we understand the treatment of refugees is not the reasonably straightforward question of whether there has been a human rights violation, but a consideration of the interaction of various groups in society and their response to the treatment.

Therefore, the ways the treatment of refugees within a discourse of state crime can be understood moves past whether human rights violations can be established as having taken place (reasonably straightforward) to how we can understand the interaction of various groups in society and their response to the behaviour in question. This is not to suggest that a coherent response from a majority audience is required to define behaviour as criminal, but rather the means by which the state seeks legitimacy must be discernible and hence its illegitimacy readable. We could extend such a reading by returning to Gramsci's reading of legitimacy, read through hegemony, as being a combination of force and consent (ideology). Hegemony is central if we are to consider the complex interactions between the traditionally-defined ideological sphere (including the media and civil society) and its role in the creation and maintenance of consent *and* the role of the traditionally coercive sphere of the state such as the police and military. Therefore, in making readings of state crime we cannot focus only on the operation of the coercive aspects of the state. We must also focus on the ideological legitimation of state practices in liberal democracies and their problematic application of human rights discourses to developing countries rather than their own.

Utilising a concept like state crime means that we have a framework in which to critique and challenge the treatment of

---

26   Ibid, p 109.

refugees by liberal democratic states. The definition means a range of state traditions are examined '[F]rom the perspective of a continuum, rather than as two discrete incomparable formations – authoritarian and democratic'.[27] From the late 1990s, Australia has retreated from its international human rights obligations and has sought to particularly distance itself from its international human rights obligations to refugees.[28] Not surprisingly this has been achieved through the diminution of human rights bodies and standards for liberal democracies. Human rights is considered an issue for developing nations: the impoverished and authoritarian nations of the world. Dropping any pretence as to the universality of human rights, it follows that human rights were only ever meant to be used to measure the performance of countries such as Burma, the Peoples Republic of China, Iraq and the like. In short what many pundits, including the 'leader of the free world', would call 'rogue states',[29] or 'government by terror' associated with decolonised 'infrahuman blackness' of some African states.[30] In other words, human rights are a tool that democracies measure others by and are not something they should be *measured by* themselves –as their very status as 'democracies' makes their behaviour legitimate. However, the 'self-evident' democratic label serves to cloud the relationship of capitalism to colonial and neo-colonial domination.[31] It also clouds the ways refugee determination can also provide moments of potent neo-colonialism.[32] International law, particularly those laws and obligations associated with the international human rights regime, have increasingly represented a challenge to the moral position of the government rather than morally affirming the liberal democratic government position. International law has become an obstacle, even a threat. The legitimacy of state action resides in the nature of these interactions – for the legitimacy of state action is not achieved

---

27 Ibid, p 101.
28 Minister for Foreign Affairs Alexander Downer, Attorney-General Daryl Williams, Minister for Immigration and Multicultural Affairs, Philip Ruddock, 'Australian Initiatives to Improve the Effectiveness of the UN Treaty Committees, MPS 042/2001, <www.minister.immi.gov.au/media_releases/media01/r01042.htm>, accessed 13 March 2002.
29 See Chomsky, N, (2001), *Rogue States*, London: Pluto Press.
30 See Gilroy, P, (2000), *Between Camps: Nations, Cultures and the Allure of Race*, London: Penguin.
31 Alexander, M and Mohanty, C, (eds), (1997), *Feminist Genealogies, Colonial Legacies, Democratic Futures*, New York: Routledge.
32 I will discuss this further in Chapter 3.

simply by concurrence with the opinion of the majority audience, but by examination against the means by which the state seeks legitimacy. These are not limited to democratic means of election, but include ideological constructs.

Emissaries from the UN have become distractions from the ultimate audience: the domestic internal audience. Recently the Prime Minister and then Minister for Immigration and Multicultural Affairs mocked surprise that the UN Commissioner for Human Rights would be interested in Australia's treatment of refugees in immigration detention centres.[33] A spokesperson for the Minister of Immigration responded to the Commissioner's request by saying '[W]e have to look at the disruption it causes',[34] with the Minister for Foreign Affairs asserting an alternative framework: 'What would be embarrassing ... would be if we were party to a policy that gave people smugglers a financial bonanza and we're not going to do that'.[35] In turn the condemnation of the international community (framed in the discourse of rights) becomes an issue of sovereignty: an attempt to undermine the policies and practices of a democratically elected government. At best the response is to rectify the 'inefficiencies' of the international system to make them more 'workable'.[36] The international community becomes a hostile domain that joins with 'rogue states', in the propagandist use of the term that includes: "[T]he defiant, the indolent and the miscreant', the 'disorderly' elements of the world who reject the right of the self-anointed 'enlightened states' to resort to violence when, where and as they 'believe is just', discarding 'the restrictive old rules' and obeying 'modern notions of justice' that they fashion for the occasion'.[37]

There remains the difficulty in the communication of those breaches of human rights (often known) within an understanding of why those breaches are deviant (ie, not acceptable and in need of censure). Such breaches satisfy the first element of Green and

---

33 'UN may be kept out of Woomera' *The Australian*, 6 February 2002, p 4.
34 Ibid.
35 'UN Scrutiny puts pressure on Howard' *The Sydney Morning Herald*, 6 February 2002, p 4.
36 Minister for Foreign Affairs Alexander Downer, Attorney-General Daryl Williams, Minister for Immigration and Multicultural Affairs, Philip Ruddock, 'Australian Initiatives to Improve the Effectiveness of the UN Treaty Committees, MPS 042/2001, <www.minister.immi.gov.au/media_releases/media01/r01042.htm,> accessed 13 March 2002.
37 Chomsky, (2001), op cit, p 6.

Ward's definition, but the challenge comes in making the second part of that definition palatable in the public domain. Moving from breaches of human rights into the deviancy of the state requires us to address the various ways, means and reasons why the deviancy of democratic states is so easily denied, dismissed and ignored. As Cohen has cogently argued, liberal democracies have developed elaborate practices of denial in relation to human rights violations at home and abroad.[38] Australia has not been responsive to the deviance label that the international community has used. Not being responsive to audiences from without means the responses of audiences from within and from below become crucial in establishing the illegitimacy of state behaviour.

The naming of state practices as 'crimes' serves important ideological and discursive functions. Being able to name 'state crime' alters discourses surrounding the treatment of refugees and asylum seekers. It brings into focus the definitions and categories of who is considered a legitimate victim and who or what is considered a legitimate perpetrator. It begins by posing the questions: Can refugees be a legitimate victim of the criminal practices of a liberal democracy such as Australia? Can the Australian government be considered a legitimate perpetrator of crime? These are important questions – the practice of naming and the use of definitions and categories are socially controlling in that they affect the ways individuals consider themselves in relation to the state. Civil society, most notably the media, has been reluctant to name government treatment of refugees and asylum seekers as a crime. However, asylum seekers, supported by NGOs, have questioned the legitimacy of Australia's treatment of refugees. They have done so by asking: What is the crime of the refugee?[39] The current interpretive frameworks surrounding refugees and asylum seekers are culturally powerful and serve to reinforce practices of violence and coercion. Being able to name an act as state crime is politically important in that it displays a rejection of the state practice and it grants a powerful discursive repertoire to those doing the naming. However, the political deployment of the term *crime* is not enough – it is easily derided or side stepped. Being able to effectively name state crime must be grounded (legitimated) in a workable and

---

38 Cohen, S, (2001), *States of Denial: Knowing About Atrocities and Suffering*, London: Polity Press.

39 'Malaria Hits Boatpeople in PNG,' *The Age*, 5 February 2002, p 2.

consistent definition of criminality for the subsequent task of developing appropriate systems of justice or the utilisation of existing systems of justice.

It is important to note that those refugees who have questioned the legitimacy of Australia's treatment of refugees have been met with swift responses from government that have served to reorder the legitimacy of the deviant act in question. A response that serves to reinforce traditional categories of legitimate victims and legitimate perpetrators of crime. For example, in 1992 lawyers sued for the release of a group of Cambodian asylum seekers who had been in immigration detention for over two years[40] (see Chapters 3 and 7). Less than 48 hours prior to the Federal Court handing down its decision, the government whisked the *Migration Amendment Act* through parliament. It retrospectively required any person who arrived by boat in Australia after November 1989 to be kept in custody until he or she was given a visa or left Australia. Therefore, the illegality of the state act became erased by the hurried legislation and this reduced the capacity of those involved to name government behaviour as a crime or to be understood as victims of state deviance. So how we can effectively engage the language of state crime when government busily reinscribes legitimacy through its control of the legislature? Moreover, how can we effectively engage the language of state crime considering the parlous state of civil society in Australia and the effect this has on the ability to censure?

Defining state crime in relation to the formal and informal censure of a range of audiences makes the diminution of civil society more difficult. As I have previously argued with Michael Gard,[41] critics of the government's treatment of refugees and asylum seekers have been branded anything from 'bleeding hearts', members of the 'intelligentsia' to being 'unAustralian'. The Federal Minister for Employment and Workplace Relations recently had this to say:

> 'If critics of the Government's policy believe that our conduct is unbecoming, can they please provide more polite ways of saying no? If they believe than an influx of 5000 boatpeople a year is not enough to justify exclusion, can they explain how permitting smaller numbers will not encourage larger numbers? ... Why do so many

---

40 See Chapters 3 and 7.
41 Pickering, S and Gard, M, (2004), 'Women in Privatised Prisons', in S Pickering and C Lambert (eds), *Global Issues, Women and Justice*, Sydney: Institute of Criminology Monograph Series.

members of the intelligentsia have so little respect for the culture that shaped them? Why have they so little affection for the society that pays their wages, appoints them to prestigious positions and often gives them a more respectful hearing than they deserve?'[42]

By Green and Ward's definition, an active civil society, including the small or grossly under-resourced, can act as one of the 'from below' or 'from within' audiences that can call into question the legitimacy of government behaviour and label it deviant. The dominant voices of government and of mainstream media do not have a monopoly on the definitional moment. The question remains, however, about the capacity of the voices of censure (particularly from below) to be effective in their own quest for legitimation within territory defined and bounded by state interests when it is often their legitimacy, rather than the substance of their challenge, that is the focus of state rhetoric, in this case called into question by the Federal Minister for Employment and Workplace Relations. Linked to this is the applicability of both formal and informal censure. While formal censure can be made in a range of ways (from the United Nations, other states and other political jurisdictions, eg, State governments), we need to consider such censure in concert with audiences 'from below' and 'from within' in defining the acts of a refugee-receiving country as state crime.

The role of non-state actors in the treatment of asylum seekers and refugees in Australia is paramount and raises questions of how human rights are realised when the state contracts out human rights obligations.

The detention of asylum seekers becomes operational matters of trans-national corporations. Therefore the realisation of rights, and indeed the violations of human rights, within immigration detention centres becomes an issue of the behaviour of both state and non-state actors. Therefore, this most concerning aspects of Australia's treatment of refugees and asylum seekers needs to be addressed in a way that can account for the behaviour of both a multi-national corporation and government. While the mistreatment of asylum seekers within immigration detention centres could be addressed by existing domestic legislation it has not been subject to such scrutiny. Rather it has been subject to various government and

---

42 'No Shame in Doing the Right Thing', *The Australian*, 7 January 2002, p 11.

non-government inquiries, most of which have outlined routine violations of human rights.[43] The potential definitional moment involves untangling the relationship between multi-national corporations and the federal government and makes possible the complicity of both government and corporations in what we may come to know as state crime.

Sovereignty: Where state crime and law and order meet the refugee

There are two key elements of (territorial) sovereignty relevant to this discussion. The first element is the sovereign right to enforce borders against all who seek to cross them and the concomitant 'right' to determine who shall enter a country.

It becomes a matter of controlling the disorderly movement of people across borders. It is from such a position that the Australian Prime Minister made this statement regarding asylum seekers on the MV Tampa:

> Those people will never set foot on Australian soil ... Never.[44]

More recently the Co-Chair's Statement of the Ministerial Conference between Indonesia and Australia on People Smuggling, Trafficking in Persons and Related Transnational Crime concluded:

> Ministers recognised that the increase in all forms of illegal migration, including overstayers and those who sought to bypass regular migration channels without resorting to smuggling networks, posed a threat to the management of countries' regular migration programs

---

43 Most recently and significantly the Joint Standing Committee on Foreign Affairs, Defence and Trade *Visits to Immigration Detention Centres* (JSCFADT), the Ombudsman's Report of an Own Motion Investigation into Immigration Detainees held in State Correctional Facilities, The Ombudsman's Report of an Own Motion Investigation into the Department of Immigration and Multicultural Affairs' Immigration Detention Centres and the Flood Report of Inquiry into Immigration Detention Procedures. In addition to these the Senate and Legal Constitutional References Committee released *A Sanctuary under Review* report in June 2000 and the Human Rights and Equal Opportunity Commission inquiry *Those Who've Come Across the Seas: Detention of Unauthorised Arrivals* was released in 1998.

44 Cited in Rundle, (2001) op cit, p 3.

and eroded States' capacity to protect their borders, regulate migration and safeguard their citizens.[45]

In response to a damning article in the *Los Angeles Times*, the Minister for Immigration and Multicultural Affairs reasserted:

> Australia is a sovereign country which alone determines who is allowed entry and who is not, and has laws which protect its borders and safeguards its citizens.[46]

The second element is the sovereign right not to experience bureaucratic and legal interference from outside the nation-state for matters occurring within the nation-state. However, there is the obvious and ongoing contradiction in the free flow of goods and information that furiously crosses borders with decreasing control and regulation while the refugee is rejected at the frontier. There is also the contradiction in how international 'interference' *is* embraced by the sovereign nation-state from what Chomsky has called an 'array of megacorporations, often linked to one another by strategic alliances, administering a global economy which is in fact a kind of corporate mercantilism tending toward oligopoly in most sectors, heavily reliant on state power to socialise risk and cost and to subdue recalcitrant elements'.[47] Moreover, the contradiction rests in the notion of the refugee at international law: a set of rules and mechanisms that oblige (by treaty and international customary law) states to numb territorial sovereignty by undertaking to protect refugees in certain circumstances. Most particularly, Article 31 (1) of the Convention relating to the Status of Refugees 1951 requires that refugees not be penalised for crossing borders unauthorised by the receiving state:

> The Contracting states shall not impose penalties, on account of their illegal entry or presence, on refugees, who coming directly from a territory where their life or freedom was threatened in the sense of article 1, enter or are present in their territory without authorisation,

---

45   Ministerial Conference Between Indonesia and Australia on People Smuggling, Trafficking in Persons and Related Transnational Crime, (2002), *Co-Chairs' Statement*, <www.dfat.gov.au/illegal_immigration/cochair.htm>, accessed 13 March 2002.

46   See <www.minister.immi.gov.au/media_releases> accessed 6 March 2002.

47   Chomsky, (2001) op cit, p 199.

provided they present themselves without delay to the authorities and show good cause for their illegal entry or presence.[48]

While Australia is signatory to the above, the Minister for Immigration made the following comment in the same response to the article in the *Los Angeles Times* in relation to advocacy groups opposed to the government's policy:

> Simplistically, they think that people who come to Australia covertly and against the law should be treated like heroes and rewarded. The result of this attitude is to encourage others to come, thus endangering more lives ... They violate those laws when they arrive illegally without any documentation.[49]

In the coming chapters it is argued that the notion of sovereignty gives law and order its decisive push into the realm of the politically unchallengeable by looking inwards. It does so by playing on the idea of the border – most literally in the recent package of Border Protection legislation.[50] The crossing of the national territorial border in unseaworthy vessels is represented as *the* challenge to public morality, decency and way of life. It is in that 'unauthorised' border crossing that the very presence of the asylum seeker becomes deviant and triggers various processes of criminalisation. It is in this moment that the asylum seeker is both victim and offender so many times over.

The criminalisation of the asylum seeker is made possible when territorial sovereignty is challenged and transgressed and then violently reinscribed by the state. Law and order reinforces the sovereignty of the nation-state. But it is also at the territorial border that we can double the question of sovereignty back on itself and ask questions about the ways notions of sovereignty can help reposition criminality and the nation-state. A state crime framework means that borders must fade (not disappear) and that the notion of the

---

48   Convention Relating to the Status of Refugees, 1951.

49   See <www.minister.immi.gov.au/media_releases> accessed 6 March 2002.

50   See the *Migration Amendment (Excision from Migration Zone) Act* 2001 (Cth); *Migration Amendment (Excision from Migration Zone) (Consequential Provisions) Act* 2001 (Cth); *Migration Amendment Act (No 6)* 2001 (Cth); *Border Protection (Validation and Enforcement Powers) Act* 2001 (Cth); *Migration Legislation Amendment (Judicial Review) Act* 1998 (Cth); *Migration Legislation Amendment Act (No 1)* 2001 (Cth); *Migration Legislation Amendment Act (No 5)* 2001 (Cth).

nation-state (as defined by sovereignty) becomes the basis upon which state responsibility and state protection turn. Sovereignty becomes the basis by which external audiences are increasingly important in censuring the nation-state and, hence, the nation-state is required to look simultaneously inwards and outwards. By beginning with the notion of state crime, sovereignty is challenged and repositioned in relation to the nation-state, particularly via the range of audiences from within, outside and across national borders. Therefore, throughout this book it will be sovereignty that provides the grounds for critiquing law and order refugee policy and sovereignty that helps apply a state crime framework to refugee policy.

The framework that I am invoking is the deconstruction of law and order and construction of state crime has a clear purpose. I seek to theoretically ground the case that the response of the Global North to refugees increasingly relies on unmitigated ideological and coercive force. It distances Western nations such as Australia from their complicity in the production of refugee flows and in their production of the refugee deviancy as justification for unbridled denunciation and violent rejection.

Chapter 2

A mundane process of criminalisation

The criminalisation of refugees has been normalised in the ordinary hum of media reporting of refugees in the Australian print media. This occurred prior to the series of scandals and incidents that took place from 2000 onwards.[1] Refugees had received considerable national media coverage in Australia prior to 2000 and inspired equally considerable social and political debate. Discussions surrounding refugees have been rooted in the taken for granted assumption that there is a refugee 'problem'. This chapter argues when asylum seekers and refugees arrive on Australian shores, the 'problem', both implicitly and explicitly, is readily shaped by the dominant theme of deviance. Refugees represent a significant 'problem' because they are a 'deviant' problem. Deviancy has been built on the discursive construction of exclusion and the polarisation of normality as being whatever refugees are not. The deviancy of asylum seekers and refugees has routinely been a matter of 'common sense'.

Using Gramscian notions of 'common sense' and the 'ideological work' of the media to question definitions of deviance, this chapter explores the ways asylum seekers and refugees transgress many boundaries: physical, geographic, language, legal, national, social and political that routinely disrupt established, although precarious, orders. Problematising the social functions of representations of deviance in relation to refugees potentially reveal the 'normality' of prevailing social orders. Four major thematic categories of representation will be interrogated: the invading deviant; the racialised deviant; the diseased deviant; and deviance aided and abetted by international law.

---

1   For example, the MV Tampa and the 'Children Overboard' incidents.

Each of the themes contributes a distinctive element in representing the 'other' within dominant orders that are grounded in racial, nationalistic and international economies of discourse. The reproduction of hegemonic relations is also an important locale to understand the orchestration of consent.

Utilising a deviancy oriented conceptual framework is by no means the only way to critically read stories about asylum seekers and refugees. However, deviancy offers a reading that begins to address the increasingly punitive regimes that are greeting those seeking the protection of developed nations. As developed nations such as Australia are making it more difficult to claim refugee status and therefore the pressure to exclude is becoming greater, one of the clearest ways to understand efforts at exclusion is the way we label asylum seekers as being unworthy of protection. Relying on ideas (and words) about deviancy contributes to the conditions that make exclusion easier.

This chapter is drawn from a thematic textual analysis of the *Sydney Morning Herald* (SMH) and the *Brisbane Courier Mail* (BCM) over the period January 1997-December 1999. These two newspapers were selected as 'quality' broadsheets from two different States to provide some range in data.[2] Broadsheets were selected over other forms of print media such as the tabloid press because often the messages produced and reproduced in the later mediums have been considered more obvious than insidious. More importantly, the 'quality' press is more often cited in regard to 'objective', 'factual' and 'tempered' reportage; an important site of interrogation for

---

2   In particular a Queensland-based newspaper was selected because it is a State that receives more asylum seekers by boat and therefore may be expected to carry a higher volume of press coverage in this regard. The *Brisbane Courier Mail* (BCM) is a News Limited publication that is the only State paper in Queensland apart from the Australian (that is the national broadsheet) and therefore caters to a diverse public. The *Sydney Morning Herald* (SMH) is a Fairfax publication and caters to a public that also has the choice of the more tabloid style *Daily Telegraph*. Articles analysed included editorials, standard news reports, descriptive pieces, features and commentary articles. The vast majority were standard news reports. Unless introduced otherwise, the extracts utilised in this paper were standard news reports. By focusing on broadsheets the examples used here often lack the sensationalist accounts of more tabloid style reporting. For an account of tabloid journalism and refugees see Ponting, S, (2002), 'Bin Laden in the Suburbs: attacks on Arab and Muslim Australians before and after 1 September", 14 *Current Issues in Criminal Justice* 43.

those concerned with the reproduction of consent.[3] Therefore this chapter addresses both the 'ordinary' and 'responsible' coverage of refugee issues.

The seductive and material power of language in the representation of deviance can be seen in the binary logic deployed in relation to asylum seekers and refugees: bogus/genuine; refugee/ 'boatpeople'; law abiding/criminal; legal/illegal; good/evil. Such logic insists on the polarisation of the subject and provides communal comfort in removing ambivalence through the forced choice of either/or. More importantly, however, is the way binary representations inform discourses of deviance and state responses to such deviance.

The power of language in the representation of deviance provides the base for not only discourses of deviance to be developed but also state responses to that deviance. Such a process removes doubt from representation and forces discursive and material choices. According to the BCM and the SMH 'we' are soon to be 'awash', 'swamped', 'weathering the influx', of 'waves', 'latest waves', 'more waves', 'tides', 'floods', 'migratory flood', 'mass exodus' of 'aliens', 'queue jumpers', 'illegal immigrants', 'people smugglers', 'boat people', 'jumbo people', 'jetloads of illegals', 'illegal foreigners', 'bogus' and 'phoney' applicants and 'hungry Asians' upon 'our shores', 'isolated coastlines' and 'deserted beaches' that make up the 'promised land', the 'land of hope', the 'lucky country', 'heaven', 'the good life', 'dream destination' and they continue to 'slip through', 'sneak in', 'gathering to our north', 'invade' with 'false papers' or 'no papers', 'exotic diseases', 'sicknesses' as part of 'gangs', 'criminal gangs', 'triads', 'organised crime' and 'Asian crime'. In response, 'we' should have 'closed doors' only sometimes having 'open doors', we should respond 'nationally' with the 'navy and armed services at the ready', 'we' should 'send messages', 'deter', 'lock up' and 'detain', 'we' should not be 'exploited' 'played for a fool', be seen as 'gullible' or be a 'forelock-tugging serf'.

---

3   Allan, S, (1999), *News Culture*, Open University Press: Buckingham; Deacon, D, Pickering, M, Golding, P, and Murdoch, G, (1999), *Researching Communications: A Practical Guide to Methods in Media and Cultural Analysis*, London: Arnold; Bell, A, (1999), 'The discourse structure of news stories', in A Bell and P Garrett (eds), *Approaches to Media Discourse*, Oxford: Blackwell; Fairclough, N, (1998), 'Political discourse in the media: an analytical framework' in A Bell and P Garrett (eds), *Approaches to Media Discourse*, Oxford: Blackwell.

As others have noted, oppositional terms are constructed in a system of value which routinely renders one normal and one strange/other.[4] The use of such terms generates a sense of commonality and simultaneously excludes (and criminalises). Through binary opposi-tions difference is established,[5] including the infinite discursive possibilities for talking about 'us' and 'them'.[6] This chapter argues that the above descriptions establish discourses of illegality and legality through positing the very presence of refugees and asylum seekers as illegal (nationally, racially, socially, bodily, criminally) and necessitates and reinforces the legality of current state res-ponses. Because the original illegality resides with the other then all responses are rendered legal. Such operations serve to reinforce the communality of the experience of 'dealing with' refugees and asylum seekers for 'all Australians'. Binary modes of analysis can also flatten out moments of struggle and resistance that Gramsci's writings argued as integral to the maintenance of consent. Conse-quently, the 'refugee' occupies a precarious and changing position in relation to legality and illegality in the press.

This chapter examines the ways that refugees and asylum see-kers have been rendered deviant and excluded through discourses surrounding: the integrity of the nation-state; the biologically gene-rated notion of racial otherness and disease; and deviance aided and abetted by judicial processes and international law.

Integrity of the nation-state

There have been a number of ways that representations of asylum seekers and refugees in the press have been underpinned by con-cerns for the integrity of the nation-state. Representations of illegal immigrants as embodying a threat to national security have a heavy investment in the representation of refugees as embodying and symbolising deviance. Such representations contribute to the validation and invocation of repressive state responses.

The ideological significance of press representations of the nation-state can be seen in the ways that immigration discourses and criminal discourses are enmeshed with discourse about tactics of

---

4   Ferguson, R, (1998), *Representing Race: Ideology, Identity and the Media*, London: Arnold; Billig, M, (1995), *Banal Nationalisms*, London: Sage; Young, A, (1996), *Imagining Crime*, London: Sage.
5   Ferguson, op cit.
6   Billig, op cit.

war. More than the SMH, the BCM has consistently made a heavy investment in eliding the vocabulary of war with crime discourses in relation to asylum seekers and refugees. For example, in a headline that read remarkably like a crime news story 'Record Arrest of Boat People – Swoop Nets 350 Illegal Boat People', the article details:

> The incident, the largest single attempted incursion on record, follows the most sustained assault on Australia's shores since the refugee tide following the Vietnam War.[7]

The article told of how 'would be migrants' paid 'huge sums of money' to 'criminal gangs' for a chance of 'a new life' but instead they will 'stay in tents at an isolated north-west detention centre'. It continued: 'more than 2000 illegal immigrants from the Middle East were *massing in Indonesia* for the short hop to Australia'. Another report,[8] citing a front page article in the BCM a few days previous, read: 'It told of an *unexpected invasion* of 2000 Iraqi and Afghan boat people *gathering to our north* for the *illegal run* to this land of hope … '. The article went on to formulate a 'temporary solution' – that reads like a 'defence plan' including putting all international treaties 'on hold', closing all immigration routes and not taking advice from 'those ethnics'. The SMH headlined 'hunts' for 'boatpeople'.[9]

The metaphor of war is considered one of the most notorious in criminology and criminal justice policy.[10] For some time a 'war on crime', or more particularly 'war on drugs' has been common parlance. A war is only won or lost and there can only be one just side. Sides are therefore demarcated, boundaries and lines are drawn. In the case of asylum seekers, the boundaries are easily identified by the discrete nation-state – not only fixed national and geographic boundaries in the case of Australia, but also those of race. In 'record arrest', 'swoop', 'incident', 'criminal gangs' and 'illegal run' criminal justice discourse becomes interwoven with that of war: 'incursion', 'sustained assault on Australian shores', 'gathering to our north', 'massing in Indonesia', all to invade the 'land of hope'. In constructing a war, identities and individualities are irrelevant and excluded– there are simply sides – 'ours' and 'theirs'.

---

7   'Record Arrest of Boat People', *Brisbane Courier Mail*, 3 November 1999.
8   *Brisbane Courier Mail*, 16 October 1999.
9   *Brisbane Courier Mail* 29 December 1998.
10   Young, (1996), op cit.

While the SMH more consistently included a range of sources, including a number from outside government, in the BCM alternative views were routinely downgraded or excluded. In one particularly alarming report there was no contesting clearly challengeable views:

> Immigration Minister Philip Ruddock has claimed tens of thousands of people 'entire Middle Eastern Villages', are planning to move to Australia.[11]

Not contesting such views suggests the idea of entire Middle Eastern villages planning to move to Australia were not at odds with 'common sense' assumptions about the threat of asylum seekers to the integrity of the nation-state. The discursive repertoire of war serves to reinforce a sense of normality that may otherwise be questioned.

Part of the common sense successfully deployed in the development of 'deviancy' through the use of war metaphors is also apparent in the implied militaristic and defensive responses required. Similar to McLaughlin,[12] this study identifies that the discourse of war promotes the need to repel whatever is hostile or threatening. The security of a strong sense of normality is used as the dramatic and discursive platform from which a navy 'Boys Own Adventure' style article was printed in the BCM. The article was primarily interested in Australia's 'need' for constant surveillance of its extended shoreline. At the heart of this surveillance, it contends, is the Royal Australian Navy. The extended article goes on to describe, in diary fashion, a 'day in the life' of HMAS Ipswitch. How it 'runs down an illegal fishing boat' with the threat of military fire power:

> Short of sinking the intruder, in effect a prime-ministerial decision, the Ipswich has one alternative – a hostile boarding.

It continues with military bravado:

> One of them, a first-timer at this sort of thing, is just a bit twitchy. What, despite the preparations, is missing from his webbing belt – torch, medical kit, tools, a police baton or a 9mm Browning pistol?

The expansion of certain forms of policing, devices of restraint and detention, affirms the normality of defence responses when anxieties

---

11   *Brisbane Courier Mail*, 20 November 1999.
12   McLaughlin, 1998

about the inviolability of the nation-state are raised. For example, the BCM[13] told how: 'The Australian customs service is *the front line of detection'*, necessitating increased surveillance and security. 'Immigration controls' become matters of 'national security' – violent responses to the threat to the security of the nation. Locating the threat and repressing it becomes a major pre-occupation. Borders (political, geographic, legal, racial) come into crisis – and where there is a threat to those borders security can be increased through vigilance and strength. The arrival of 'illegal immigrants' is a 'national emergency'[14] that calls for the 'full deployment' of the armed forces in protecting those borders:

> Protecting the *integrity of our shores,* even from *rag-tag illegals* in rusty fishing boats, might soon become a *prime defence mission.*[15]

The SMH reported the introduction of extensive radar and surveillance systems for 'detecting *incursions into our* territorial waters'.[16] Debate on these matters becomes narrowed and flattened into the framework of nationhood – alternative voices become voices against the nation, while the nation remains an uncontested concept. The reinforcement of the integrity of the nation through the deployment of the intermeshed discourses of war and deviance confirms Billig's argument that the 'reasonableness' of nationalism draws heavily on the 'syntax of hegemony' by which the part claims to represent the whole.[17]

Integrity of the nation-state and deviancy can also be considered in terms of the ability of the state and institutions of civil society to attribute legality or illegality, often in the assertion of sovereignty, but importantly in this study in the use of the term 'refugee'. The official United Nation's definition of who is a 'refugee' was marginal to press coverage. Rather, constructions of deviancy have consistently been more concerned with casting 'genuine' refugees in opposition to the 'bogus' and 'phoney'. This bifurcation routinely saw 'genuine' (normal) applied to those who sought asylum in another nation before embarking for Australia, while 'bogus' and 'phoney' was readily applied for those who arrived in

---

13   *Brisbane Courier Mail,* 3 December 1997.
14   *Brisbane Courier Mail* 10 November 1999.
15   *Brisbane Courier Mail,* 3 November 1999.
16   *Sydney Morning Herald,* 27 November 1998.
17   Billig, op cit.

Australia, by whatever means and then applied for asylum. The latter are routinely described as 'queue jumpers', 'boat people' and even 'jumbo people' and the press has made a heavy investment in distinguishing the two groups in order to distribute legality and illegality (deviancy) in their coverage. Therefore, it is not just the discourse of the tactics of war that invokes 'invasion' in terms of deviance and illegality but also and simply, the very act of being present without prior refugee status is portrayed as an aggressive *deviant* act against the nation-state that is inherently illegal. For example, in commenting on new legislation on temporary visas and the sentencing of three Indonesian fishermen, such measures were considered to:

> [H]ave an impact over time and send a strong message to the world that Australia was tough on illegal immigrants. He said that with boatpeople jumping queues, genuine refugees around the world obeying Australian laws could lose their places to clients of people smugglers.[18]

Genuineness is elided with law abiding. It completely negates the conditions of flight in the country of origin and the right to seek and enjoy asylum under international law. In this report two new regulations proposed by the government were outlined and supported – they included the increased identity testing of illegal immigrants using fingerprinting, DNA testing and face and palm recognition and stopping illegal immigrants who have been granted or refused refugee status elsewhere: in essence, criminalisation. While an Amnesty International spokesperson and a member of the Democrats condemned the regulations, this was at the end of the article and after the majority of the article was given over to bipartisan government and opposition comment leaving little room for debate.

The SMH routinely used concepts of being genuine with law abiding:

> *We* are entitled to decide how many immigrants *we* want, and to lay down at the very least the requirement that they ask first … Genuine refugees are a different matter, but no one is helped by the ingenious attempts of lawyers to classify the rest of the world as potential refugees.[19]

---

18   *Brisbane Courier Mail* 23 November 1999.
19   *Sydney Morning Herald*, 3 October 1998.

One of the few spaces in which alternative voices on asylum seekers and refugees entered media discourses in relation to the integrity of the nation-state was during the annual International Refugee Week and in the initial stages of the UN bombing of Kosovo and Indonesian brutality after the East Timorese vote for independence in 1999.

During these periods the inviolability of the nation-state was sidelined as the rhetoric changed with altered political imperatives. 'Genuine' was interchanged with 'grateful' while 'bogus' and 'phoney' with the 'ungrateful'. The explanatory frameworks became altered in relation to these political developments, however, only inasmuch as the objects of representation (refugees and asylum seekers) remained passive. Such explanatory power shifted because refugees and asylum seekers were represented as 'acceptable' (and hence not deviant) in a number of ways. They were not deviant 'queue jumpers' and were not destined to spend weeks, months or years in detention centres (even though the conditions in army barracks may be considered less than ideal). Therefore it became possible for the media to deploy the language of humanitarianism and justice because these people were clearly 'worthy'. Indeed, Kosovar refugees were also the subject of nationwide jostling on the part of state governments to 'welcome' and 'house' them. 'Disappointment' was repeatedly expressed by those state governments that 'missed out' on the opportunity to grant 'safe haven' to the refugees.

The BCM headlined a story 'Refugee Hopefuls Pack up their Troubles' that told of the refugees 'putting on a remarkably brave, almost serene face'. Later it told of:

> War-weary Kosovo refugees are beginning to arrive on our shores grateful for sanctuary.[20]

Despite the history of Australian government complicity in atrocities in East Timor,[21] when the East Timorese began to arrive in Darwin after the 1999 vote in East Timor the BCM described:

> As the aircraft's rear ramps clattered down on Darwin airport tarmac, a bus driver witnessed one little Timorese boy, aged no more than four, who went down on his knees and kissed the hot asphalt.

---

20 *Brisbane Courier Mail*, 15 May 1999.
21 Graydon, C, (1998), 'East Timorese Asylum Seekers: Close to Home but No Justice in Sight', 36(Aug–Sept) *Arena Magazine* 24.

The gesture said it all 'thank you' ... Old people, bent with age, young mothers carrying babies. They had one thing in common, they were a bewildered people, a frightened people ... .[22]

This depiction 'says it all' in relation to the ideal refugee: very young or very old, afraid; persecuted by internationally proclaimed oppressive state; acts of invitation by the Australian government integral to their presence in Australia; they originated from 'wars' and 'conflicts' in which Australia had a current political and publicly proclaimed interest; and they were visibly grateful to be in Australia. Overall, such stories were constructed in opposition to the more routine reliance on deviance.

Erring from the script of being the passive invited refugee, however, was met with a swift return to more conventional representations of refugees and asylum seekers – ungrateful, aggressive, demanding, draining and different. Potentially indicating that asylum is an act of charity rather than a legal humanitarian obligation. A case in point is the BCM coverage of the Salihu family, initially joined by dozens of other Kosovar refugees, who refused to get off a bus at the Singleton Army Barracks because of a lack of heating and other facilities. The BCM told:

For more than a day, about 80 refugees *thumbed their noses* at frustrated officials by refusing to get off buses at Singleton army barracks north west of Sydney.[23]

The article went on to say:

Not even pleas by embarrassed fellow Kosovars that most of the problems were being fixed could make them budge.

This is an attempt to promote that even some of 'their own' saw how 'ungrateful' they were being:

Immigration Minister Philip Ruddock said the Federal Government *refused to be dictated to by refugees* with *'unreasonable'* complaints.

'Dictated to' is an assertion of 'us' and 'them' – that 'they' will not dictate the terms and infringe upon Australian sovereignty. Repeatedly described as *'disgruntled'* – there is no sense of legitimacy attributed to their protest. In a later article, the BCM told:

---

22   *Brisbane Courier Mail,* 15 September 1999.
23   *Brisbane Courier Mail,* 16 June 1999.

Twelve days after being welcomed to Australia, the unhappy Salihu family has quietly bid farewell from *the comfortable economy seats of a Qantas jumbo.* But the seven Kosovo family members *who outraged many Australians* during their short stay *have no idea* to what they are returning.

It further told:

The *ringleader* of the *disgruntled* Kosovars in Singleton took his sick mother from hospital, broke off negotiations with the Immigration department then *accepted a free taxi ride* to Sydney last night.[24]

He was problematised by the media: he 'snubbed' help; was the (criminal) 'ringleader'; who exploited Australian generosity in a range of ways including 'accept[ing] a free taxi ride'.

The racialised deviant

An investigation of banal opinion or the doxa of common sense[25] in relation to the 'deviance' of asylum seekers and refugees also calls for the examination of race: the biologically-generated and socially-constructed notions of racial otherness that informs the 'threat' of the deviant refugee in media reporting.

Extensive research has noted that news media representations of race in Western nations are continually posited within dominant white cultural attitudes, which also suggests that racial prejudice is politically dangerous as well as prevalent in both tabloid and quality papers.[26] Authors have highlighted the need to expose the discursive reaffirmation of race.[27] Ideologies of racism have long been considered some of the most fundamental in the production and reproduction of 'common sense' and 'normality' in the press. Deviancy can play an important part in the construction of racial 'common sense'.

As raised earlier, the inherent deviancy of asylum seeking in media discourses and the implied need for deterrence is heavily encoded in assumptions about race. Sometimes this is explicit in terms of 'us' and 'them'. In reference to Iraqi asylum seekers, a BCM

---

24 *Brisbane Courier Mail*, 24 June 1999.
25 Billig, op cit.
26 Allan, op cit; Ferguson, op cit.
27 Hall, S, (1990), 'The whites of their eyes: racist ideologies and the media', in M Alvarado and JO Thompson (eds), *The Media Reader*, London: British Film Institute.

editorial suggested: 'They should stay elsewhere until we decide to let them in'.[28] The BCM further reported:

> Mr Fischer said that more than 500 boat people had arrived in Australia last year. ``People ought to be aware of that and let that message ripple up the bamboo grapevine so that people can desist from this dangerous and foolhardy queue jumping," he said.[29]

According to the grammar utilised, the 'people' that 'ought to be aware' about the numbers of 'boat people' are internal to Australia. The message is not meant for an audience external to Australia. However, the next sentence talks about the message rippling up the 'bamboo grapevine'. Potentially, this is a racially derogatory term (insinuating 'backward', 'uneducated', 'poor') that attempts to suggest that the message is travelling externally to Australia. However, the message is clearly about race and is primarily directed towards an internal Australian audience that invokes a cultural division between 'us' and 'them' that is discursively anchored in a preferred inflection of a homogenous Asian identity that is 'foreign' and 'other'. This arguably potent race message offered by the Deputy Prime Minister went unchallenged.

It is not just those seeking asylum that can be read as the subject/object of such deviant discourse. Such discourse is also readily transferable to wider ethnic communities. In shoring up the inherent illegality of race, ethnicity becomes interwoven with criminality on a wider scale:

> Ethnic communities helping to fund illegal arrivals and some boat people are arriving with cash of up to $US50,000, expensive travel luggage and first class air tickets to Indonesia.[30]

Ideologies and explanatory themes of race, however implicit or explicit, promote the broadest application of threatening discourses often expressed in terms of criminality or potential criminality. The ethnic citizen is a precarious part of 'us' as 'they' border on the inherent criminal problem of immigration and asylum. Ethnic communities can be quickly rendered homogenous, unfamiliar and strange within such discourses.

---

28   Brisbane Courier Mail, 22 November 1999.
29   Brisbane Courier Mail, 16 June 1997.
30   Brisbane Courier Mail 13 October 1999.

'Let's make a quid from our asylum' headlined a feature in the BCM[31] that argued the Australian government should set aside 'a few thousand' places in Australia's annual refugee intake to be sold to 'the highest bidders'. Justification of this position is possible through the invocation of a legal/illegal asylum seeker:

> People claiming to be refugees are paying crime syndicates to bring them to Australia illegally, and to instruct them in the most effective ways of taking advantage of our comparatively liberal immigration and welfare programmes. As there are only a fixed number of refugee places available, wealthy asylum seekers are displacing those in genuine need who are too poor – or perhaps too scrupulous – to jump the queue.

This implies that those who do not 'queue', that is, have their applications for refugee status processed in a country other than Australia, are automatically cast as suspect. Their means of transportation to Australia criminalises them by association with 'people smugglers' and their 'willingness' to pay. However, pecuniary and fiscal concern is not necessarily the crux of the matter, race is. The BCM writer recommends:

> [I]f the large sums that illegal entrants seem ready to pay went into Australian public coffers where they could help provide a higher level of post arrival services so as to *integrate* needy refugees more effectively into the community.

And then went on:

> While I believe we should maintain a generous immigration and refugee programme – though one that gives due consideration to *social harmony* and the *national interest* ...

Social harmony, national interest and integration become the basis on which 'genuine' refugee status is determined, rather than the persecution from which a refugee is fleeing. It goes on to say:

> Those who were able to buy places would obtain a comfortable risk-free trip to Australia, secure in the knowledge that on arrival they would be given the benefit of the doubt, and treated as though they might actually be refugees.

Genuineness and benefit of the doubt are tied up with the ways and means that one arrives. What this report also promotes is that genuineness is linked to legality/illegality– and that this duality can be dissolved fiscally. The invocation of the cultural division between 'us' and 'them' permeates the construction of press representations that express the

---

31   *Brisbane Courier Mail*, 27 November 1999.

fears of internal (white) audiences towards (Asian, black, coloured) external groups. Imagining 'us' is dependent on imagining the 'foreign', or as Kristeva has, the foreigner becomes the one who does not belong to the state in which we are and instead becomes something against which 'we' can measure 'ourselves' as a representative of normality.[32]

In this critical reading of the BCM and the SMH, the naturalisation of racism was also fluid and contradictory. Indeed, reportage that offered some alternative positions indicates that there is no singularly racist conception of the world and that there are some spaces for resistance to dominant views. Reports that offered alternative views to those outlined above, however, were mostly human interest stories. Invariably they would focus on the plight of a handful of cases often in an attempt to personalise the issues at stake. They would often offer a direct challenge to government positions and mainstream views on race. In asking why Australia was so afraid of asylum seekers, an article in the BCM[33] described the government position on asylum and immigration as 'cautious, clinical and defensive'. Local political contexts are also important in understanding the engagement of alternative views, particularly when they came together in response to the racism of the One Nation party. It was one of the few spaces where race was overtly linked to asylum and immigration and many common sense assumptions presented and questioned.

Race assumes a naturalness which is contingent upon ruling out counter-hegemonic voices as illegitimate. Normality and (overt and covert) racism operate in a symbiotic relationship. The 'national interest' is served in maintaining consensus, in turn consensus is equated with normality. Allan argues in relation to race that:

> To engage with the power of this discourse, it follows, it is necessary to recognize its capacity to constrain what can and cannot, be said about issues of race and ethnicity. [34]

This was clear in the SMH.[35] In an article headlined 'Laying down the law on refugee status', it argues that a high level of consensus on race is not only desirable but essential to national stability:

---

32 Kristeva, J, (1991), *Strangers to Ourselves*, Hemel Hempstead: Harvester/ Wheatsheaf.
33 *Brisbane Courier Mail*, 22 May 1998.
34 Allan, op cit, p 159.
35 *Sydney Morning Herald*, 3 October 1998.

Immigration and race have, happily, not been central issues during the election campaign. Win or lose, this should be held to the credit of John Howard, who ... defused them. The only people playing the race card have not been on Howard's side.

This may be read as de-legitimising the arguments of any group (not just from the opposition, but other interested groups) that challenges bipartisanship on any issue in which race plays a part. In endorsing consensus, the article also attempts to depoliticise it – it is not a political matter but a matter of common sense.

The SMH article goes on to unreservedly endorse consensus politics:

> But nothing will be settled in this election with respect to either of these issues; in both cases they are better treated as areas of bipartisan consensus – but there has to be a genuine consensus, not the imposition of an orthodoxy by the political elites, as has been the case over the past 15 years ... Thus it is sensible to devote a great deal more effort to ensuring that social tensions are not exacerbated by high rates of immigration at times of high unemployment; it is not sensible to turn immigration to political ends, as Labor has so often done. Even less acceptable is to allow ethnic lobby groups to make immigration policy.

There is no acknowledgement that the predominantly middle-class, white, middle-aged, males that make up federal parliament constitute a particular group.

Disguised as a defensive response to the attack that alternative views are continually and mistakenly, making on 'common sense', the SMH article says:

> A new attack on the bipartisan approach to refugee policy has just been published by the Centre for Independent studies ... They accuse the policies of Labor and Coalition governments towards illegal refugees as being a kind of racism, tantamount to 'soft Hansonism'. They, along with some religious and legal lobby groups, consider that mandatory detention is unacceptable.

The article notes 'they' have a point but then dismisses such views:

> Again, the word would soon get back, especially to those who run a profitable trade in boat places, and the problem would quickly burgeon.

The depoliticisation of common sense and the deligitimation of alternative views provide a fertile ground for racially challengeable views to be aired:

> Of course, the majority of detainees will be Asian, for geographical reasons. It is not a kind of racism or Hansonism to apply a consistent non-discrimination policy to all illegal immigrants.

The unquestioning assumptions in presenting race as a consensus issue actively legitimate mis-readings of race and criminal justice/ immigration responses to asylum seekers. In constantly redrawing lines of common sense with heavy investments in discourses of race, asylum seekers are implicitly, explicitly and routinely rendered deviant in the press. The endorsement of consensus becomes a discourse of legitimation, any contradictions are smoothed over or ignored.

The diseased deviant

The interpretive frameworks of race and the integrity of the nation-state may also be read as informing the use of the metaphor of disease in representing the deviancy of asylum seekers and refugees and the need to repel and exclude them from Australia.

The implicit 'threat' of sickness was often not far from the surface. Both papers repeatedly described the need for 'health screenings' and 'medical checks' even though details of what people were being screened and checked for were largely absent. Sometimes the words and descriptions were more explicit: asylum seekers were 'health hazards' and their vessels 'disease ridden'. But it was the BCM that can be read as developing the theme of diseased deviancy in an explicit sense. It has been noted by others that militaristic metaphors are often used to represent disease and media reporting of refugees is no exception.[36] The BCM told:

> To call it *'war'* would be stretching things a bit. Mostly flyblown, rat and cockroach-infested little craft, the Indonesian and Taiwanese *intruders* are at best an increasingly worrying *health hazard,*

---

36 Sontag, S, (1996), *Illness as Metaphor and AIDS and Its Metaphors*, Harmondsworth: Penguin; Park, K, (1993), 'Kimberly Bergalis, AIDS and the Plague Metaphor' in MGarber, J Matlock and R Walkowitz (eds), *Media Spectacles*, London: Routledge; Young, A, (1996), *Imagining Crime*, London: Sage.

potentially a nightmare for *quarantine* officials. But *shots across the bows, armed boarding parties* and a cockier, even belligerent attitude by the illegals no longer are rare incidents.[37]

In another report, the BCM[38] told of how 'this country is losing a war against the introduction of many of the *'world's worst pests and diseases'*. The article outlined:

> Farmers *fear illegal boat people* will bring in *exotic diseases* that could *decimate* Queensland's multibillion-dollar rural sector. The major concern is a foot and mouth, screw worm fly or blue tongue outbreak that would force meat off the international market. The fruit and vegetable industry export trade could be wiped out by the papaya fruit fly and Newcastle disease would ruin the chicken trade. ... 'It is not so much the people, though obviously that is worrying, as what they are bringing with them,' Mr Armstrong said. 'The boats are not just anchoring off shore. They are running ashore for any animal or pest to hop off'.' ... 'It may sound alarmist but it is a fact that it would take only *one diseased beast* to *jump ship* to immediately endanger our entire industry'. Queensland Cattle Council president Mike Hill said the recent arrival of two boats on the east coast demonstrated that *urgent* action was *necessary*. 'It is not unreasonable to suggest *that Australia's defence forces should be used* as a stop-gap measure'.

Disease is considered a threat to the health of the Australian country and in particular to the health of the traditional heartland of Australia: the land, its animals and its farmers – with grave fiscal consequences. Disease sees asylum seekers constructed not only as problems, but as deadly problems. In becoming linked to the transmission of disease an analogy is created: asylum seekers threaten the life of the host society. Australian society is repeatedly presented as the healthy and the robust and the asylum seeker as the foreign (the pest), the polluted enemy that potentially compromises the health and endangers the wellbeing of the healthy nation. Like the criminal, asylum seekers become parasitic, preying on the health of the nation, corrupting and contaminating the fabric of society. The response to this, according to Young,[39] enlists technological rationality – through this the problem of the diseased deviant will be dealt with. Quarantine, detention and isolation become central

---

37   *Brisbane Courier Mail*, 12 January 1998.
38   *Brisbane Courier Mail*, 18 April 1999.
39   Young, (1996) op cit.

responses of the host society that also serves to construct the host society as the clean, the objective, the scientific and the normal.

Disease has also informed media discourses surrounding the deviancy of asylum seekers in other ways, including the 'exploitation' of the health system. Repeatedly, the BCM told of asylum seekers preying on the Australian health system:

> A *loophole* in Australia's immigration laws means anyone who arrives on a valid tourist visa can apply to become a refugee. This instantly allows them to work here and be covered by Medicare. The Immigration Department has heard accounts of people travelling to Australia and claiming refugee status with the sole intention of receiving free operations under Medicare.[40]

Asylum seekers are not only invading with foreign diseases and pollutants but in seeking to have them treated are impinging upon the ability of the health system to treat the native local sicknesses of full (read tax-paying) citizens. The elision of the diseased and the invading discourses in the fiscal arena also had an investment in the denigration of the 'rights' of individuals, especially of non-citizens. Their 'exploitation' was not only of the health system but also of the legal:

> Mr Ruddock said that as soon as some boat people were on dry land they were *demanding lawyers and expensive medical treatment*. 'They are coming here with life threatening disease like cancer and motor neuron disorders' he said.[41]

Deviance aided and abetted by the courts and international law

Refugee deviancy aided and abetted by both domestic and international law came to be all encompassing when the Federal Court rejected the government's plan to not allow asylum seekers on board the MV Tampa to disembark in Australia. Although the Full Court of the Federal Court overruled this decision on appeal, the intervening media commentary proved to be a defining moment in how the press positioned refugee policy along a continuum of deviancy. While the Tampa incident is discussed further in the following chapter, it is important to acknowledge not all reportage

---

40 *Brisbane Courier Mail*, 11 January 1998.
41 *Brisbane Courier Mail*, 13 October 1999.

of asylum and the law has been so blunt – it is often nuanced and complex. This section examines the definitions of deviance that underpin the reportage of asylum seekers utilising domestic and international law. In particular it examines the ways refugees are routinely considered as aided and abetted by international law and domestic judicial processes. The embodiment of original deviance in the refugee has been augmented by the utilisation of domestic and international law and systems. Extending 'justice', the rule of law and the doctrine of the separation of powers to non-citizens invokes ideas and representations of deviance.

Significant media, activist and academic work has lauded the role of the media in the promotion and protection of human rights. In relation to a range of conflicts and mass refugee movements, the media has been considered an important ally in precipitating change. This is not to suggest, however, that the role of the media in relation to refugees has been ambiguous. Some have argued that the media reinforces representations of refugees as hapless and helpless victims in need of paternalistic, benevolent 'civilising' support and aid. As Harrell-Bond has noted, 'Agencies vary in the degree of dignity with which they transmit images of refugees, but all rely on funding from a public which responds to media portrayal of extreme human suffering, starvation and helplessness'.[42]

Critical literature on international relations and the role of the media has often centred on the concept of civil society and increasingly, the globalisation of civil society. While 'global civil society' may in itself be a contested concept, what is not contested is the integral role the media has in transmitting stories and images across borders, regimes and conflicts and hence its centrality to ideas of 'globalisation'. Alongside the role of the media, human rights have also been understood as being at the forefront of globalisation, particularly in relation to the creation of a 'global civil society' and its 'universalising mission'. Considering human rights as performing such a 'globalising' role raises the inherent contradiction to the post World War I notion of the centrality of the nation-state. The implicit and explicit sovereignty of the nation-state has been the basis upon which the peoples of the world have been represented in United Nations' human rights mechanisms and processes.

---

42 Harrell-Bond, B, (1999), 'The experience of refugees as recipients of aid' in A Ager (ed), *Refugees: Perspective on the Experience of Forced Migration*, London: Pinter Publishing, p 149.

Nation-states have been represented as discrete sovereign entities with unequal standing in processes of international governance.[43] While increasing economic globalisation, (privatisation, unfettered systems of trade and transfer of wealth, the International Monetary Fund and the World Bank), has effectively repositioned and diminished the role of nation-states in international financial systems, the nation-state has retained definitional power within discourses of human rights. In short, despite the economic disruption to the centrality of the nation-state, its hold over the conceptualisation and representation of rights has not been equally disrupted. This paradoxical definitional relationship between human rights, the nation-state and changing world systems has left some elements of media work (as ideological work) less than straight forward.

For example, the reportage of human rights and international law has been problematic when the subject and object of the media gaze arrives from the Global South on the shores of developed nations such as Australia. This section investigates the ways that refugees have been rendered deviant and excluded through discourses surrounding human rights, international law and the legal system. The deviance implied in the co-option of the legal system by asylum seekers has been the final act in the inherent illegality of asylum seekers in media representations.

The fiscal deviance of judicial review

The costs involved in asylum seekers seeking asylum has been considered evidence of their inherent deviance. In particular, the use of judicial and administrative review by asylum seekers has been presented in the press as a fiscal drain and an abuse of Australian legal and administrative systems.

Media reporting concerned with changes to judicial review, the legal status of asylum seekers and their recourse to legal aid, routinely returned to explanations that posited the inherently illegal presence of the asylum seeker as the catalyst for administrative and judicial change. According to the BCM,[44] the pressure for changes to judicial review emanate from the increasing numbers of illegal immigrants arriving on Australian shores:

---

43 For example, see Sassen, S, (1999), *Guests and Aliens*, New York: The New Press.

44 *Brisbane Courier Mail*, 18 November 1999.

Driving the need for reform is the soaring cost of illegal immigration.

Highlighting the 'cost to taxpayers', it tells that:

> Under the Government's plan, illegal immigrants and Australian citizens questioning the department's decision will never get their day in court ... if they then apply to the Refugee Review Tribunal or appeal to the Federal Court and are finally deported they will cost the taxpayer a minimum of $20,500 each. That does not take account of the final avenue to the High Court.

The article reports the government's solution is to:

> [L]imit the scope of appeal to the courts, citing the United Nations High Commission for Refugees requirement that there be one process of appeal – either court or administrative ...

This adheres to the letter rather than the spirit of international law as well as shifting responsibility for repressive law onto the external UN body. The article quotes the Minister for Immigration saying that the new Bill:

> [W]ill make the umpire's decision final, cutting out expensive and time consuming court battles.

The Minister and the article simultaneously deploy the language of fairness when actually removing procedural fairness from the application process. Even when members of the opposition were interviewed and made their reservations clear, they still relied on the language of 'rorting' and wanting people to have their 'day in court' but do not want them 'abusing' the system. The language of reasonableness being used at the moment procedural fairness is being attacked:

> Department figures show more than 130 foreigners, despite failing to gain refugee status from the Immigration Department and the independent review tribunal, are fighting court battles to stay in Australia after being told to go. Ruddock is also aware from departmental debriefings of illegal immigrants that people-smugglers are advising their passengers to use Australia's courts to prolong their stay.

Such discourse is about making the case that Australia is being manipulated by the devious and cunning other – and that we ought to get smart and put an end to it. The article outlines the 900 per cent increase of applications to Refugee Review Tribunal and an assessment of public 'sympathy' in order to render marginal the concerns of human rights and refugee groups:

> What these organisations may not understand, however, is the public anger about the cost to taxpayers from legal battles. Public sympathy may rest with the 60,000 genuine refugees waiting patiently in line around the world for a chance of a new home.

Consequently, 'our' sympathies are with those abiding by the process, not the ones jostling, 'jumping the queue' and 'being impatient'.

Throughout the press examined, there remained attempts to reaffirm Australia's position within the international community. International agreements remained something Australia worked within and a system that others abused. Eventually this would turn to 'reforming' and making more 'effective' and 'efficient' such international instruments and processes.

As judicial review can reject departmental decisions, the judiciary has often been charged as colluding in the illegality of the refugees. Consequently, the government often contested judicial and administrative oversight. The BCM reported:

> Mr Ruddock said the independent refugee tribunal had upheld about 94% of appeals by illegal Iraqi and Afghan migrants despite departmental assessments that they were not genuine.[45]

Similarly the SMH reported:

> A Federal Government plan to deport the two Kenyan stowaways as illegal migrants was thwarted at the last minute when the two men obtained a court order, after the plane had taken off, banning the deportation. A furious Mr Ruddock said last night he had been trying to limit the ability of the courts to interfere with the Government's handling of the immigration system.[46]

The courts *thwart* and *interfere* while the government *plans* and *handles*. The legislation, clearly directed at limiting the power of the judiciary in immigration matters, raised questions about the immediacy of the relationship between the judiciary and the parliament. Crock has described this as a most extraordinary battle between the government and the courts over the issue of who should have the

---

45 *Brisbane Courier Mail*, 3 November 1999.
46 *Sydney Morning Herald*, 4 August 1998.

final say on 'legal' decision-making in this area.[47] The courts have engendered resentment in both the parliament and the bureaucracy and have been considered as appropriating the refugee policy-making role of the parliament and threatening the 'very fabric of immigration control'. Both of the above passages imply that the primary issue is the way judicial review is allowing non-genuine refugees to remain, rather than the questionable nature of departmental determinations: legal processes are represented as undermining the Executive and the parliament rather than as fulfilling a desirable and necessary expression of procedural fairness and accountability in a liberal democracy.

The knowledge and language of rights as deviance

Discourses of rights have not been embraced by Australians generally.[48] Utilising the court system has been routinely linked to having a knowledge (and language) of human rights, and the exhibition of human rights knowledge and language is often read as both undermining the integrity of the nation-state and common sense assumptions about what it is to be part of Australia.

In representations of refugees, knowledge and language of the law has often been mediated by the lawyer, often working for community legal centres or even *pro bono*. The role of the lawyer has been integral to positioning access to the courts and international mechanisms as deviant. It has been represented as another way that the Australian public is victimised by predatory lawyers. In particular, lawyers have been widely considered as colluding in the 'abuse' of the court system and this has consistently been couched in terms of financial cost. The SMH reported:

> [M]any lawyers have argued that people who are not permitted to have more than one child under China's population policy thereby qualify as persecuted and, therefore, legitimate refugees.[49]

The article goes on to say:

---

47 Crock, M, (1993), 'Climbing Jacob's Ladder: the High Court and the Detention of Asylum Seekers in Australia' 15 *Sydney Law Review*, 338-356.
48 Charlesworth, H, (2001), *Writing on rights: Australia and the Protection of Human Rights*, Sydney: University of New South Wales Press.
49 *Sydney Morning Herald*, 3 October 1998.

> Why are the would-be refugees detained so long? ... Does the government want to punish these people? No, the fault is with the lawyers and do-gooders who engage in interminable litigation as they try to drive holes through our immigration policy.

The report describes a struggle for power between the judicial and Executive arms of government as 'conquering new territory'. The reporter calls this the 'rule of lawyers':

> The main beneficiary is, of course, the legal profession on both sides, and the main losers are the Australian taxpayer and detainees who are the gun fodder for the lawyers' high principles.

Consequently, the fiscal imperative negates any legal or humanitarian principle. By 'establishing' such realities the report has then cleared the space to locate the root of the problem:

> If the detention of claimants is too long, it is unacceptable. If the detention is under bad conditions the same is true. But make no mistake about it: the main fault lies with the people who would impose their own beliefs about race, immigration and population policy on the rest of the community.

The article ends by saying:

> We are entitled to decide how many immigrants we want, and to lay down at the very least the requirement that they ask first. Genuine refugees are a different matter, but no one is helped by the ingenious attempts of lawyers to classify the rest of the world as potential refugees.

Judicial review is considered disingenuous and adverse to effecting and sustaining immigration control which is constituted by detention, swift hearings and swifter still deportation. Moreover, it cannot be a matter of rights – it is a matter of courtesy and control.

Illegality and the deviance of international law

Much of the reporting on the role of judicial review in determining refugee applications commented on the role of international law generally and the Refugees Convention specifically. Part of this commentary has been preoccupied with discourses of illegality. The use of international law has been offered as further evidence of the inherent illegality of asylum seekers. In turn international law has been represented as undermining national sovereignty and the decision to include and exclude, to render legal and illegal.

Rights have been talked about in a number of ways in the reportage studied. For example, on the one hand, the Australian government has repeatedly 'defended Australia's human rights record'[50] in relation to asylum seekers and refugees. On the other hand, those who land on Australian shores without appropriate documentation are deemed to have no rights:

> This latest group ... had no right to be here.[51]

The power of rights is recognised and considered dubious when used by individuals and groups considered external to Australia. For example, an article in the BCM headlined 'Magic Words' reported how 83 Asians had been found on a boat and transferred to Port Headland. It said:

> But it could be months before they leave Australia because they had learned to say in English on their capture: 'I am a refugee'. Without those words, Australia has no obligation to offer protection or entitlement to legal advice. Being able to say 'I am a refugee' triggers access to legal services, blocks a speedy deportation and gives the right to have a refugee claim assessed.[52]

Rights in this report are defined only a hindrance to Australia, which subvert a speedy process and the ability of a nation to make its own determination about inclusion and exclusion. The language of rights also becomes the language of vulnerability whereby international agreements serve to undermine national sovereignty and they guide and support those seeking asylum. For example:

> Andreas Schloenhardt of the University of Adelaide told the AIC that Australia and New Zealand were among the most viable destinations for illegal migrants because both had signed international agreements protecting refugees. While their humanitarianism is laudable, the practical effect was 'more refugees'.[53]

'More refugees' constitutes an undesirable result that needs to be avoided as do international agreements that compel nations to take more refugees. There is no mention that Australia and New Zealand are geographically undesirable and protected (so to speak) by a lack of land borders – borders that have seen most other nations around

---

50   *Brisbane Courier Mail*, 16 May 1997.
51   *Brisbane Courier Mail*, 30 December 1999.
52   *Brisbane Courier Mail*, 19 May 1999.
53   *Brisbane Courier Mail*, 11 November 1999.

the world subject to considerably higher numbers of refugee arrivals regardless of whether they are signatories to the Refugee Convention.

Human rights, therefore, are a matter of 'principle' rather than a matter of 'policy'. Rights must be subsumed to issues of 'national security' and 'social harmony' and can be meted out to those who are 'genuine' and withheld from those who are not. In so doing, the 'universality' of rights is diminished:

> Where, perhaps surprisingly, there has been the greatest degree of bipartisanship has been on refugees. First of all, both parties agree that in principle we should, for humanitarian reasons, accept a substantial number of refugees from civil war or ethnic persecution. More to the point, both parties agree that policy towards refugees who have been accepted after genuine displacement (as in Vietnam or former Yugoslavia) should be different from that towards those who, without permission, arrive in Australia and then claim to be refugees. These have fairly tough tests applied to them, and they are subject to detention until their status is resolved. A distinction is drawn between refugees from actual persecution and those who are unhappy about their home country and think they would be better off in Australia.[54]

The paragraph immediately following reads:

> But there are those in the community who believe that anyone who turns up in Australia claiming to be a refugee is in need, and we should be open and charitable towards them. A fine principle but not a workable one when, as it must, it becomes known and the numbers of self-styled refugees arriving without prior permit swell to huge proportions.

In 1997 Australia was found by the UN Human Rights Committee to be in breach of its obligations under the International Covenant on Civil and Political Rights. Reporting this, the BCM was primarily concerned with re-asserting Australia's decency. Australia had a 'right' not to uphold human rights and rather had a 'right' to assert sovereignty of the nation through the act of granting refugee status and determining conditions of asylum:

> The UN committee's findings do not and cannot challenge the decisions by the Government and the courts that the boat people were not entitled to refugee status under the relevant UN

---

54 *Sydney Morning Herald*, 3 October 1998.

convention. Australia, as much as any country in the world, has been scrupulous about observing its humanitarian and legal responsibilities to refugees.[55]

The article continued:

Australia has every right to be suspicious of people claiming to be refugees who arrive surreptitiously, without seeking permission. The law approved by the Parliament regards them as illegal migrants until they can persuade the Minister they should be given refugee status. They have no moral or legal claim to be at large in the community. There is nothing improper about their detention under civilised conditions. Nor is there any reason Parliament should not limit (so long as it does not completely eliminate) their right to contest in the courts any decision by the Minister rejecting a claim for refugee status ... Australia is entitled to establish a regimen which makes it clear that it will grant asylum only to genuine refugees. There is no reason to provide a welcome mat for people who arrive in Australia without having shown that they are entitled to refugee status. Australia cannot afford to be thought of as providing a haven to all the boat people of eastern and south-east Asia.

This may be considered a weak form of deviancy when contrasted with another piece in the BCM:

The story illustrated the weakness of Australia's political masters to bite the global bullet and tell the United Nations to get stuffed for a change instead of grovelling before that UN international elite who would force their views on any forelock-tugging serf willing to listen. Do you recall that great English comedy *Dad's Army*? I see that as the world stage with Australia reincarnated as silly old Corporal Jones who runs around in diminishing circles shouting 'Permission to volunteer, sir. Permission to volunteer', for every insane edict coming down from above. We must break out of that circle because in it we have become one of the world's most gullible nations ... I have a temporary solution that will frustrate the criminal gangs, illegal immigrants and those ethnic communities that are financing boat people, and give our boffins time to work out a foolproof plan to bring common sense to a system thriving on greed, deception and criminal intent on one side and blind, bleeding heart compassion on the other. First of all tell the UN we've put all its refugee treaties on hold. Then close all immigration routes, legal and illegal for as long as it takes to sort out the foolish mess we've created through years of misdirected compassion. Let it be clearly known that anyone arriving

---

55   *Brisbane Courier Mail*, 16 May 1997.

on these shores without authority will be deported immediately with no hope of ever gaining legal entry. In the process, be very wary of advice from those ethnics who have badly misled governments on immigration in the past. Remember in 1994 how some ethnic groups appointed to advise the Federal Government on immigration used their positions to promote their own communities?[56]

Again we are returned to issues of common sense to rectify easily exploited acts of misguided benevolence. *Those ethnics* remain marginal to the white Australian majority, are devious in the ways they have accumulated (and are now spending) their wealth to allegedly finance the arrival of those who will undermine the kind of society we live in. Australia's role in drafting and negotiating international obligations fades.

Amid such reporting, some articles continue to prioritise the personalising of asylum issues through the language of rights. For example, following a BCM article headlined 'Refugee's call to aid human rights':

Basic human rights are being violated in Australia, according to a multicultural worker who came to Brisbane 11 years ago as a Chilean refugee.[57]

However, the article, a human interest story, is on page seven. It was small and ends:

All Queenslanders are being urged to support Amnesty International's Candle Day ...

In short, this piece was acting as a small public service announcement. Similarly, during International Refugee Week in 1997 the BCM headlined: 'Our duty to greet refugees'.[58] The article went on to say:

AUSTRALIA has had as good a record as any country in receiving and resettling refugees since World War II, and we should continue to do so as part of our international obligation to assist displaced people. Unfortunately there are always pressures upon governments in times of economic hardship or unemployment to reduce the annual overall migrant intake ... it needs to be strongly asserted that our moral responsibility to settle refugees is a qualitatively different issue to the determination of general migration levels. There is clear

---

56 *Brisbane Courier Mail*, 16 October 1999.
57 *Brisbane Courier Mail*, 23 October 1998.
58 *Brisbane Courier Mail*, 19 October 1997.

justification for any government regulating the supply and demand of labour for economic reasons, but the matter of meeting international moral obligations comes in a quite different category.

There remains some space for such alternative reportage, but again it was an ambiguous space, one tucked away in the incessant hum that is refugee deviance in the media.

Conclusion

Examining the press as a site of the reproduction of hegemonic relations suggests that the deviancy of asylum seekers is continually reproduced in relation to discourses surrounding: the integrity of the nation-state; the biologically-generated notion of racial otherness; disease; and the courts and international law.

With the exception of a handful of interviews during International Refugee Week, what is absent from the press examined is any consideration of seeking asylum from the point of view of the asylum seeker or in reporting issues such as home country conditions or the conditions of flight. Instead, the issues prioritised in the press are debates over the deviant problem that asylum seekers and refugees constitute and how a strong state is required to regulate this problem. There are occasions in which reports challenge these dominant news themes. However, these were the exception and not the norm and when clearly at odds with broader views they were only invoked on grounds of human interest.

The choice of vocabulary revealed the ways in which language that challenged the status of refugees was used by the press, without questioning the assumptions upon which debateable terms such as 'phoney' and 'bogus' are based. Being 'genuine' and grateful become a newsworthy question, demanding frequent comment and discussion. Blatantly racist images were not widespread, however, the legacy of racism has manifested itself in subtler and perhaps equally powerful ways. The quality press can construct and sustain discourses 'with a veneer of sophistication',[59] which if you examine reveal attempts to normalise the close relationship between those media discourses which feed on concepts of normality and those discourses which are overtly racist.

---

59   Cf Ferguson (1998), op cit.

The range of metaphors used in relation to the integrity of the nation-state; race; disease; and the role of courts and international law collectively designate a state of normality. Mainly through appeals to 'common sense', ideological representations of refugees often go unchallenged. The embodiment of original deviance in the asylum seeker remains unchecked in the majority of press coverage. Consequently, it is with relative ease that such rule breakers are expelled from the community. But such exclusion is not always automatic, it is contingent and often negotiated – there seem to be some spaces for resistance and the reconstruction of borders and boundaries. The discourses investigated here support the sacrificing of the other for the sake of our normality. The act of sacrifice is realised through the asylum seeker being 'recaptured', subject to 'police lock up' and a matter of 'security'. The act of sacrifice is important in the categorical distinction of 'us' from 'them': imagining, either implicitly or explicitly, ourselves requires that we imagine 'them'. The discourse of deviancy in relation to asylum seekers and refugees has ultimately been a discourse of legitimation. It has repeatedly served to justify and pre-empt repressive state responses that, couched in the language of common sense and normality, have been largely reproduced and sustained rather than challenged by the press.

Chapter 3

The spectacle of refugee deviancy

> The spectacle presents itself simultaneously as all of society, as part of society, and as *instrument of unification*.[1]

> No one today can reasonably doubt the existence or the power of the spectacle; on the contrary, one might doubt whether it is reasonable to add anything on a question which experience has already settled in such a draconian fashion.[2]

The incessant hum of refugee deviancy has primarily been the business of the mundane and increasingly everyday reporting of refugee issues outlined in the previous chapter. But refugee deviancy has also been constructed through the refugee spectacle. That is, the dazzling national coverage of key refugee 'events' – moments when other national and international issues struggle to steal front pages away from refugee coverage. This is not for a moment to suggest that the spectacle of the refugee is not incrementally built, but rather to nominate key moments when the refugee has gained intense and concentrated attention. The moments of spectacle selected for examination are the Cambodian asylum seekers of the early 1990s, the case of the 'Chinese Woman', the Woomera crisis of 2000, the MV Tampa and the 'Children Overboard' incident. These are just that, a selection. An examination of editorial, feature and general news items in the SMH, *The Daily Telegraph*, *The Australian*, *The Age*, *The West Australian* and *The Courier-Mail* form the basis of this chapter. Letters to the editor were excluded from selection, as were photographs.[3] The articles selected were analysed using the

---

1   Debord, G, (1983), *Society of the Spectacle*, Detroit: Black and Red.
2   Debord, G, (1990), *Comments on the Society of the Spectacle*, London: Verso, p 5.
3   Each newspaper was systematically searched over the identified spectacle period. All articles were read and a sample of between 12 and 30 articles for each spectacle was made. The sample was formed in order to make a comparison across articles and across at least two newspapers for each incident. The sample could never be exhaustively representative.

tenets of critical discourse analysis as outlined by Fairclough and van Dijk.[4] Principally they were analysed through an examination of lexical items, categorisation, nominalisations, modality, transitivity, theme/rheme and process types as well as identification of the topics of discourse that relate to refugees. This chapter draws on Fairclough's more recent writings on the need to analyse text both paradigmatically and syntagmatically:[5] Paradigmatically analysed by examining the range of alternative possibilities in the choice and use of language in particular texts; and syntagmatically analysed by examining the use of words in phrases and sentences. The following discussion that draws on that analysis is divided into two sections: the emergence of the spectacle and the spectacle *par excellence*. The spectacles chosen, while not discrete, were all moments where state practice could figuratively or literally be considered deviant. All were moments when resistance to dominant narratives of refugee deviancy were possible. However, such resistance has not occurred in any comprehensive fashion and instead with each spectacle the discourse of refugee deviancy seems to become more complex and impervious.

The spectacle

Refugees are continually produced and reproduced as an event, a scene, a spectacle.[6] Most of all, the spectacle has been about the frenzied and deliberate public dismembering of the criminal refugee. By examining spectacles across the past decade I am interested in what changes have taken place in the representation of refugees as criminals in the Australian press. This chapter makes the connections between language and the creation and sustenance of the refugee spectacle. It is with some irony that I use the term spectacle

---

4   Fairclough, N, (1992), *Discourse and Social Change*, Cambridge: Polity Press; Fairclough, N (2001), 'The Discourse of New Labour: Critical Discourse Analysis', M Wetherell, S Taylor and SJ Yates (eds), *Discourse as Data: A Guide for Analysis*, Sage: London; van Dijk, T, (nd) *Ideology and discourse: A Multidisciplinary Introduction,* Universitat Oberta de Catalunya: Online at <cf.hum.uva.nl/teun/ideo-dis2.htm>, accessed 9 September 2002; van Dijk, T (nd) *Racist discourse,* online at <www.discourse-in-society.org/Racist%20Discourse.htm> accessed 5 January 2003.

5   Fairclough, N, (2001) op cit.

6   Young, A, (1996), *Imagining crime*, London: Sage. Young uses this description in relation to HIV and AIDS.

in relation to refugees in Australia considering their ongoing small numbers (in absolute and relative terms) and their general invisibility (little chance to photograph on the high seas or within detention centres).

The dissection of the spectacle in order to discover its mechanisation – the way it functions – is not my purpose here. Rather the dissection of the spectacle offered is an attempt to use the largest and grandest of media moments on refugee issues to return the discussion to some of the smallest building blocks of language so as to understand how discourses of refugee deviancy are so easily sustained. What do moments of great spectacle reveal, in their detail, about the ideological case against the deviant refugee and the ideological case that is still to be made against the deviant state? Examining the spectacle, the flurry of activity around an event, can tell us much about the construction of that event, purported responses to it and of course the consequent repositioning of victims, offenders, sovereignty and rights. Attending to the detail of the media spectacle ensures that the choices made in the presses of a liberal democracy do not become lost amid the frenzied attention to its object. It may well be trite, but the spectacle, like the mundane hum of the ordinary coverage of refugee issues, can reveal much more about society at large and the media particularly, than it ever can about the people and issues it purports to be about.

The spectacle is about stepping inside the power to create a crisis – in this case the power to produce the criminality of the refugee and to deny, delay or downgrade the criminality of the state. The spectacle is the impossibility of the collective imagination to place the state as criminal and the ease of imagining the refugee as criminal. It is about the unanswerability of the spectacle – the public, the media and the government have all remained unaccountable for the ramifications of the spectacle. As a moment of convergence, the spectacle is also a moment of concentration and, as Debord has argued, unification: 'The spectacle presents itself simultaneously as all of society, as part of society and as *instrument of unification[s]*'. Moreover, the spectacle, as Baudrillard has argued, is but another moment of consumption – the spectacle is consumed, discarded, recycled, reused and so on.[7] How is this cycle of unification and consumption engaged as media discourses reproduce the spectacle of the refugee?

---

7   Cavallaro, D, (2001), *Critical and Cultural Theory*, London: The Athlone Press.

Round 1: The emergence of the *refugee as criminal* spectacle

The reporting of the case of the Cambodian asylum seekers in the early 1990s, the case of the 'Chinese woman' in 1999 and the Woomera crisis of 2000 were key turning points in the construction of refugee deviancy in the press. Each of the incidents represented a moment of spectacle in the national and continued level of media coverage of refugee issues.

In 1993 a group of Cambodian refugees took their ongoing detention, of eventually four years, to the High Court.[8] On the eve of a court decision that found the government exceeded its powers, the Federal Parliament legislated to 'make legal' government actions.

In 1999 it was found that in 1997 Australia had returned to China a woman who had unsuccessfully claimed asylum. Ms Zhu was eight-and-half-months pregnant with her second child when the Australian government 'removed' her. Under China's one child policy she was forced to undergo an abortion upon return to the People's Republic of China.

In 2000 the spectre of internment without trial, otherwise known as administrative immigration detention, captured the attention of some Australians. Importantly, many in the press began to ask why a liberal democracy such as Australia needed to breach many of its own laws and international laws by imprisoning thousands in the desert.

The Cambodian asylum seekers

In what has become known as the second wave of 'boatpeople' who arrived in Australia in the late 1980s (the 'first wave' being those who arrived in the late 1970s and early 1980s after the fall of Saigon), refugees from Cambodia, China and Vietnam arrived in Australia. From the time of this second wave, the government instituted a policy of mandatory detention for asylum seekers who arrive by boat.[9] The case of the Cambodian refugees resulted in a judicial challenge in the High Court and a complaint to the United Nations.

---

8   See Chapter 7 for a detailed discussion of the case.
9   See also Chapter 7 for a discussion of the *Chu Kheng Lim v Minister for Immigration, Local Government and Ethnic* (1992) 110 ALR 97 (Case of *Lim*). For further discussion of this case and the policy of detention at that time see Poynder, N, (1994) 'An Opportunity for Justice Goes Begging: Chu Kheng Lim v Minister for Immigration, Local Government

The case of the Cambodian refugees was *the* most important turning point in the development of refugee deviancy discourses in the press. What made this case a spectacle? The Cambodian case involved Sino-Vietnamese refugees arriving by boat, it introduced consistent media discourses of the refugee as being in some way deviant and it involved the use of the courts by the powerless to condemn the actions of the powerful. Moreover, the case saw the formal introduction of mandatory detention of 'unauthorised arrivals'. The Cambodian case was a moment in which the rise of refugee deviancy occurred and the very moment the courts were to find the government deviant. At the instant the government should have been cast as criminal, the tables were turned and the criminal was now the refugee seeking protection.

'Hapless adventurers' was the initial depiction of the Cambodians who arrived by boat: they 'risk all' to 'make a remarkable voyage', they are 'venturesome souls'. Such a seemingly sympathetic portrayal is at odds with the deviancy discourses utilised consistently in the press by the end of the decade. However, these sympathetic depictions occurred simultaneously with discourses of deviancy relating to the incursion of the sovereignty of the nation-state and the deviancy of the diseased asylum seeker. The term 'illegal entrant' was used more consistently, the term 'economic refugee' was introduced and most importantly detention was justified in terms of deterrence, that is, deterring deviant refugees. Importantly the choice of vocabulary altered – refugees became genuine or fake and the heavy media investment in the 'queue jumper' came into sight. International obligations were constructed in the passive, Australia had no choice or control and on the whole that was acceptable. Once the court case began, however, depictions of the refugees quickly changed and the most consistent issue in the demarcation of deviancy for the entire decade – the role of the courts – was flagged. As immigration remained a matter of bipartisan

---

(*cont*)
and Ethnic Affairs', 1 *Australian Journal Of Human Rights* 414; Poynder, N, (1993), 'Marooned in Port Hedland', 8(6) *Alternative Law Journal* 272; Poynder, N, (1997), 'The incommunicado detention of boat people: A recent development in Australia's refugee policy', (1997) 2 *Australian Journal of Human Rights*, 2 p 53; Mathew, P, (1994), 'Sovereignty and the Right to Seek Asylum: The Case of the Cambodian Asylum Seekers in Australia', 15 *Australian Year Book of International Law* 35; Poynder, N, (1997), 'A(name deleted) v Australia: A milestone for asylum seekers', (1997) 29 *Australian Journal of Human Rights*, p 155.

support, the left was now represented in the press by the judiciary. A significant body of media reporting was dedicated to the role of the judiciary in developing policy rather than the role of the judiciary in keeping the powers of the Executive in check.

The term 'boat people' was repeatedly used during this period but there are no instances of the collocations of the word 'refugee' with adjectives intimating illegality ('illegal migrant', 'illegal immigrant' or even 'illegal boat people') that have become common place a decade on.

Other than references to 'boat people', refugees were referred to by their nationality/race/ethnicity or as 'refugees', 'arrivals', 'refugee type arrivals' and 'latter day refugee arrivals'. While the latter two choices in vocabulary raise questions of refugee authenticity, they are still a far cry from 'illegal immigrant'. Typically articles of this period focus on the 'refugee problem', a form of nominalisation that backgrounds the people and foregrounds the effect of the refugees – refugees are a problem. Importantly, refugees are accorded political reasons for fleeing (eg, the fall of Saigon to Communist forces in 1975).

Articles regularly drew on a range of statistics regarding the numbers of refugees. The use of numbers is a common practice aimed at enhancing the credibility of an argument. It is also a common strategy in immigration debates to focus attention on the number of people arriving in the country. By stating numbers frequently and reporting them as raw figures rather than percentages (which are likely to be insignificant) the numbers of people seems large and therefore a threat:

> Numbers and statistics are the primary means in our culture to persuasively display objectivity. They represent 'facts' against mere opinion and impression. Especially in discourse about immigration, also in the mass media, therefore, the frequent use of numbers is well-known. The very first attribute applied to immigrants coming to the country is in terms of their numbers.[10]

Numbers are coupled with a concern for the financial burden of refugees. For example, 'Australia is spending millions of dollars to supposedly protect our coastline but nothing has changed' and '[t]here should be an investigation into all the money that has been

---

10   van Dijk, T, (nd), *Ideology and discourse: A Multidisciplinary Introduction*, op cit.

spent to such little effect'.[11] This again returns the journalist to one of the 'safest' anti-immigration discourses. van Dijk has said this is an argument often put forward with the implicit message that refugees are drawing hostility not because of their colour or race but because of the potential (unproven) financial burden.

Sovereignty attracts heavy overwording of associated terms – 'Australia's coast', 'our shores', 'shoreline" as well as references to Coastwatch and patrol boat systems. Overwording is the proliferation of different words in the same area of meaning and may be indicative of 'intense ideological preoccupation' – suggesting that a particular area of meaning is especially significant or problematic.[12] The repetition of these terms taps into the perceived vulnerability of Australia's coastline to invasions.

Australia's international obligations, namely the Refugee Convention and the International Customary Law of *non-refoulement*, were also constructed through the use of a modalising expression indicating obligation: 'Australia had to guarantee fair and reasonable processing …'.[13] Australia had no choice or control over these obligations, nor should it. However, this is in contrast to many south-east Asian nations who are not signatory to the Convention and are constructed as active agents with a choice as evidenced by the verbs associated with them: 'other Asian nations had adopted …'; 'They had agreed …'; 'but would withhold …'; 'They opted …'.[14]

Adjectives and nouns associated with these actions, 'comprehensive' and 'plan of action', give the impression of careful consideration, planning, detail and action. Their status as active agents, underpinned by verb choice, is in contrast to Australia who is a passive player which has to accept refugees who 'are still landing at will'.

This article is seemingly sympathetic in its understanding of the plight of refugees. It raises discourses of deviancy in relation to disease and sovereignty, but most notably uses a range of strategies to make the case for what are essentially illegal state practices. This article was written before the Cambodian asylum seekers in detention sought relief through the courts.

---

11   Aisbett, N, (1992), 'Boat People Risk All, Including Repatriation', *The Age*, 17 January.
12   Fairclough, N, (2000) *New Labour, New Language?* London: Routledge, p 163.
13   Aisbett, op cit.
14   Ibid.

In *'Boat People Caught in the Rush'*[15] legal discourses are amp-lified, the passivity of the refugee is highlighted and the (positive) action of the government reaffirmed. Terms used to describe refu-gees include: 'the most vulnerable of people', 'so-called boat people', 'the Cambodians being held'. There are numerous collocations of refugee with adjectives describing their illegality: 'illegal migrant', 'other illegal entrants', 'the Cambodians have arrived illegally and without papers' and 'people who arrive here illegally'. The nomi-nalisation of the adjective 'illegal' to 'other illegals' removes any common terms to refer to people and focuses attention entirely on the outcome of the action of entering the country illegally.

Lexically the government is identified with 'tough immi-gration legislation', 'Governments second most senior Left minister', 'the toughest immigration lines' and with a 'legal right to intervene'. While the application process/judiciary is identified with 'lawyers', 'access to all court action', 'delays', 'tardy lodging of applications' and 'the wrong message'.

In English, verbs often display a socially or ideologically significant choice between different process types: actions, relations of being or having, mental processes and verbal processes. Action processes can be either transitive (they have two participants, ie, an agent and the person or thing which is affected by the actions of that agent, a goal) or intransitive (they have only the one participant).[16] As in the previous article, the verbs in the text denote refugees as the affected or goal of actions by others:

> legislation ... which will affect the Cambodian boat people (goal)

> lawyers trying to use the courts to free the most vulnerable of people to seek asylum, the so-called 'boat people' (goal) ...

> to consider the release of 37 Cambodians (goal) ...

> many of the Cambodians (goal) have been in custody ...

Where the refugees are the agents the process types are mental (wanting) or relational (having) rather than action processes. The (mostly transitive) verbs associated with the government and Mr Hand indicate control and power – all action processes. Routinely the court process is described as 'delaying', 'hampering',

---

15   Easterbrook, M, (1992), 'Boat People Caught in Rush', *The Age*, 7 May.
16   Fairclough, N, (2000), *New Labour, New Language?*, London: Routledge, p 163.

'congested', while the legislature are action oriented and decisive – "being tough', 'motivating force', 'intervene', 'obligations'.

A seemingly empathetic portrayal is betrayed by the word 'but': '[c]oncerns about racist undertones are being quietly harboured by lawyers. But Mr Hand has been quick to quash this, saying that it is not a matter of a particular group being singled out, but of ensuring that people who arrive here illegally are held in custody until processed'.[17] There is, however, considerable ambivalence in this text. Statements such as: 'Who other than these people, with access to money for a plane ticket and a passport to travel, would choose the treacherous route by sea?' and then ' … the Cambodians will have to continue their bid to be freed'[18], run counter to the rhetorical strategies that insist on the passivity of the refugee and the strategic undermining of empathy.

The case of the Chinese woman

Ms Zhu arrived in November 1994 by boat and was held in detention until July 1997. She had fled the People's Republic of China. She was deported from Australia with her 20-month-old daughter and de facto husband, after two unsuccessful applications for refugee status.[19] At this time she was in the final month of pregnancy. When Ms Zhu returned to China she was forced to undergo an abortion. When news reached Australia of the forced abortion there was public outcry. A Ministerial Inquiry was initiated in response to questions raised by Senator Harradine and the Senate Legal and Constitutional References Committee investigated the case.[20] The Inquiry found Australia had breached its obligations under the Convention Against Torture and recommended that special protocols be put in place with regards to the removal of pregnant women. Moreover, it recommended that pregnant women be brought for special attention by the Minister: in short, that pregnant women be encouraged to seek the exercise of Ministerial discretion to stay in Australia on humanitarian grounds. Scholars have consistently

---

17   Easterbrook, op cit.
18   Ibid.
19   Senate Legal and Constitutional References Committee, (2000), *A Sanctuary Under Review: An Examination of Australia's Refugee and Humanitarian Determination Processes*, Canberra: Commonwealth of Australia.
20   Under its terms of reference for its report, *A Sanctuary Under Review: An Examination of Australia's Refugee and Humanitarian Determination Processes*.

questioned whether China's one-child policy constitutes grounds for refugee status. In this case, the press coverage turned on the complicity of the Australian government in the human rights violation. Human rights are incompatible with the depiction of refugee deviancy, yet human rights came to dominate stories on Ms Zhu. My concern is how such clear human rights violations are embedded within predominant discourses of refugee deviancy in the rush of the spectacle.

In the coverage of this case, Ms Zhu was mostly referred to with a series of lexical items that identified her as an illegal immigrant and indeed that there was something quite deviant in her becoming pregnant in detention. China was also depicted by a series of deviancy metaphors. However, the only depictions of Canberra as deviant came from articles which operationalised heavy over-wording and dramatisation. This designated the woman as victim and the government as perpetrator. This was a strategy at odds with many other articles which acknowledged the incident not only as a failure of compassion, but as an inevitable glitch. Notably, Ms Zhu was removed from Australia as part of 'Operation Ox'. The deconstruction of the name of the operation to remove a pregnant Chinese woman is unnecessary.

When the case of Ms Zhu emerged in 1999, the established discourses of refugee deviancy were diverted rather than disrupted. Discourses of refugee deviancy became gendered and implicit in the case of Ms Zhu.

The article 'Inquiry Into Forced Abortion' begins 'A Chinese mother'[21] – not Chinese woman nor an illegal immigrant nor an asylum seeker. This acts to connect refugees with the roles that we all know and many perform (as opposed to the refugee whose plight is endlessly unknown by most). Throughout the article Ms Zhu is only referred to by nouns which categorise her as a woman, a mother and/or Chinese – she is not named and she is not identified as a refugee.

The author firmly establishes the Australian government's role in the situation by giving them agency in the opening clause of the article. This negative self-presentation is offset by a greater negative other presentation of the Chinese authorities who are more consistently named as the agents in the abortion of Ms Zhu's baby.

---

21 Symons, E, (1999), 'Inquiry Into Forced Abortion', *The Daily Telegraph*, 6 May 1999.

Even when Ms Zhu is the agent in a clause it is in a most passive act, 'sobbing', as the action 'is seen': 'The woman is seen sobbing and holding up the certificate for the abortion ...'.[22] Ms Zhu could not simply sob, she had to be seen as sobbing. Her sobbing could only be rendered real through its visibility.

Ms Zhu is only given an active voice towards the end of the article. When she is given agency, quotation marks are used to diminish any authority she may have: For example:' ... accusing the Immigration Department of '"cheating her"'.[23] Ms Zhu was consistently undermined with framing techniques that influenced the ways her words were reported: 'According to the woman ...'; 'Allegedly ...'; 'She claimed ...'. Such techniques were largely not used to question the truthfulness of what the government spokespeople were saying.

When reporting on the Australian government's position and the response from the Immigration Minister, Philip Ruddock, the author avoids negative presentation of both Australia and China through the use of a nominalisation, 'Ruddock could not confirm the forced abortion'.[24] In doing so, the author effectively removes both the agent and the process, focusing our attention on the outcome or effect. In this case who forced the abortion is missing and Australia's responsibility in the act is obfuscated. The use of nominalisation also works to separate the harm from the woman: it is the foetus and forced abortion that is the focus.

The article 'Our Hypocrisy in Compassion Can Prove Fatal' begins: 'For one dead baby, Australia proved a land of no opportunity'.[25] The opening statement equates refugee protection with opportunity (usually read as a 'better life') rather than being the application of human rights norms and international legal obligations. Opportunity immediately locates refugee protection within the realms of generosity and compassion (as the headline illustrates). Importantly, it locates it within moral rather than legal responsibility: 'it lies in the realm of the collective responsibility which we must accept in a democracy' and 'Refugees are a collective responsibility for a nation, akin to adoption on a grand scale'.[26] 'Adoption'

---

22 Ibid.
23 Ibid.
24 Ibid.
25 Shanahan, A, (1999), 'Our Hypocrisy In Compassion Can Prove Fatal', *The Australian*, 24 May.
26 Ibid.

returns refugees to motherhood, the mothering role of a nation. 'As a mother, as a citizen' the author moves the reader to the implicit recognition of women as bearers and reproducers of the nation.[27] The author has located herself with Ms Zhu, as a mother she shares the pain and the victimhood: 'distress', 'haunt me', 'move me to tears'. It is through the author's distress that we come to know the object of our gaze: the Chinese woman. Indeed, in some ways the object of this article becomes the distressed author. For example, the article ends with the following: 'One poor child does matter. One bereft mother matters. They haunt me and move me to tears of pity and sorrow'.[28]

The abortion and the human rights abuse endured by the mother is not enough to finish the argument. Their horror can only be complete via the compassion/sorrow/distress of the author. Can we not talk about refugees and humanity and rights without having to locate our Western selves at the centre? Is it so impossible to condemn the state without such recourse? Without locating 'ourself' at the centre of the story, as this author does, the deviancy of the refugee cannot be eradicated. Without it, the malpractice of the state cannot come into view.

This is also evident in relation to the author's shifting use of pronouns and the alternation between the pronoun and the noun. The central issue for the author is that human rights do not stretch to the unborn child. Indeed it is legal rules that have caused the violation: 'cruel, amoral legalism by Australians'. The author uses the inclusive 'we' throughout the text (taking the readers with her) but the frequent use of 'I', 'me' and 'my' tends to separate her from 'us'. Further, one asks why it is that the 'cruel, amoral legalism' is performed 'by Australians', rather than 'by us'? She goes on to say: 'Australian policy is to blame and we stand condemned as a nation'.[29] Those who created Australian policy appear to be separate from Australians generally (the readers and herself) and as such the author and the readers do not stand among those who are to blame. There is also dissonance between Australia and 'we'. 'Australia' must be incompatible with 'we' to recognise the illegality (or immorality in this case) of state action. The deviancy of the state depends upon its separation from the 'us'.

---

27   Yuvul-Davis, N, (1997), *Gender and Nation*, Macmillan: Basingstoke.
28   Shanahan, op cit.
29   Ibid.

The spectre of all Chinese women claiming asylum on the grounds of China's one-child policy was raised in an article by Padraic McGuiness in *The Age*, two years prior to the deportation of Ms Zhu and her subsequent forced abortion.[30] This article established the tone for many implicit assumptions for the reporting which surrounded the case of Ms Zhu. The article is of note as it confirms the importance of hyperbole and dramatisation in discourses that ward off the ever-dangerous and threatening woman of the global south. A woman, along with her many countrywomen, will simply bide their time to use their bodies to access (the always too lenient) immigration (read refugee) channels.

Dramatisation is a way to exaggerate the facts in one's favour. 'Positions in immigration debates, thus, tend to represent the arrival of a few thousand refugees as a national catastrophe of which we are the victims'.[31] This time it was the case of individual women that heralded the influx:

> 'It would mean that any Chinese woman, or couple, who disagreed with China's population policy could claim the status of refugee under Australian law that is, the potential number of refugees that the Federal court would admit into Australia from China has now increased by some tens of millions'.[32]

Notably, the dangerousness of pregnant women, or would-be pregnant women from Asia, was underpinned by the deviousness of the judiciary in general and the Federal Court in particular. Legal procedures are a 'trap', 'legal maze', 'arbitrary' and 'ad hoc'.

Hyperbole, similar to dramatisation, is a semantic rhetorical device used to enrich meaning. The interpretation of hyperbole may depend on one's political point of view: 'What is exaggerated for one group, may be the simple and objective truth and the 'correct' way of referring to an issue, for another group'.[33] Hyperbole (100 million) underpins the sleight of hand that moves the recognition of refugee status to an infringement on the (implicit sovereign) right of another country to make seemingly sensible laws: 'if Australian law does not recognise China's right to operate its own population control

---

30   McGuiness, P, (1995), 'Population Poser Drops Back in Government's Lap', *The Age*, 20 January.

31   van Dijk, T, (nd), *Ideology and discourse: A Multidisciplinary Introduction*, op cit.

32   McGuiness, op cit.

33   van Dijk, T, (nd), *Ideology and discourse: A Multidisciplinary Introduction*, op cit.

policies, then Australia must accept some of the resulting problem. Thus if 100 million extra Chinese are born every year as a result of no population controls, we might well be asked to accept a substantial proportion of the increased population'.[34]

The case of Ms Zhu was an opportunity to at least acknowledge the deviancy of the state, however, the deviancy became understood as a problem with the administration of compassion. In this spectacle human rights were marginalised from refugee issues in the press and the age of gratuitous humanity had arrived.

Woomera 2000

By 2000, refugee deviancy had become a matter of common sense.[35] During 2000 a series of child abuse allegations were made regarding the treatment of children inside immigration detention centres. Indeed the detention of refugee children became a major focus of refugee advocates. However, allegations of mistreatment of refugees by ACM guards, as well as riots, self-harm and suicide became central features in the reporting of refugee detention. Woomera was the site for the majority of these incidents.

The child abuse incidents in Woomera came in a period where the term 'refugee' was rarely used and instead reports often referred to 'detainees'. When the word 'refugee' was used, it was with negative other presentations such as 'who earlier this month accused refugees of double-dipping on welfare'. Such negative other presentations often had little to do with the current story.

Incidents within Woomera were often overworded and dramatised with little information of any injuries sustained by refugees. While refugees remain passively assigned in most of the language, there were moments when they become agents. Unfortunately this was usually the case when they were the agents of dangerous behaviour: when they 'pose a risk' and were 'pelting' and 'burning'.

Many reports during this period, including a sustained series by The Australian (Woomera In Crisis), represented refugees as members of families and as people in need of protection. However, the substantive issue at stake remained incidents of child abuse.

The notion of choice was routinely highlighted in the reporting of Woomera: refugees 'chose' to take this journey to Australia,

---

34   McGuiness, op cit.
35   See previous chapter for further discussion.

they 'chose' to board boats on which children were not segregated and they essentially 'chose' their own detention. Similarly, the response of some refugees to detention, riots, escape attempts etc, equally underlined the issue of choice – an unacceptable choice according to the majority of press reporting. The spectacle of Woomera 2000 was one of simultaneous child abuse, riots, escapes, suicide attempts and self-harm.

By the time the series on Woomera in *The Australian* was published, deviancy narratives were embedded. The whirl of deviancy and punitive responses to refugees was like a magnetic force that equally repelled talk of rights and humanity. Sustained critiques of the private companies, criticism of the Minister or the government, even challenges to the language of the press itself, did not seriously dislodge the trajectory of deviance narratives. From Woomera 2000 onwards anything was possible.

Much reporting of Woomera critically examined the reasons why people sought refuge by boat and challenged many of the prevailing myths, including that refugees are able to choose the boat and the people they travel with. For example: '[t]he pleasantly middle-class assumption – that refugees arriving here by boat carefully choose their travelling companions ...'.[36]

In 'False Basis for Woomera Safety Policy', far from undermining the notion of choice in the conduct of child abuse, the article problematically recycles 'choice'. The article grants considerable space to the arguments of the Minister for Immigration which reflect the standpoint that refugee parents have made a series of choices that endanger their children, including the danger of child abuse. Central to this argument is that parents choose which boat they come to Australia on and therefore choose the company their children will be forced to keep on unsegregated boats. This argument does not fall into disrepute when the Minister notes that refugees are housed in detention in unsegregated groups made up of the refugees' 'travelling companions'. Refugee choices are represented as in some way responsible for the system of (state) responses to their arrival. In short, through the combination of the series of choices made in the 'illegal' act of coming to Australia to seek protection, as well as the inherent illegality of the refugee, child abuse is positioned as unsurprising.

---

36   Spencer, M, (2000), 'False Basis for Woomera Safety Policy', *The Australian*, 18 November.

In this article refugees are represented as families, as people in relationships – mothers and sons, fathers and children, husbands and wives. Such representations remain reasonably rare in coverage of refugee issues in the Australian press. However, the instances of sexual abuse are positioned within those families. Parents are either exposing their children to abuse or abusing their children themselves. The article raises the need to segregate children from other 'detainees' to 'limit' sexual abuse, but notes that such abuse 'often occurs among family members'.[37] Notably, the article reads, 'Australia's policy to limit the sexual abuse of children at Woomera Detention Centre ...'.[38] The choice of the verb 'limit' is particularly revealing. Under what circumstances would the verb 'limit' be more appropriate in relation to the act of child abuse than perhaps 'prevent', 'eradicate', or even 'stamp out'? 'Limit' suggests some kind of inevitability, some kind of residual presence, regardless of efforts to remove the practice, as well as an acceptance of a 'relatively small' number of those incidents. This acceptance of a limitation rather than eradication of child abuse is evident in the closing sentence of the article: 'The number of reports of child sex abuse in Woomera was "relatively small", but the government would investigate any fresh allegations, he said'.[39]

The 'but' betrays the government's attitude towards and acceptance of previous reports of child sex abuse. Moreover, child abuse is represented as 'rape' when used in sentences concerning the refugee and the refugee family, 'child sex abuse' in relation to ACM and 'inappropriate behaviour' when discussed by the Minister.

The unresolved nature of the argument in this article operates at two levels. First, it rests on the passive representation of refugees (equated with cargo) that slips into the frame of the inevitability of child abuse (sexual deviancy) aboard refugee boats and among groups of refugees. The passivity of refugee representation envelops the passive act of ('private' realm, insidious, unspoken, unacknowledged, dirty) child abuse. This reaffirms the already steadfast knowledge of refugee deviancy but ratchets it up a notch – refugees somehow collude (however passively) in the abuse of their children. Ironically perhaps, the article advances, albeit reluctantly, the rhetoric of choice while resolutely representing refugees in the passive.

---

37   Ibid.
38   Ibid.
39   Ibid.

Secondly, the absence of the state casts a large shadow over the other agents in the piece. While the Minister for Immigration gets considerable space, he is nonetheless positioned at a distance from the main issue: the child abuse. The deviant act resides with the refugee, the problematic procedures reside with the privatised prison contractor. The article finishes by raising the criminal track record of the private prison company in the US. While crucial to the issue at hand, it keeps the role of the state as a bystander, similar to the reader which is encapsulated by the Minister's comment: ' Their parents have chosen to bring the children and have also, I guess, had some say about whom they will travel with'.[40] The colloquialism, 'I guess', is a tool to position the Minister as part of the general public making common sense assumptions about the decisions strangers make in seeking protection.

In reports of Woomera, the refugee was not only routinely represented as the illegal immigrant, of having inherent illegal status, but also slipped to become primarily defined by detention. While arguing for faster refugee application processing times and questioning the expansion of the immigration detention regime, 'Detainees Appeal for Better Deal'[41] lexically redefines the refugee by their incarceration. Refugees are described as detainees in the headline thus positioning them in and of detention. Never are they referred to as 'refugees' or 'asylum seekers', rather they are 'boat-people' (interestingly, now established as one word rather than two words or hyphenated), 'people whose refugee applications had been refused', 'internees', 'inmates', or 'demonstrators'. Detention defines their status, engulfs them.[42]

'Boatpeople' who 'breach barriers' establish discourses of sovereign incursions as illegal acts and the collocation of 'illegal immigrant' underlines the illegitimacy of detained refugees versus refugees in the community. The article shifts to nominate refugees as 'internees', denoting a political reason for their detention, only to then describe them as 'inmates'. Importantly, they are 'internees' when they riot, a clearly political act. 'Demonstrators' are returned to their 'barracks'. 'Such people' should be 'segregated' and 'depor-ted'. Although the author attempts to argue against the use of immigration detention, notably on the grounds of economic cost,

---

40 Ibid.
41 *Brisbane Courier Mail*, 'Detainees Appeal for Better Deal', 29 August 2000.
42 Ibid.

this argument is swamped by the linguistic power of penal lexica-lisation.

The discourse of common sense is set up through the use of presupposition throughout the article. For example: 'Few people would question the need ...'; 'Most Australians would support a policy where ...' and '[h]owever a great many people are disturbed by the way in which ...'.[43] Presupposition is a potent way to estab-lish common sense; establishment as a matter of 'fact'. The author has used quantifiers 'few', 'most' and 'a great many' to indicate the argument being made is typical and it is not simply his opinion but the opinions of all reasonable people.

Initially these factors appear to present an opportunity for representation to move away from descriptors of basic crimina-lisation and introduce critique of the application of penal politics to refugees. However, upon closer examination the article moves the refugee into an equally troubling penal realm that expands distur-bing representations. The article does not focus on allegations of child abuse, but rather on attempts of refugees to escape detention and protests within immigration detention centres. In so doing, the refugee as criminal is known afresh.

A common tactic in arguments is to use specific examples and generalise from them to illustrate that they are not exceptional but representative. Anti-refugee discourse repeatedly generalises crimi-nal behaviour in ways that portray all refugees as criminal. In this piece, the Minister of Immigration attempts to reverse this trend with a retreat to a softened 'bad apple' type argument. The role of the government and ACM in child abuse is downplayed by the Minister who turns the argument around to attack 'detractors' by saying they should not generalise the illegal behaviour of individual refugees to all refugees: 'One of two specific instances relating to specific individuals ought not to be used as a basis for generalised changes and claims which reflect upon the generality of the people who have been detained'.[44]

This attempt to unwind the general flow of (official) commen-tary that relies on generalising the criminal behaviour of refugees is followed by the Minister's positive self-presentation of those working for the Immigration Department. This is in contrast to

---

43 Ibid.
44 Mallabone, M, (2000), 'Inquiry Ready to Check Child Sex Allegations', *The West Australian*, 28 November.

the preceding negative other presentation of those who criticise them: 'Nor do I think it is reasonable for people who have a view about detention policy and are seeking to unwind it to unnecessarily and inappropriately reflect upon the integrity and the professionalism of officers of the department'.[45]

Round 2: Spectacles of refugee deviancy *par excellence*

Two incidents saw the spectacle of refugee deviancy explode: the MV Tampa and the 'Children Overboard' incident. Both occurred in the lead up to the federal election of 2001. Similar to the spectacles examined in Round 1, I want to examine how the refugee as criminal is produced in moments of spectacle and investigate whether there is space for understandings of state illegality amid the flurry of reporting.

The MV Tampa, a Norwegian vessel, rescued 433 asylum seekers from a sinking boat in the Indian Ocean, approximately 140 kilometres from Christmas Island on the 26 August 2001. The Australian government, after requesting the MV Tampa rescue the asylum seekers, declared that the MV Tampa could not disembark the asylum seekers at Christmas Island. However, the MV Tampa headed for Christmas Island. The Australian government insisted that the MV Tampa stay outside Australian waters, ordered the port at Christmas Island closed and prevented contact between those onboard the MV Tampa and lawyers. On 29 August 2001, Captain Rinnan of the MV Tampa declared his ship in distress – being licensed to carry 50 people it was now unseaworthy and moved into Australian waters. The government sent 45 members of the Special Air Services to take control of the vessel. The Norwegian Ambassador boarded the ship and received a letter from the asylum seekers. On Friday, 31 August 2001, proceedings were commenced by the Victorian Council for Civil Liberties in the Federal Court of Australia against the Commonwealth of Australia, the Minister for Immigration and Multicultural Affairs, the Attorney General and the Minister for Defence (see Chapter 7). Meanwhile, the government was developing what was to become known as the 'Pacific Solution', whereby Nauru and Papua New Guinea would allow the detention of Australia's asylum seekers and the processing of their claims on

---

45   Ibid.

their territory. These arrangements meant that the asylum seekers aboard the MV Tampa and those on other boats interdicted by Australian authorities would not be brought onto Australian land. The government also sought to introduce legislation in the form of the Border Protection Bill that, if passed, would have placed government action outside the rule of law (see Chapter 7 for a detailed discussion). The Bill was defeated in the Senate. The proceedings in the Federal Court were for the writ of habeas corpus. The case was successful in the Federal Court on 11 September 2001, but was defeated upon appeal to the Full Court of the Federal Court (although with a very strong dissenting judgment from Black CJ). The timing of this tragic event was terrible. Within days of the rescue and within hours of the initial Federal Court decision the World Trade Center and the Pentagon were attacked.

MV Tampa

The lexical classification of the refugees on board the Norwegian boat evidences a shift in the categorisation of refugees in media reporting. In 'Refugees Trapped at Sea',[46] refugees are primarily described as 'survivors'. Survivor is of course an empowering word, as opposed to the usual 'victim' designation (similar to situations of violence against women and recourse to 'survivor of domestic violence' rather than 'victim of domestic violence'). Importantly this includes both the crew and passengers from the rescued boat. While 'they' and 'them' still features, as does 'the problem', the refugees are identified by gender, age and nationality, described as 'asylum-seekers' and depicted in relation to a humanitarian reading of their situation: 'in distress', 'people who could need protection', 'sick and starving'.[47]

Refugees, despite what may be described as a largely positive lexical identification, are generally accorded agency only with a negative or aggressive depiction such as 'threatening to jump overboard', being 'aggressive and highly excited' and lacking 'proper documents'. So while lexical identification denotes a shift in this article on the Tampa in relation to broader media coverage of refugee issues, the active refugee remains the deviant refugee.

---

46 Garran, R and Carson, V, (2001), 'Refugees Trapped at Sea', The Australian, 28 August.
47 Ibid.

Refugees and the situation they are in are nominalised into 'the plight of the boat': 'The Prime Minister said Australia was discussing with Indonesia the plight of the boat, but considered it an issue for Jakarta and Norway to resolve' and 'Indonesia was undecided how to respond and was still 'discussing the problem with Australia', said a spokesman for its embassy in Canberra'.[48]

No longer refugees, but a boat and 'the problem'. These nominalisations effectively remove all aspects of agency, process and objects. Not surprisingly, it follows that the discourse of fairness invoked by the Prime Minister, the selective use of international law and the (at best) partial deployment of 'humanitarian help' remains unproblematised.

Returning to a lexical classification, 'Australia Delivers A Message'[49] is at odds with the previous article in its description of the refugees onboard the Tampa. Unlike the previous article, there are no references to the refugees as 'asylum-seekers' or 'refugees' – they are exclusively 'boat people'. The single instance of 'refugee' is in relation to whether assessment would determine if there were any 'genuine refugees' among the boat people. International law is read in a narrow and emaciated form to make the argument that Australia had no international legal obligations to those on board the MV Tampa and that any moral obligation should equally be attributed to Indonesia. The refugees are therefore to be made an example of under deterrence strategies and thus Australia's sovereignty remains intact. Detailed work is required to make such a distorted reading of international legal obligations and the operation of deterrence 'logic' (see the following chapter for a more in-depth discussion). The flawed argumentation remains dependent upon the lexical classification of refugees as illegal and the resort to describing their status as 'boat people'.

The legality of government action is the focus of 'Asylum Strategy Starts to Unravel,'[50] which sets it apart from the majority of reporting on the Tampa spectacle. It regards the government position as part of a strategy, not merely a response to refugees, but a proactive strategy with dubious legality. The failure of the government's strategy is foregrounded and described as being 'in disarray' and 'is a mess'. The author uses various modalising techniques to

---

48   Ibid (my emphasis).
49   *The West Australian*, (2001), 'Australia Delivers a Message', 29 August.
50   *The Age*, (2001), 'Asylum Strategy Starts to Unravel', 12 September.

raise doubt regarding the government's recognition of their actions. For example:

> At the very least, they will *need to* be confident that any policy they decide upon will have a sure foundation in law, and as of yesterday that confidence *must* be lacking.[51]

> It *may* even have been lacking when the cabinet first decided to refuse the Tampa permission to land the asylum seekers on Christmas Island and then sent Special Air Service troops to board the ship. The government quickly introduced into parliament the Borders Protection Bill, which Labor and the minor parties blocked in the Senate. The legislation would, among other things, have retrospectively validated the use of the SAS, which *suggests* the government recognised that it was on dubious legal ground.[52]

> Now it has foreshadowed legislation that *presumably* reflects a similar concern about legality.[53]

The article casts doubt on the motivation of the Prime Minister and Minister of Immigration:

> Prime Minister John Howard and Immigration Minister Philip Ruddock *may* gain some political advantage from this decision *by portraying it as* yet another instance of courts being used to frustrate their aim of preventing people from entering Australia illegally.[54]

The modal auxiliary verb 'may' expresses a degree of possibility or probability, suggesting that the Prime Minister and the Immigration Minister knew there was the possibility of making political gains out of the situation.

In addition, the expression 'portraying it as' could be read as a kind of framing device, in the same way as using 'claim' rather than 'said', to negate the force of the argument of the Prime Minister and Minister and imply that they are presenting an image of something they themselves have constructed. Significantly, the first part of a conditional clause establishes the collocation between humane action and legal action:

---

51   Ibid. My emphasis.
52   Ibid. My emphasis.
53   Ibid. My emphasis.
54   Ibid. My emphasis.

Simply, it is a mess, and it could all have been avoided *if the govern-ment had chosen to act humanely, and within the law,* by allowing the asylum seekers' claims to be processed in Australia.[55]

Children Overboard

On 6 October 2001 the HMAS Adelaide intercepted an Indonesian fishing boat approximately 100 nautical miles north of Christmas Island. On 10 October the 223 passengers onboard the boat were transferred from the custody of HMAS Adelaide to the Australian Federal Police on Christmas Island. A report that a child had been thrown overboard from the fishing boat arose from a conversation between the Commander of the HMAS Adelaide and Brigadier Mike Silverstone on 7 October 2001. The government (notably the Prime Minister, Minister of Defence and Minister for Immigration) seized upon this information and released to the media photographs allegedly showing children thrown overboard. Within days of that release, it was made clear by the navy that no children had been thrown overboard but were in the water because their boat was sinking. The Senate Inquiry convened to investigate the matter found that the government failed to alter the public record when information contravening the initial report came to light and that the Minister of Defence had misled the public. The Senate Inquiry was also highly critical of the bureaucracy that handled the matter, notably the People Smuggling Taskforce and Ministerial advisers. The allegations were made during the 2001 federal election cam-paign. Politicians seized upon the spectre of refugees throwing children overboard to explain the need for border protection and to justify their actions in relation to the MV Tampa specifically and refugees generally. The Children Overboard incident was *the* defini-tional moment that established the government's stand. Government rhetoric was ratcheted up, any lingering overtures to international law ceased and the refugee had proved her ultimate deviance: throwing a child overboard.

The micro-management of the Royal Australian Navy and the over-management of public (mis)information fractured some relations between the government/bureaucracy and the media. Indeed, a group of journalists gave evidence to the Senate Inquiry as to the ramifications of the government's misinformation campaign. The coverage of the Children Overboard incident has also seen some

---

55   Ibid. My emphasis.

enduring linkages between this incident and what has come to be known as the SIEV X and the drowning of 353 asylum seekers on 19 October 2001. Both incidents have seen questions of government illegality raised in the media.

Through much of the reporting of the Children Overboard incident, children are informationally foregrounded – not as refugees or asylum seekers – but as children. In 'Children the Victims in Refugee Exodus'[56] children are constructed as the 'victims' of the 'refugee exodus' more than anyone else.

The only instances of 'refugee' are in the headline and in relation to government policy: 'The Howard Government, with Opposition support, has a refugee policy ...'.[57] Refugees are humanised through their association with family and parenthood and their depiction as children and as humans: 'Surely not, for to believe they would is to demean not only them as humans but to believe they would risk their lives so the strangers who follow in their wake could find it easier'.[58]

The article then tackles head on two aspects of the dominant discourse on refugees: that they are not in need of protection and simply seeking a better life and they are impinging upon Australia's 'generosity'. The only alternative discourse is the inhumanity of Australian refugee policy:

> If these stranded people were simply selfish enough to buy a better life, or rort our immigration system, or in a conspiracy to intimidate Australia, would they would throw their children overboard? Surely not, for to believe they would is to demean not only them as humans but to believe they would risk their lives so the strangers who follow in their wake could find it easier.[59]

> The Howard Government, with Opposition support, has a refugee policy based on treating indecently those it catches in the forlorn hope that this will deter others, most of whom have genuine claims for asylum.[60]

Despite the author's sympathy for this particular group of refugees, we can see in the excerpts above that there is still the suggestion that

---

56 *The Australian*, (2001), 'Children the Victims in Refugee Exodus', 8 October.
57 Ibid.
58 Ibid.
59 Ibid.
60 Ibid.

there are non-genuine refugees. This position retains an investment in the bogus/genuine dichotomy rather than considering everyone has a fundamental human right to seek asylum (even if they are found not to be refugees under international legal obligations). Importantly, however, the article clearly denounces deterrence for its purpose and for the fact that it has not worked. 'in the forlorn hope that this will deter others ...'; and 'Yet deterrence has not worked'.[61]

Notwithstanding the sympathetic tone of the article towards the refugees and an emerging impatience and frustration with refugee policy, the article continued to deploy an 'us' and 'them' polarisation (eg, Australians and 'this lot of refugees'). However, 'they' are not portrayed in negative terms except for one instance in the rhetorical question posed in the second paragraph.

> If these stranded people were simply selfish enough to buy a better life, or rort our immigration system, or in a conspiracy to intimidate Australia, would they would throw their children overboard?[62]

Significantly, there appears to be a degree of polarisation between 'us' (Australians) and the Howard Government/Ruddock (although their remains some slippage as to whether the 'our' is inclusive or exclusive of the government in some parts). For example: 'our immigration system'; 'our policy'; 'our problems'; and 'our decency'.

In foregrounding the discredited photo and its political use, the article '*Photo Sinks Howard's Claim*'[63] continues to depict refugees as children, but notably not as refugees but as 'asylum seekers' and 'boatpeople'. However, they traveled on a refugee boat and there is no mention of 'illegal immigrants'. The article offers a greater ambivalence towards those at the heart of the incident. This article deploys significant overwording of children being thrown overboard despite the article being about the fraudulent claims of the government. For example:

> allegedly showing refugee women and children *thrown into the sea* ...

> the Government claimed asylum seekers ... had *thrown children overboard* ...

---

61 Ibid.
62 Ibid.
63 McPherson, I and Madigan, M, (2001), 'Photo Sinks Howard's Claim', *Brisbane Courier-Mail*, 9 November.

his claim that asylum seekers had not *thrown children into the sea* ...

he stated it did not appear the *children* had been *thrown in* ...[64]

For an article that disputes the veracity of government claims and reports that, in fact, the children were not thrown overboard, variations of 'throw', 'throwing' and 'thrown' are used extensively. The choice and use of 'throwing' keeps the focus on the action of throwing and the disputation of the government is weakened. Official discourses of refugee deviance depend upon appropriate victim designation. In the Children Overboard spectacle, despite evidence of state duplicity and misinformation, the emphasis on the 'throwing' allegation mitigates against refugees being considered victims. At best the Australian public had been deceived but the default state of refugee as deviant remained undisturbed. Coupled with this overwording, a series of framing devices further impairs its criticism of the government. Such framing allows the author to influence the way the reader interprets the discourse, in this case through the use of 'claimed' and 'allegedly' as well as the modalising expressions of 'believed', 'it did not appear' and 'might' adding to the conditionality of the claims. Finally, the article depicts government misinformation as passive and through agent deletion the responsibility of the government for that misinformation is not featured, for example: 'when it was revealed a photo allegedly showing refugee women and children thrown into the sea had been taken after their boat had sunk'.[65]

Even when the government is identified as responsible for misinforming the public, the agency of the refugee in relation to the violence of throwing children overboard overwhelms any sense of government illegality:

> Reith had issued the photograph after a drama at sea an October 7, in which the Government claimed *asylum seekers* (agents) on a refugee boat intercepted by the navy *had thrown children overboard* in an attempt to generate sympathy.[66]

In the article '*Truth Sinking in a Sea of Hyperbole*',[67] a lexical classification indicates that the discourse of refugee deviancy is only ever

---

64 Ibid. My emphasis.
65 Ibid.
66 Ibid. My emphasis.
67 Akerman, P, (2002), 'Truth Sinking in a Sea of Hyperbole', *The Daily Telegraph*, 19 February.

suspended and never overcome. The refugees are illegal and their boat is illegal, for example: 'illegal immigrants'; 'the people smuggler's craft'; 'the illegal craft'; and 'the illegal craft's passengers'.[68]

Refugee deviancy also depends upon the demonisation of refugee advocates specifically, for example: 'present themselves as the defenders of the truth'; 'some of the more hysterical commentators'; and 'members of the commentariat' who conduct 'The witch-hunt'; 'the hyperbolic furore' and 'conspiracies'.[69]

Negative other presentation is established through the allocation of agency and throughout much of the second half of the article refugees are presented as agents of violent/criminal acts.

For example, the following excerpts make an argument that even if 'technically' a child was not thrown overboard as initially reported, there was still enough refugee criminality going on to suffice the demonisation of those onboard as capable of throwing children overboard:

> But the chronological narrative then notes that a number of the illegal craft's passengers then *'threatened to commit suicide* and *throw children overboard* unless taken to Australia' and that there was a disturbance aboard their vessel during which *its navigational equipment was destroyed* and *an aerial ripped off and jettisoned*.[70]

> A number of illegal immigrants then began jumping into the ocean while others continued to *destroy their ship's upper deck fittings*.[71]

The positive self-presentation of the Royal Australian Navy is established through the various actions they took in response to the deviant actions of the refugees:

> The warning was ignored, as was a note sent to the illegal craft early on Sunday which was followed by four 5.56mm warning shots, another notice and a burst of .50 calibre fired into the water.[72]

Such positive self-presentation is maintained through the designation of the RAN in the passive with agency deleted: 'a note was sent to the illegal craft', 'the note was followed by shots', 'another notice

---

68   Ibid.
69   Ibid.
70   Ibid. My emphasis.
71   Ibid. My emphasis.
72   Ibid.

was sent', 'a burst of .50 caliber was fired'.[73] The passives avoid negative self-presentation in aggressive/ugly actions on the part of the Navy/government who are deleted as the agents of these actions.

Conclusion

The moment of the refugee spectacle was increasingly accompanied by more critical (read sympathetic) reporting of refugees and more critical questioning of state practices. Journalists banded together to denounce the misinformation of government and the small 'l' liberal came to the fore in the name of human dignity, compassion and decency. But the detail of words, the structure of sentences, the location of passive and active voices betrays the role that such critical reporting plays in moments of crisis. It is not simply the mundane hum of refugee deviancy, nor is it in the conservative or racist corners of the press that drives the refugee as criminal spectacle. Critical reporting also reproduces the spectacle – eternally preparing fertile ground for the next great refugee (as criminal) scene.

From this analysis the spectacle of refugee deviance has been affirmed but increasingly the possibility of state deviance has been raised. Not that state deviance then cancels the falsely constructed deviance of refugees. Indeed, in some ways it further amplifies the identification of refugees with practices of illegality and deviance. The press has been one of the mediating realms by which the public has spectated the refugee and through which the state has sought to legitimise its actions. It is through the spectacle that state crime can be recognised in a way that it is not within the everyday reporting of refugee issues. In some ways it is the spectacle of the refugee as criminal that may provide a moment of judgment (or at least acknowledgement) in which the insistence of the refugee as criminal becomes evidence in the construction of the state as criminal. The refugee spectacle is a moment whereby everyday people are drawn into the extraordinary world of forced migration and the legitimate/ illegitimate expression of state. However, I do not wish to overstate the case. Across the incidents covered, the spectacle, to a greater or lesser extent, dissolved the deviancy of the state. But the more recent moments of spectacle provide some limited evidence that the spectacle of state illegality may increasingly capture some part of a sustained media imagination.

---

73   Ibid.

This chapter has been mostly concerned with the language rules that amplify refugee deviance and obfuscate state illegality, coercion and violence: how discourses of rights have been neutralised and territorial sovereignty valorised. Both Arendt and Cohen have argued that language rules have ensured that the violent intent of the state is brutally clear while simultaneously launching instructions on how to disguise its reality with lies, concealment and euphemism.[74] This chapter has examined how the most basic language rules (in the form of grammar and sentence structure, lexical classification, the designation of agency and the like) have obfuscated the role of the state and left the spectacle of the refugee as a spectacle of refugee criminality.

Most of all the spectacle of the refugee as criminal concerns the performativity of the state and its stasis. As Said has noted in relation to Kifner, hidden comparisons between 'Islam' and the West are made without danger of appearing wrong or absurd.[75] The hidden comparisons between the culpability and illegality of the state and the normality of the refugee, at best, inhabit the default position of the 'absurd'. The crude and essentialised caricatures of refugees exist in the detail of language which ensures the ongoing vulnerability of refugees to state retaliation and the (increasingly) proactive authoritarian state. It is also the default position from which state criminality becomes the exceptional rather the ordinary condition of the liberal democracy.

Capital has made new claims on nation-states. These claims guarantee the domestic and global rights of capital. The nation-state has responded to these claims with the production of new forms of *legality*. However, when the individual outsider has made rights claims on the nation-state the state has responded with new forms of *illegality*. The ascendance of this regime of illegality depends on a series of practices that propels forward the refugee as spectacle and places the refugee subordinate to interests of capital and free flowing information. My argument in this chapter has been that a series of intricate language practices obfuscate this subordination of the person in need. At best these language practices in moments of spectacle shepherd through market-centred regulation of capital and rebuff human rights to insist upon state-centred migration control

---

74 See p 80 of Cohen, S, (2000), *States of Denial*, London: Polity, for further discussion.

75 Said, E, (1979) *Orientalism* New York: Pantheon Books p 177.

under which the refugee disappears. At worst, these language practices not only veil but become a constituent part of state violence. The conferral of respectability on government action/inaction, the sanitisation and use of palliative terms, according to Cohen, acts to deny or misrepresent harm. The spectacle of the refugee as criminal by and large is the product of the anaesthetising function of political language in the placement and structure of words. While the anaesthetic may be wearing off in some parts, the spectacle of the state as criminal lays beneath the ongoing paralysis.

Chapter 4

Deterring refugees

Despite recent compassionate inflections, deterrence is the discourse upon which current refugee policy rests. It is the legitimising framework for immigration detention, temporary protection visas, the 'Pacific Solution' and all other aspects of border protection. It is a normalising discourse. It attempts to normalise practices that if carried out against ordinary citizens would be considered not only immoral or unjust but also illegal. The purpose of this chapter is to examine the normalising discourse of refugee deterrence. This chapter does not attempt to 'discover' or 'reveal' the *real* truth of practices that hide behind the deterrent discourse, but rather to argue without such discourses certain practices could not exist. Systematic state violence cannot be sustained without normalising discourses, therefore to take apart deterrence equally takes apart the violence the state inflicts upon refugees, as well as upon the body politic. Deterrence is primarily about race and more particularly has come to be about those of Middle Eastern origin and Muslim faith. When deterrence is the narrative, it is almost always the Muslim Arab that is the contemporary focus. Race inflects all elements of deterrence because it is only particular races that have been forced onto boats to seek onshore asylum in Australia. The boats that arrived from the late 1990s were largely full with Iraqis, Afghans and Iranians and deterrence policy was, and continues to be, aimed exclusively at them.

Towards deterrence

How has deterrence been established in refugee policy in the Global North generally and Australia specifically? Deterrence has appeared in various facets of immigration legislation and practice mostly across Europe and the US, however only Australia has explicitly made refugee deterrence a pre-eminent and high profile legislative, policy and media issue.

Deterrence in refugee policy has been an overtly simple, if a somewhat slippery, rationale. This is especially the case in recent times when the hard line of refugee repulsions has been questioned from within government circles, particularly government representatives of rural and regional seats where refugees are an important labour source. Deterrence logic has it that refugees can and should be deterred from seeking protection onshore and this requires nations to undertake unilateral and bilateral action that makes a country a 'less desirable destination'. It is premised on the presumption that nations, particularly developed nations, can effectively control aspects of global migration which have the consequence of refugees seeking protection at the borders of the developed world. Nations, usually through militarisation, unilateral action and bilateral agreements with poorer nations, can stop people seeking protection, or at the very least treat them differentially if they seek protection onshore. There is no doubt that such an approach is in breach of the spirit and letter of the Refugee Convention Article 31 which imposes an obligation against deterring refugees from seeking protection:

> The Contracting States shall not impose penalties, on account of their illegal entry or presence, on refugees who, coming directly from a territory where their life or freedom was threatened in the sense of article 1, enter or are present in their territory without authorisation, provided they present themselves without delay to the authorities and show good cause for their illegal entry or presence.

Article 31 actually uses the word 'illegal' itself and thus does not suggest that crossing borders without authority is simply legal, but that in seeking refugee protection any illegality should be trumped by them showing 'good cause' for their entry.[1]

Underlying deterrence has been the rhetoric that the humanitarian core of refugee protection is preserved and indeed strengthened by practices that can now effectively determine the 'genuine' from the 'bogus' refugee. In many ways, deterrence has been positioned as the bridge that will take international refugee protection into a new era. While some have characterised deterrence developments as the tension between push and pull factors, others have pointed to the impact of constituencies and anti-immigrant feeling as being the driving force in moves towards deterrence. Too often, however, the debate appears to rest upon whether we believe the nation-state can effectively influence global migration or

---

1   I am grateful to conversations with Michael Gard on this point.

whether conditions in sending countries can be the only causal factors of refugee flows. Some have argued that individual nations cannot control the mass movement of people and at best deterrence measures will simply displace the issue to poorer transit nations (who already bear the brunt of forced migration). Others have suggested that legislative reform can impact on the number of asylum applications, that the human rights framework that has governed refugee protection has overly compromised the sovereignty of the nation-state, and that the increasing mobility of peoples and realisation of positive 'welfare outcomes' in the developed world is the true driver of refugee movement.

Not surprisingly, the limited research suggests a more subtle set of issues at work. Most studies argue that nation-states are 'not prisoners of the internationalisation of migration' and that 'even the most restrictive measures [do] not influence refugee inflows from certain states'.[2] More importantly, studies generally agree that the impact of deterrence measures differs across sender countries, and that the unilateral measures that usually govern deterrence dramatically 'undermine the liberal international asylum regime'.[3] In the most comprehensive study of the effects of legislative deterrence in Switzerland it was found that in abandoning the liberal refugee regime of the post World War II era, small industrialised countries like Switzerland can only influence the flow of refugees some of the time and that deterrence measures are useless if the refugee-producing conditions in nearby regions reach a critical level. Interestingly, they also note that the rise of deterrence has been accompanied by the development of temporary protection and a move away from the individual treatment of asylum cases. Most importantly they concluded:

> The analysis also demonstrates that governments have been successfully controlling the number of asylum applications through their manipulation of the relative number of recognised refugees. The interrelationship between recognition rates and the number of asylum seekers is objectionable insofar as it contradicts the right of an individual to receive a fair treatment of an asylum application irrespective of the general asylum situation. ... [W]ith regard to future legislative measures, that the trade off between international

---

2   Holzer, T, Schneider, G, and Widmer, T (2000) 'The impact of legislative deterrence measures on the number of asylum applications in Switzerland (1986-1995)', 43(4) *IMR* 1182.

3   Ibid, p 1184.

commitments and unilateral measures is one of the crucial conflicts in the asylum policy of western European states.[4]

There are three main concerns that emerge from this literature. First, the duality of push/pull factors rarely captures the complexity of forced migration and responses to it and 'push' or 'pull' cannot solely justify deterrence. Secondly, unilateral deterrence measures systematically undermine international systems of refugee protection. Thirdly, there has been relatively little focus upon the conditions underpinning the development of deterrence in refugee policy in developed countries. It is this last point that this chapter takes up. The concern of this chapter is not whether deterrence itself is achievable or effective (both of which are arguably immeasurable and unknowable) than with the manner in which deterrence is enthused and sustained in the domestic context.

Narratives of deterrence

Deterrence as a normalising discourse depends on a series of familiar and convincing narratives. These narratives are not necessarily ordered, and certainly they do not conform to any straightforward rational system. However, they are punctuated by the ideologies of the new right, neo-liberalism, deviancy and the sovereign nation-state. Most of all they rest on implicit racial knowledges. This examination of the narratives of deterrence precedes discussion of the sites where deterrence most notably takes place.

Narratives of the bordered state

Australia is a sovereign nation. We have the legal and moral right to protect our borders and coastal waters. ... If we do not demonstrate that we will defend our coastal waters from illegal intruders, we will not be respected in the region ... We will continue to be at the mercy of illegal entrants who exploit our vulnerability ... [5]

The importance of a managed outcome is critical and is brought sharply into focus when we look at the way in which migration issues are managed – or more properly – mismanaged around the world ... Border control and the management of people movements.

As well as our determination to safeguard the integrity of our Immigration program, we are also determined to safeguard the

---

4   Ibid, pp 1205-6.
5   Aldred, Liberal Party, Migration Legislation Amendment Bill (No 4), 8 March 1995, House Hansard, p1845.

integrity of the nation's borders and to protect the Australian public from the entry of people who have serious criminal backgrounds.[6]

Deterrence, by necessity, rests on narratives of a closed, fixed state against which deviations may be recognised and repelled. Once this fixed state is recognised there is indeed a range of forms deterrence may take – from the more gentle 'discourage' to the harshness of repulsion. Ultimately, deterrence seeks to reinforce the narrative of the homogenous bordered state. It is a narrative because it largely exists within the spoken and written word as the feel, the look, the touch of the homogenous, bordered state is sometimes difficult to find – unless of course you look for the marks now drawn upon the raced body of the refugee, for that body is now the only canvas onto which narratives of the homogenous, bordered state can be fixed.

The alleged reassurance of the contained, controlled nation-state is the fiction of states seeking to reassure their role in a rapidly changing order of transnational organisation. But it is as much about organisational concerns as it is about the kinds of identity politics at work when the nation-state confronts the potential of difference and the importance of borders in human communities. And it is the clashing cultural, racial, political and territorial boundaries that govern discussions on refugees. While this clashing is uncertain and highly unpredictable, it is represented as a stable state of being that reaffirms the need for stable territorial borders. The crisis of racial, cultural and legal borders remain afterthoughts to the 'integrity' of the immigration system and the 'integrity' of the nation. The bounded nation-state, and the identities therein, is what is in crisis:

> The principle is that everyone who resides permanently in the terri-
> tory should share a common national identity, and that this identity
> should override other characteristics that might cause social boun-
> daries to be drawn differently, whether within the state or between
> states. So nationality is to take precedence ... [7]

There is a contradiction at the heart of such understandings – that the external border must be upheld to prevent borders/fractures from appearing internally. There is a crisis in Australia in as much as the territorial nation-state does not map onto the cultural, racial,

---

6   Ruddock, Philip, (1998), *Australia's Immigration Policies – An Inter-
     national Perspective*, Address, Victorian Press Club, 26 March.
7   Miller, D and Hashmi, S (2001), 'Introduction', in D Miller and
     S Hashmi (eds) *Boundaries and Justice: diverse ethical perspectives*,
     Princeton: Princeton University Press.

political or legal nation-state. Or perhaps even, as Bigo has described we are coming to the 'limits of our political imagination'.[8] It is a crisis because mapping the social onto the territorial has been a distinctive feature of the modern state: converging social and territorial boundaries.[9] Now deterrence is the method mobilised to force this convergence long after its potential has dissipated and is now only possible through a reliance on a coercive border imagination.

A border imagination is in large part what sustains discourses of inclusion and exclusion, order and disorder, protection and attack, definition and division.[10] McCorquodale quotes Oppenheim's International Law when he eloquently argues for a radical reconfiguration of sovereignty:

> Boundaries of State territory are the imaginary lines on the surface of the earth which separate the territory of one State from that of another, or from unappropriated territory, or from the Open Sea.

McCorquodale goes on to argue that these lines are not simply imaginary: 'they are invented and created by the international legal system'. The imagined lines upon the surface of the earth and the open sea may have been invented by international law, but they are believed, in relation to the movement of peoples, like a dogma by domestic regimes. Such fervent belief in the border as a marker of territory is necessary for states to be able to recognise themselves. The belief is repeated over and over, like a mantra, in discourses of deterrence. We are witnessing a highly complex area of thought, sovereignty, being reduced to its most crude bordered form.

The popularly-used definition of sovereignty as a territorial matter in refugee debate reaffirms the centrality and power of the homogenous state, diminishes alternate voices and holds on tight as globalisation rushes around it. The bordered territorial state is able to define and redefine those within it and marshal forces against those outside, or those considered internal enemies. By their very mobility and statelessness, refugees are always in breach of both territorial and identity borders and the recreation of borders upon

---

8   Bigo, D, (2001), 'The Möbius Ribbon of Internal and External Security(ies)' in M Albert, D Jacobson and Y Lapid (eds), *Identities, borders, orders: rethinking international relations theory*. Minneapolis: University of Minnesota Press.

9   Miller and Hashmi, op cit, p 5.

10   McCorqudale, R, (2001), 'International Law, Boundaries and Immigration' in D Miller and S Hashmi (eds), op cit, p 137.

their very presence has been a socially and culturally reaffirming practice for those who seek to exclude. By their presence the refugee creates a moment to fight, to reaffirm, and to recapture what shared identity is meant to mean to a people apparently under threat. The nation becomes convinced of its own victimisation when its every action is one of aggressor. But of course it is not the dispossessed refugee that is considered vulnerable, rather it is the robust bordered state. At the very moment territorial borders reinforce the strength of the sovereign state they also contribute to narratives of the vulnerable (but wealthy) state. Refugees become a matter of national and international security and states must deter insecurity. Deterrence brings together a simultaneous recognition (and contradiction) that a robust and strong state must be defended, but that same state is still inherently vulnerable to the transgression of borders that fracture identity and belonging. Deterrence promotes the primacy of the bordered state over the individuals who seek to enter or the individuals that seek to dissent. We are seeing narratives of sovereignty being collapsed and folded to fit ad hoc notions of deterrence as states confront the limits of their border imaginings.

Seeking to exclude, keep out, refuse entry, and deny those that seek protection from the bounded nation marks a return to a most crude form of control at the very moment sovereignty is shifting from what Pangalangan describes as the territorial to the decisional.

> 'Modern' international law actually emerged from an earlier shift in the concept of sovereignty from the decisional to the territorial, from command over people's allegiances, to title over land. Today we are completing that cycle, as we recognise that control over *territory* has served merely as the doctrinal proxy for control over *resources* – natural, economic or strategic- and correspondingly, that while susceptible of more sophisticated modes of control, generally decisional in character, and thus more easily subject to overlapping claims by non-state groups and to communal regulation by a putative international community.[11]

If sovereignty, under this interpretation, is to be seen as moving from a source of power to a basis of responsibility, we can think of deterrence as a bridge between the security of the spatial in territorial sovereignty and deterrence as a means to stave off (pan national) decisional sovereignty. The spatial element inherent in

---

11   Pangalangan, R, (2002) 'Territorial Sovereignty: Command, Title, and Expanding claims of the commons' in D Miller and S Hashmi, (eds), op cit, pp 137, 164.

territorial sovereignty also remains principally connected to the use of force and the re-emergence of jurisdictional exclusivity. When deterrence is deployed on the basis of the homogenous bordered state, it is played out as a dogma, it is fought in connection to a notion of territory but grounded in fractured and wounded identities, it is all about insecurity at the very moment it defines existing security.

The most disturbing aspect of deterrence, however, does not just take us to the edges of border imaginings or the crude use of force to hang onto the spatial that is inherent in territorial expressions of sovereignty. The narrative of the homogenous state stifles collectivities within and across states, and most of all deters 'people from reaching out and finding common cause (eg, human rights) with others beyond national borders'.[12] When we rely on the narratives of the bordered nation to support ideas of deterrence, understanding and commonalities across borders are diminished.

Narratives of deviancy and choice

Narratives of deviance reinforce the legality and necessity of the responses of the homogenous bordered state. That response has largely been deterrence. As the original illegality resides with the asylum seeker, there is an obvious need to repel such deviance that in turn re-affirms the legitimacy of state responses. Deterrence becomes part of the techno-legal and bureaucratic response of control. When we deter asylum seekers, we are in control. Deterrence represents a way of responding to refugees that is orderly and has integrity, both of which assume that controlling the movement of persecuted people is both possible and desirable. Importantly, deterrence does not simply rest on narratives of deviancy and control but also discourses of choice and individual responsibility.

The press has routinely constructed refugees and asylum seekers not only as a 'problem' but as a deviant problem (see Chapters 2 and 3). Deviancy has been constructed through the deployment of legality and illegality in relation to the very presence of the asylum seeker. *Non-citizens* become *illegal entrants*. *Illegal entrants* in turn become *illegals*. *Illegals* in turn become *parasites* and burdens upon the health and legal systems. Very quickly a vocabulary of deviance becomes interchangeable with the notion of the queue jumper. The *queue jumper* is understood as an individual who

---

12   Ibid, p 164.

makes a choice to subvert appropriate procedures and hence col-ludes in their own illegality. Similar to law and order accounts of street crime, in which individuals must be deterred from making bad choices to offend, deterrence in refugee policy rests upon the common vocabulary of choice. In having a choice, asylum seekers should choose to be part of the offshore program, they should choose not to jump the queue and invoke onshore protection obligations. In their 'choice', it is as if the asylum seeker is able to opt for one side of the deviance binary such a vocabulary allows: they can be genuine or bogus, decent or dangerous, parasites or in need. The *choice* is *theirs*. With such a discursive repertoire at hand, shifting talk of deterrence to the bureaucratic and sanitised 'forum shoppers' seeking 'migration outcomes' seems an almost liberal reading:

> The people arriving on the boats are seeking to migrate to Australia as their destination of choice. There is increasing public sentiment that we should detect them and send them packing. The fact is, however, that many of these people are refugees. This means that we must carefully assess their claims and honour our obligations to those who are refugees. But many of these refugees have left coun-tries where they already have effective protection. They are seeking to choose their country of protection; they are forum shoppers seeking a migration outcome. The minister has now announced further measures to deal with this aspect: measures to reduce the perception by those people that Australia is both a highly attractive destination as well as a soft touch.[13]

Narratives of deviancy ensure that refugees are not fleeing persecution but are making decisions about lifestyle or different kinds of migration outcomes. They must be deterred from making decisions that involve travel to Australia. The structural issues that underpin forced migration do not, and indeed cannot, be engaged with. Individual responsibility becomes the only focus. Responsi-bility, or even understanding, of refugee producing states or refugee receiving states cannot fit within this narrative. Indeed, deterrence narratives of deviancy and choice ensure that the state fades from view, as if forced migration is a matter for individuals.

Deterrence in refugee policy centres on the construction of the refugee making a series of choices to come to Australia. The idea of

---

13 Chair, Legal and Constitutional References Committee: Operation of Australia's Refugee and Humanitarian program: Discussion, 22 November 1999, Canberra, Senate Hansard, p 777.

choice means the responsibility for refugee flight is located with the refugee. Narratives of deviancy and choice become even more familiar when they are coupled with narratives of punishment. This is the moment where the most familiar, the most commonsensical, stories about refugees are told. Deterrence is a narrative of punishment from deep within the criminal justice system: a system, unlike the system for international refugee protection, which ordinary people have a basic understanding of and connection to.

Narratives of punishment

Narratives of punishment in the criminal justice system underpin the familiarity of deterrence when used in relation to refugee policy. Deterrence is a key component of sentencing legislation throughout Australian State jurisdictions. In this sense deterrence is often considered necessary 'to deter the offender or other person from committing offences of the same or a similar character ...' (s 1A, *Sentencing Act* 1991 (Vic)). The rationale for this aspect of the sentencing smorgasbord[14] has been understood also in terms of a dessert or denunciation which broadly understands deterrence in terms of rationality or choice:

> In many cases before the courts, the offence may be motivated by malice, greed, thoughtlessness, stupidity or momentary anger, but may not be the product of some underlying psychological, psychiatric, social or other pathology. In these cases, the appropriate response is proportionate punitive response which addresses the retributive, deterrent and denunciatory aspect of punishment.[15]

Within such an understanding, the duality of rationality and irrationality is reinforced. Offending is a rational activity and the state must respond rationally to deter the offender and others from such acts. Criminologists have long been interested in the rationales for sentencing and punishing offenders. Notably they have made a range of contributions about the scope, nature and workability of deterrence in the criminal justice system. The most recent review of sentencing legislation in Australia contends that the sentencing system cannot, by itself, reduce crime and increase community

---

14 Noting that deterrence is but one of the rationales for sentencing along with rehabilitation, incapacitation, retribution, denunciation.
15 Frieberg, A, (2002), *Pathways to Justice: Sentencing Review 2002*, Victoria: Department of Justice, p 34.

safety.[16] Deterrence is considered but one component of the sentencing framework, a component overshadowed by concerns for proportionality and parsimony. In order to promote sentencing transparency and improve deterrence the proposal to develop guideline judgments for the judiciary was recently put forward in the State of Victoria. However, it was rejected because it limits the discretion of the judiciary to individually tailor sentences to individual offenders and in acknowledgment of the fact that offenders do not fall into neat categories.[17] Moreover, studies in a range of jurisdictions have found that deterrence does not have clear or measurable results. The rate of crime is seemingly unrelated to rates of imprisonment. The clearest examples of this are studies that have consistently found that the operation of the death penalty does not deter the most serious crimes. Nonetheless, deterrence has become one sentencing component over which public concern has been paramount. More so than rehabilitation, and alongside incapacitation, deterrence has been the focus of media and broad public criticism of so called lenient sentencing by the judiciary. Research has found that the public has a high expectation of the sentencing process, especially in terms of deterrence and that public confidence is best addressed by improving the public's knowledge of the system and making the process more transparent:

> Research into public opinion and sentencing consistently finds that the more information that is provided to respondents the less punitive are their responses, especially when the polling takes the form of sentencing vignettes or simulated sentencing exercises.[18]

In short, criminologists have challenged and critiqued the notion of deterrence as it operates within the criminal justice system. Seriously questioning its workability, criminologists have offered complex arguments for its ongoing but diminished inclusion in a principled criminal justice system. In so doing, they have helped to prepare the ground for the critique of law and order upon which deterrence as a principle is popularly sustained. Deterrence within refugee policy is only just being opened up to a similar critique to counter its deployment as an unquestioned frame for state responses to refugees.

---

16   Ibid.
17   Ibid.
18   Ibid, p 42.

Where the narratives are told: Sites of deterrence

> I applaud the government on the recent advertising and the harsher measures taken to ensure that illegal boat people do not come to Australia or that they are deterred in the strongest possible way ... These changes send a message to other people considering illegal travel to Australia that we are certainly not a soft touch, and that queue jumpers will be dealt with very harshly indeed.[19]

In as much as deterrence relies on a series of familiar and convincing narratives, it also operates across a series of key sites. While discourses of deterrence rest on very familiar and comforting notions, the sites upon which deterrence is played out are not familiar and can only exist if we refuse to imagine what daily realities they involve. Sites of deterrence are isolated, they are at sea, they are within communities that are not passed through, they are within communities of other nations. Narratives of deterrence may be very familiar but the sites of deterrence are isolated and apart from community imaginings.

Site 1 – Immigration Detention: Creating the intra-territorial frontier I

> This will provide a disincentive for people to put their lives at risk by boarding unseaworthy boats to come to Australia.[20]

Legislation has provided for forms of immigration detention since before Federation in 1901. Before 1992, legislation outlined two main reasons for detention, embodied in the *Migration Act* 1958 (Cth) and *Immigration (Unauthorised Arrivals) Act* 1980 (Cth), both of which were concerned with the means of arrival. First, a prescribed authority could order the detention of a prohibited immigrant for up to seven days with the possibility of extension. Secondly, passengers who arrived without authorisation needed to be brought before a prescribed authority within 48 hours of arrest.[21] After 1992 this changed radically. The *Migration Reform Act* 1992 (Cth), effective

---

19   Gambaro, Liberal Party, Migration Legislation Amendment Bill (No 2) 1999, 6 March 2000, House Hansard, p 13993.
20   *Minister Ruddock's comments regarding the building of a permanent immigration facility on Christmas Island* Minister, Press Release, Permanent Immigration Facility for Christmas Island, 12 March 2002.
21   Adrienne Millbank, (2001), *The Detention of Boat People*, Department of the Parliamentary Library, 8 *Current Issues Brief* 2000-2001.

from September 1994, categorised those arriving in Australia as either lawful or unlawful non-citizens and introduced mandatory detention for unauthorised non-citizens. Mandatory detention can also apply to visa overstayers as well as unauthorised arrivals. In practice, however, overstayers seeking refugee status are usually given a bridging visa. In 1997 the operation of immigration detention centres were contracted out to Australasian Correctional Management, 'to improve service delivery and to test value for money, the operation of detention facilities …'.[22] In October 1999 a range of measures were introduced that legislated for temporary protection, broadened a range of powers for Customs officers to board and detain boats, to restrict access to the courts for refugee applicants, and in 2001 legislation was introduced which gave greater powers to authorities in immigration detention centres. The Migration Legislation Amendment (Immigration Detainees) Bill 2001 increased punishment for escaping from a detention centre, introduced new offences relating to the possession and manufacture of home-made weapons, and allowed strip searches. Since major initiatives introduced in June 1999, refugee policy has allegedly focused on the factors that 'encourage those who select Australia as a target'.

The battle over the meaning and purpose of mandatory immigration detention can be traced to its introduction in 1994 and parliament's continual struggle in understanding, justifying and challenging the practice. Its introduction was underpinned by a determination to deal with what had already been constructed as the deviant choices of refugees:

> The purpose of the Migration Legislation Amendment Bill (No 4) is to ensure that Australia's onshore refugee determination system is not open to the abuse of forum shopping by asylum seekers …. [23]

However, the very legality of deterrence was repeatedly brought into question by Independent senators, while government and opposition members worked tirelessly to keep questions of illegality and injustice pointed at the individual refugee they were seeking to deter:

---

22 Border Protection, Unauthorised Arrivals and Detention – Information paper, February 2002, <www.minister.immi.gov.au/borders/detention/2002paper_2.htm>, accessed 5 September 2002.
23 Crosio, Australian Labor Party, Migration Legislation Amendment Bill (No 4) 1994: Second Reading, 8 November 1994, House Hansard, p 2830.

It may be that the Government wants to set an example – this seems to be the underlying assumption – so as to deter others from entering Australia in this way. But how can we, in all conscience, accept this? In the criminal system, the principle of general deterrence ... violates justice. ... Much more so is it an offence against justice when no offence has been committed and people have simply sought refuge on our shores. Detention in this situation for people who are being processed for refugee application status is a crime against humanity.[24]

[W]e are not talking about protecting the rights of those who arrived here illegally – and we are not distinguishing between citizens and non-citizens: we are distinguishing between those who come to Australia legally and those who come to Australia illegally. We are protecting those who, in many cases, probably are not even in this country and who under our processes have been rejected as refugees. We are doing so in a way that does not allow this government to act in accordance with international law. That is the advice we have had. What we are doing is in accordance with international law; we are doing it in accordance with the principles governing our constitution. Why is that the case? Because we are overcoming a technicality.[25]

In response, Senator Chamarette[26] noted:

Senator McKiernan said that this – and I assume he is referring to the policy of detaining the boat people – had not deterred the boat people who continued to lodge applications on legal technicalities while the Government had paid for expensive legal defences. ... This is an extraordinary admission from the senator who, as chair of the Joint Standing committee on migration, insisted that the detention policy must be upheld even though no evidence was provided to the committee to suggest that detention deters anybody from coming. Indeed, the arrival earlier this year of a group which had already been in detention in Australia once, had been deported and decided to risk the journey again, shows how pathetic a justification of deterrence is. It is quite apart from the fact that deterrence is not a just principle upon which to act.

Even while numbers in IDCs stabilises and even decrease, for many Australians immigration detention represents a loss of compassion.

---

24 Chamarette, Independent, Migration Laws Amendment Package 1992:
    Second Reading, 7 December 1992, Senate Hansard, p 4304
25 Bolkus, Australian Labor Party, Migration Legislation Amendment Bill,
    (No 3) 1994, 9 November 1994, Senate Hansard, p 2716.
26 Australian Democrats.

For others it is a necessary evil, for others a shining jewel in the exertion of 'immigration control'. The immigration debate, as it has largely played out in the press, but also in the parliament, and across a range of government and NGO sectors, has often missed the subtlety of immigration detention for the competing purposes of deterrence. In attempting to peel back the layers of deterrence rhetoric that make illegal state practices acceptable, I suggest immigration detention may have garnered exceptional levels of attention (particularly in the last few years) but is still poorly conceptualised. It is my purpose here to locate immigration detention as a site of deterrence through its contradictory rationales and explanations or what I will refer to as the *competing irrationalities* of immigration detention as deterrence. In some ways this is an attempt to bring good order to the irrational, but it is also to point to the ways immigration detention has developed meanings well beyond notions of incarceration and processing. The preamble to a recent report by the envoy of the Human Rights High Commissioner on immigration detention in Australia, and the response to it by the Immigration Minister, provide an interesting starting point for this examination.

The preamble stated:

> Justice Bhagwati was considerably distressed by what he saw and heard in Woomera IRPC. He met men, women and children who had been in detention for several months, some of them even for one or two years. They were prisoners without having committed any offence. Their only fault was that they had left their native home and sought to find refuge or a better life on the Australian soil. In virtual prison-like conditions in the detention centre, they lived initially in the hope that soon their incarceration will come to an end but with the passage of time, the hope gave way to despair. When Justice Bhagwati met the detainees, some of them broke down. He could see despair on their faces. *He felt that he was in front of a great human tragedy.* He saw young boys and girls, who instead of breathing the fresh air of freedom, were confined behind spike iron bars with gates barred and locked preventing them from going out and playing and running in the open fields. He saw gloom on their faces instead of the joy of youth. These children were growing up in an environment, which affected their physical and mental growth and many of them were traumatized and left to harm themselves in utter despair.[27]

---

27 Report of Justice PN Bhagwati, Regional Advisor for Asia and the Pacific of the United Nations High Commissioner for Human Rights, Mission to Australia 24 May to 2 June 2002. My emphasis.

The response from the Minister was:

> The report of the UN High Commissioner for Human Rights into immigration detention is fundamentally flawed. It misconceives the Government's policy and ignores the fact that people in immigration detention have arrived in the country illegally. Almost all have passed through countries in which they could have sought protection en route to Australia.[28]

The Minister's response went on to say:

> They have had access to due process in Australia and many have exhausted the avenues available to them and have been found not to be in need of protection. They are free to leave immigration detention and return home at any time ... It is quite clear under international law that the process of detaining unauthorised arrivals is consistent with those human rights obligations. Immigration detention is an essential element underpinning the integrity of Australia's migration program and the protection of our borders. The policies reflect Australia's right under international law to determine who will enter our borders and be permitted to remain, and the conditions under which they may be removed.

Minister Ruddock was correct when he stated that the report misconceives the government's policy. The misconception occurs because different frames are being applied to the one deterrence landscape. One frame, largely utilised by the UN and by many refugee groups, is the frame of international law and human rights. The second frame is that of border protection. Both rest on assigning the legal and the illegal: but one focuses on state illegalities while the other focuses on the illegalities of the individual non-citizen, or the individual abuse of powers by an ACM officer. As the admittance and exclusion of non-citizens has always been at the heart of the powers of a sovereign state, it is not surprising the operation of those powers in relation to immigration detention that consideration of illegal government action has not been forthcoming. Moreover, the government works actively to dismiss and diminish such claims. The frame of border protection and the issue of immigration detention, rooted in a law and order genre, does not depend upon the legal rationality of the human rights frame, and in fact is its antithesis, thriving on the inconsistencies of invoking a protection

---

28 Minister, Press Release, *Government Rejects the Report of the UN Human Rights Commissioner's Envoy into Human Rights and Immigration Detention*, 31 July 2002.

system that promotes the moral virtues of the offshore program and extols the deviance of those seeking onshore protection. Indeed, deterrence depends upon the irrationalities of this system. For example, asylum seekers are considered illegal under the domestic regime even though under the international refugee regime the means of arrival and a lack of documentation should not be considered against an asylum seeker. Another example is a reliance on rhetoric of choice of destination negating the need for protection when refugees transit countries on the way to Australia regardless as to whether those countries have signed the Refugee Convention. Immigration detention is most convincing in relation to its connection with the protection of borders and expressions of sovereignty. It is here that the inconsistencies of deterrence become more complex.

The crisis in utilising human rights in relation to immigration detention is the difficulty of mobilising a rights discourse in Australia specifically, and a rights discourse in relation to refugees generally. Deterrence works against a rights framework. It centrally locates sovereign rights which act as what Dauvergne calls 'trump rights'.[29] Neither substantive nor procedural rights can outdo the discursive pre-eminence of sovereign rights. To subordinate sovereign rights, that are at the heart of border protection and in turn immigration detention, is to subordinate the nation to the individual, a wholly unpalatable situation in the contemporary context. The exertion of sovereign power embodied in immigration detention cannot be undermined by talk of substantive or procedural rights. Even the courts have shied away from such determinations (see Chapter 7).

What is also interesting in the Minister's response is probably just an editing slip but it points to something much greater in relation to understanding the border: 'who will enter our borders ...'. A border in a traditional sense is something that is crossed, but what this turn of phrase suggests is that borders are a place, a space that can be entered. And of course this is the space where deterrence takes root. It is where the sites of deterrence exist – in a border space, a borderland. Deterrence has helped to create spaces which ordinarily would have been considered a line. It is within the borderland that immigration detention as border control takes root. It is also within the borderlands that the irrationalities of deterrence are overlooked.

---

29   Dauvergne, C, (2000), 'The Dilemma of Rights Discourse For Refugees', 23(3)*UNSW Law Journal* 56.

The deterrence function of immigration detention allows the state to exert itself on the body of the dispossessed refugee in denying him or her the legality of his or her existence as a person seeking protection. In locking up the refugee, the state, which in so many other areas has become a disembodied and even distant presence, is able to move swiftly and harshly against a group of individual bodies that have no means of traditional defence.

When their means of defence are mustered they are the defences of the individual bodies that the government seeks to mark as criminal, and reinforce the representations of their criminality. When the only, not just the last, but the only mechanism of defence is to suture lips, to deprive yourself of food, the body becomes acknowledged as the battleground for the assertion of state sovereignty. Within one feeble, malnourished, dehydrated, black body, the white state seeks out the final fight of deterrence. Not only will asylum seekers be locked up if they come to Australia by boat, some would prefer to self-harm or die rather than stay in the state they are in.

However, the grave contradiction is in the hidden spaces of the borderland that such protests and such acts of state violence take place. The sutured lips and the starving bodies occur in the unseen border spaces that deterrence and border protection open up, but only the refugee, the state and a few others are allowed to enter. The violence of deterrence in immigration detention depends on our inability to see, to hear or to touch the suffering, let alone acknowledge its existence.

Deterrence cannot be divorced from punishment, because deterrence is a rationale for punishment. As mandatory immigration detention impacts upon people largely from Middle Eastern countries and largely of Muslim faith, it could equally be argued that immigration detention is a punishment for race or for religion. However, I would rather suggest that immigration detention is better understood as a punishment in order to deter people of particular races and religions from accessing Australia's protection obligations.

In order to deter 'would-be' asylum seekers the punishment is detaining asylum seekers who have arrived here by boat in immigration detention. While the Minister has repeatedly denied immigration detention is a form of punishment, he also has repeatedly said some version of the following:

People being held in immigration detention have broken Australian law, either by seeking to enter Australia without authority, or having entered illegally, failing to comply with their visa conditions.[30]

You cannot have it both ways. As the parliamentary library has recently noted:

Immigration authorities have denied that the objectives of detention include 'punishing' illegal boat arrivals. However information material prepared for distribution in source and transit countries, designed to discourage people from resorting to people smugglers, would appear to be maximising the potential deterrent effect of Australia's mandatory detention regime. Recent information kits have included a forbidding picture of Woomera detention centre, and the warning that illegal entrants are held in detention far from Sydney. [31]

Acknowledging that immigration detention centres are sites of punishment as well as methods of deterrence, is then officially interpreted as a matter of controlling 'detainees'. If an immigration detention centre takes on the appearance and functions of a prison it is because of the behaviour of the detainees: 'The department and ACS and ACM fully appreciate that immigration detainees are in administrative detention not a correctional setting like a jail. They therefore rely on the cooperation of the detainees to ensure the smooth running and good order of the centres'.[32] It is the refugees who produce their own legality or illegality and hence it is in the hands of the refugees that the legality of state responses are crafted.

The tensions identified above by the parliamentary library also point to the way the national debate over immigration detention has been a battleground for 'truth' and 'fact'. In response to the investigation of the Human Rights and Equal Opportunity Commission (HREOC) Children in Detention Inquiry, the Minister released a number of publications: 'This information is a response to issues raised in media reports of the HREOC public hearings that misrepresent many issues regarding immigration detention'.[33] The Minister remains the holder of fact: '[a]s these public hearings progress, these

---

30 Ruddock, P (2002), *Border Protection, Immigration Detention Centres*, 22 July.
31 Adrienne Millbank, op cit.
32 Border Protection, Unauthorised Arrivals and Detention – Information paper, February 2002, www.minister.immi.gov.au/borders/ detention/ 2002paper_2.htm> accessed 5 September 2002.
33 Ruddock, P, (2002), *Border Protection*, Children in Detention, HREOC Children in Detention Inquiry Public Hearings – fact versus fiction, <www.immi.gov.au>, accessed 25 July 2002.

pages will be updated in an effort to replace the inaccuracies in the current debate, with the facts'. More importantly, in asserting his facts, the Minister also seeks to move and keep debate away from the embodied experiences of those detained, the same experiences inquiries such as that conducted by HREOC make central. The body of the detained refugee becomes dangerous to discourses of deterrence that are primarily geared towards the so-called protection of the nation. The site of deterrence must remain the nation because if it is shifted to that of the refugee, deterrence is lost, because our focus returns to the common human body, and not a collective national body.

Deterrence ensures the illegalities of the state cannot be countenanced, and the illegalities of the individual refugee remain the only focus. In thanking the South Australian police for their assistance in recapturing 'escapees' from Woomera in 2002, Minister Ruddock said 'it is important that detainees and their supporters are reminded by the State government that this is a country where the rule of law applies'.[34] The illegalities of detention and what goes on inside immigration detention centres, moves away from individual rights and reaffirms the absolutism of sovereign rights and our inability to conceive of the sovereign nation as criminal.

Site 2 – Temporary Protection Visas: Creating the intra-territorial frontier II

The second site of deterrence has been the establishment of temporary protection for those that are successful in making onshore asylum claims. In short, for those that make their way to Australia by boat, their protection will, at best, be temporary. Those who are settled under the offshore refugee program continue to receive permanent protection. This deterrence site is also the second major intra-territorial frontier.

In 2004, with a federal election in sight, the government introduced changes to the TPV regime that enabled refugees on TPVs to apply for permanent migration status under the non-humanitarian migration program. While initially welcomed by refugee advocates, it quickly became clear that the changes were to rhetoric but not to practice. Pressured by rural and regional backbenchers to retain rural refugee workforces, the federal government

---

34   Minister, Press Release, (2002) Minister Commends SA Police for Assistance, 30 June 2002.

announced that refugees on TPVs would now have 18 months to prepare for deportation under a new return-pending visa (instead of the previous 28 day provision) and to apply for permanent migration status. However, the majority of the 9,500 refugees on TPVs[35] were not being offered permanent protection, but rather a capacity to compete for migration places that in all likelihood they would not be successful in accessing. This new aspect of the TPV regime, if ever successfully utilised, would shift refugees from a protection scheme to a migration skills scheme thus continuing to avoid any sense that refugee protection could be permanent (rather only migration offered permanency). In short, permanent protection for those qualifying as refugees would continue to be withheld. Upon reflection, commentators noted that such changes to the TPV regime were little more than electoral opportunism and a reflection in the shift of Ministerial personalities from Mr Ruddock to Ms Vanstone. This is but the latest chapter in the elaborate development of temporary protection as frontier zone. In making the case that temporary protection continues to be the second intra-territorial frontier, I will first turn to the developing literature on temporary protection in Europe before outlining the Australian case.

Forms of temporary protection have been used increasingly over the past decade. The first significant use of temporary protection in the 1990s was in relation to the former Yugoslavia and then more recently the Kosovars. However, forms of temporary protection were also used in relation to refugees fleeing Spain during the Civil War in the 1930s, Hungarian and Czech Refugees in Austria in the 1950s and 60s, Vietnamese refugees in Hong Kong, in Thailand and Afghan refugees in Pakistan, in Iran, and with Iranian refugees in Turkey.[36] However, the experience of refugees from Bosnia-Herzegovina was the catalyst for a number of European countries formulating a harmonised temporary protection regime,[37] and it is from this experience that the most salient lessons and diverse scholarship has emanated. The European experience has much to tell

---

35 National Council of Churches in Australia (2004), 'TPV Changes are not enough', Media Release, NCCA, 14 July, <ww.ncca.org.au>.
36 Kjaerum, M, (1994), 'Temporary Protection in Europe in the 1990s', 6(3) *International Journal of Refugee Law* 444. See also Gibney, M, (2000) 'Between Control and Humanitarianism: Temporary Protection in Contemporary Europe' 14 *Georgetown Immigration Law Journal*689.
37 Koser, K, Walsh, M and Black, R, (1998) 'Temporary Protection and the Assisted Return of Refugees from the European Union', 10(3) *Internal Journal of Refugee Law* 445.

about the use of temporary protection as the foundation for a new refugee regime[38] as well as the compromised version of temporary protection now being utilised in Australia. In making this brief examination it is important to remember that temporary protection has long and disputed histories with no single expression, rationale or outcome.

Scholars have debated whether temporary protection is more or less than what the drafters of the Refugee Convention envisaged. In deference to the retention of sovereignty and the power of individual states to include and exclude, there has never been a right to asylum but rather a right to seek and enjoy asylum (Art 14 UDHR). However, sovereignty is severely curtailed under Art 33 of the Refugee Convention which requires states not to return refugees to a country where they will be persecuted. *Non-refoulement* is now well-established customary international law and the use of temporary protection, particularly by European states, has been considered the link between *non-refoulement* and a durable solution.[39] Some have argued that refugee status by nature is temporary and protection is linked with the persistence of the causes of persecution. Thus, protection is provided for a limited period of time that is dictated by the conditions in the country of origin.[40] Those advocating this view point to Art 1C of the Refugee Convention where the cessation clauses are listed under which repatriation can take place.

The use of temporary protection, particularly by European states, has been overwhelmingly used in response to mass influx. Temporary protection has thus been considered an exceptional response to exceptional numbers of refugees from a major conflict or upheaval. Temporary protection enables the international community to respond in ways that ordinary asylum procedures would disallow because they would go into administrative meltdown, or that the Convention definition does not adequately cover the kinds of harm refugees are fleeing and would therefore prevent countries from offering protection. Most notably, temporary protection has not utilised the Convention definition of who is a refugee and rather has been the outcome of administrative decisions on groups of people determined to be in need. Thus, temporary protection has largely developed alongside the Convention definition and status determination. Therefore temporary protection has utilised a

---

38   Gibney, op cit, pp 689-707.
39   Kjaerum, op cit, p 445.
40   Kjaerum, op cit, p 446.

broader understanding of persecution and offered protection to larger numbers of people than the Convention would reach, but at the same time has been distanced from international law:

> [T]emporary protection represented variously a mechanism for circumventing or suspending established asylum procedures, as well as granting fewer rights to those allowed to stay; for shifting decision-making to procedures locating in administrative edict rather than conforming to international law; and for granting status to 'war refugees' who were seen by some host States as falling outside the increasingly strict requirements for asylum under the 1951 Convention.[41]

Temporary protection has usually been used in relation to mass influx and part of efforts of international burden sharing (even if these have not been harmonised or poorly co-ordinated): 'the fortuitous aspect of being on the receiving end of a mass influx tends to stimulate demands for international solidarity'.[42] Some states have utilised temporary protection as a temporary status *en route* to a more permanent status, while others have viewed temporary protection *en route* to return.[43] In the case of Europe, temporary protection has been considered very much a regional issue. Commentators are in general agreement that temporary protection addresses three main consequences of the mass influx of people into developed nations: First, it saves resources as it avoids the expensive refugee determination procedure of assessing individual claims. Secondly, it places repatriation on the table from the outset, thus making the realisation of return of the refugee easier. Thirdly, the intake of refugees is communicated to the public at large as a temporary situation.[44]

Notably, in both Europe and the US, temporary protection (TPS in the US) has not resulted in return and has rather been an intermediate step to a form of permanent status.[45] The link between temporary protection and return has been found to be evident only in relation to particular groups of refugees. Moreover, as Koser, Walsh and Black have noted, there is significant variance between passive and active policies of return.

---

41 Koser, Walsh and Black, op cit, p 445.
42 Fitzpatrick, J, (2000), 'Temporary Protection of Refugees: Elements of a Formalized Regime', 94 *American Journal of International Law* 278.
43 Koser, Walsh, and Black, op cit.
44 Kjaerum, op cit, p 450.
45 Koser, Walsh and Black, op cit, p 455.

In terms of application, temporary protection has been found particularly wanting in two main ways: safe return and integration. Commentators have repeatedly highlighted the difficulties in gaining safe and legally justifiable withdrawal of temporary protection:

> Because the legal right of TP beneficiaries to refuge may be insecure, their protection against precipitous and dangerous involuntary return may be correspondingly weak. In the absence of agreed and legally grounded criteria for withdrawal of temporary protection, the international community is likely to witness a further downward spiral in refugee protection, as states may increasingly reject asylum seekers summarily, without a pretence of voluntariness or a plausible expectation of security for returnees.[46]

The internal exclusion of temporary protection refugees has been considered important in preventing integration or assimilation and hence not hampering efforts to return refugees to the country of origin when conditions change, for example, by limiting rights to work, education and the like. Conversely, others have suggested that integration into the host community will best prepare refugees for return as they will have economically, socially and culturally participated in a community and largely provided for themselves in preparation for return.

> It is difficult, however, to create a policy which allows the refugee to live a fruitful life in the country of asylum without being marginalised from the rest of the community, on the one hand, and which, on the other hand, keeps his or her mind open to the possibility of returning home.[47]

Some states have actively prevented the integration of refugees particularly in relation to participation in the labour market.[48] Moreover, commentators have noted the potential psychological impacts that uncertainty can cause and that extended periods of temporary protection are at best undesirable.[49] Under the European Convention on Human Rights, European states have acknowledged the right to

---

46 Fitzpatrick, J, (1999), 'The End of Protection: Legal Standards for Cessation of Refugee Status and Withdrawal of Temporary Protection', 13 *Georgetown Immigration Law Journal* 343.

47 Kjaerum, op cit, p 447.

48 Fitzpatrick, J, (2000), 'Temporary Protection of Refugees: Elements of a Formalized Regime', 94 *American Journal of International Law* 278.

49 Ibid.

respect private and family life and that the denial of family reunion is in violation of Art 8 of the ECHR.

Within the broader context of refugee protection, temporary protection has not been a consistent legal category.[50] The divergent evolution of temporary protection in Europe has occurred alongside, but separate from, the established refugee protection system and has been located within the administrative rather than the legal realm, with decisions being made within the bureaucracy with great discretion. Often temporary protection has been considered another way to move asylum out of the gaze of international law while at the same time claiming to be more liberal in the application of human rights. For the refugee, temporary protection effectively places them outside the ordinary range of rights that would assist their settlement and integration into the host society all with the aim to cleanly repatriate them: 'The allocation of rights thus impacts directly upon the question of control: the more rights-respecting the conditions faced by the temporarily-protected, the more reluctant the refugees will be to depart when the time comes to do so'.[51]

The introduction of temporary protection reflects the preoccupation of the developed world with the cessation of refugee protection and a move away from other established and permanent models of refugee settlement.[52] Temporary protection has been pioneered by countries who continue to receive far fewer refugees than the developing world but grow increasingly impatient 'even with interim palliatives' of temporary protection in situations of mass influx.[53] A useful way to consider the use of temporary protection in Europe is offered by Gibney. He argues that temporary protection has attempted to simultaneously achieve two aims. First, the aim of *control* characterises temporary protection's attempt to prevent permanent migration and integration of refugees into the host society. The host society defines the period of refuge and locates responsibility for the refugee with the country of origin and underpins this relationship with the actual or potential use of coercion (deportation etc). Notably, temporary protection grows out of a period of restrictive immigration in the 1980s characterised by increased visa requirements and carrier sanctions on the one hand and the destruction of internal European borders (and concomitant

---

50   Koser, Walsh and Black, op cit, p 445.
51   Gibney, op cit, p 697.
52   Fitzpatrick, (1999), op cit.
53   Fitzpatrick, (1999), op cit, p 344.

strengthening of common borders) on the other. From a control perspective, any attempt to permanently settle refugees in a host country under a temporary protection regime threatens the downfall of the regime that believes asylum need only ever be temporary and therefore the stakes are raised with the spectre of forced deportations to ensure the integrity of the venture. The second aim of temporary protection is recognition of the *humanitarian* needs of mass influxes of refugees and the obligation not to *refoule*. Temporary protection has been used by European states to receive large numbers of refugees while not alienating conservative/racist/ xenophobic public opinion. Almost universally, refugees under temporary protection regimes have not had access to the full range of economic and social rights essential for their integration into the host society with commentators arguing that without the realisation of such rights temporary protection can not claim to be humanitarian: 'The dominant view of control regards the vesting of rights in the temporarily protected as at odds with the state's desire to prevent permanent integration. Host states must be like a cheap hotel room – decent enough to consider spending a night, but not the kind of place one would want to call home'.[54] It is the control objective that is more clearly articulated than the ill-defined and often-contested humanitarian objective. Gibney argues that squaring these two aims lies at the heart of temporary protection's popularity in Europe.

Temporary protection, in its most recent Australian manifestation, emerged after Operation Safe Haven under which temporary protection was granted to around 3900 Kosovars in 1999 and then to around 1800 East Timorese escaping the violence of the post-referendum period. The conflicts they were escaping had received unprecedented media coverage and there was both a governmental and public desire to contribute to an international humanitarian effort to provide protection in a moment of disaster. The temporary safe haven visa class extended protection to groups of people who may not have had any treaty-based entitlement, but at the same time 'diminished access to Australia's protection for those non-citizens entitled to protection and the Convention Relating to the Status of Refugees ... the Convention Against Torture and Other Cruel, Inhuman or Degrading Treatment or Punishment ... and/or the International Covenant on Civil and Political Rights'.[55] The Safe

---

54   Gibney, op cit, p 705.
55   Taylor, S, (2000), 'Protection or Prevention? A Close Look at the Temporary Safe Haven Visa Class', 23(3) *UNSW Law Journal* 75.

Haven visa was effectively placed outside judicial review and repatriation was mishandled resulting in over 500 Kosovars existing on month-to-month visa extensions as support services were gradually withdrawn.[56] As Taylor has argued, the withdrawal of temporary protection in relation to Operation Safe Haven and subsequent repatriation may not have been in breach of international law but it was at odds with international standards

> [C]onsidered in its political context, Australia's practice to date suggests that, as long as the ability of persons, who are, or have been, safe haven visa holders, to make protection visa applications is controlled by a Minister, who is politically, but not legally, accountable for decisions made, the likelihood is that Australia will induce or force the repatriation of some individuals in breach of its treaty-based obligations.[57]

In short, the Safe Haven Visa engaged Australia in a feel-good humanitarian gesture which had little basis in international law, depended on the absence of rights and ended with what has been described as involuntary repatriation.

Regardless of the numerous downfalls of the temporary safe haven visas, introduction of the temporary protection visa utilised much of the lingering public good feeling surrounding the 'temporary protection' offered to the Kosovars and East Timorese. However, it offered a fundamentally different sort of protection that would spearhead a more compromised protection regime to address situations fundamentally different to the causes that drove the Kosovar and East Timorese crises. The introduction of the Temporary Protection Visa in October 1999 added an important weapon to the deterrence armoury in warding off the mostly Iraqi, Afghan and Iranian on shore asylum seekers at which it was aimed. Articulating the reasons for the introduction of the Temporary Protection Visa the Minister for Immigration clearly locates it as a deterrence measure:

> The regulations remove the additional benefits that had been encouraging misuse of the protection process by unauthorised arrivals and the use of people smugglers to assist people to travel unlawfully to Australia. Unauthorised arrivals often abandon or bypass protection in other countries in travelling to Australia. Under these regulations, unauthorised arrivals found to be refugees only have access to a three year temporary protection visa, in the first

---

56 Ibid.
57 Ibid, p 102.

instance. TPV holders are taking the places in the Humanitarian Program from refugees and others who are often in greater need of resettlement.[58]

The TPV is not only a measure to deter. It also condemns those who do not conform to the administrative organisation of the Australian protection regime as if it should be the administrative organisation that drives the protection regime rather than any notion of persecution. Moreover, it imposes a punitive outcome on those who qualify as refugees because of their mode of entry: 'People who arrive legally in Australia and successfully seek asylum continue to be able to access permanent residence'.[59] In deploying the TPV as a deterrent, the scheme reinforces the legality and illegality of two groups of people who have satisfied the same rigid criteria for determining refugee status.

The TPV is only granted where an applicant is a non-citizen to whom Australia owes protection obligation under the Refugee Convention and its Protocol. Therefore, the grant of temporary protection does not widen the net of protection but rather utilises the same strict formula to a restricted period and only to a certain group of refugees. In 2001 the regulations governing TPVs changed. Whereas refugees on a TPV could apply after 30 months for a Permanent Protection Visa if they had a continuing need of protection, after September 2001 some TPV holders who did not lodge an application for a PPV before 27 September 2001 may be barred from being granted a PPV and would, if they were found to be still in need of protection, continue onto another TPV.[60] The relentless

---

58 Minister for Immigration and Multicultural and Indigenous Affairs, (2002), Border Protection: Temporary Protection Visas, <www.minister. immi.gov.au/borders/detention/fs_64_tpv.htm>, accessed 27 July 2002.

59 Minister for Immigration and Multicultural and Indigenous Affairs, (2002), Border Protection: Temporary Protection Visas, <www.minister. immi.gov.au/borders/detention/fs_64_tpv.htm>, accessed 27 July 2002.

60 The September 2001 regulations apply to those who did not lodge an application before 27 September 2001 and fall within one of the following categories:
    • Since leaving their home country, they have resided in a country for a continuous period of seven days or more; and they could have sought and obtained effective protection either from: a) that country; or b) from the offices of the UNHCR located in that country.
    • Refugee and Immigration Legal Centre Inc, (2001), *Recent Changes in the Law for Temporary Protection Visa Holders*, Information Flyer.

uncertainty of having only temporary protection is compounded by the limited range of entitlements of TPV holders. They have no right to family reunion or to the full range of settlement services. Many, have not been able to access Commonwealth-funded education or health services, which has often meant they have no English language training. While they are able to work, there are a range of secondary restrictions because they are unable to access many federally-funded employment and training schemes. Settlement services withdrawn by the Commonwealth have been picked up by non-government organisations, under threat of having their more general Commonwealth funding cut, or by State governments. The restriction on this range of entitlements makes the Temporary Protection Visa a punitive venture. Refugees on temporary protection visas, in all possible ways, have their existence manoeuvred away from 'legitimate' refugees as well as from society at large.

Despite the shift in rhetoric in 2004 towards a more 'compassionate' approach towards refugees on TPVs, adjustments to the TPV regime have not seriously redressed the deleterious situation of refugees. The introduction and continued implementation of the Temporary Protection Visa has created two classes of refugees, specifically aimed at Middle Eastern refugees, creates lives of uncertainty, dilutes refugee protection, stands at odds to notions of human rights and locates protection within acts of begrudged generosity. European approaches to temporary protection have been developed in the face of mass influx and with an understanding that mass influxes are genuinely temporary.[61] Repeatedly, commentators have argued that temporary protection is only justifiable in the face of an overwhelming mass influx and should only serve as an interim solution.[62] But the Australian model was not developed in the face of such numbers. It has been positioned as a deterrent to a non-existent invasion. Moreover, deterrence has impacted on public debate in a way that the ordinary Australian could only imagine such measures being necessary if the well being of the nation was at stake. In other words, temporary protection has been developed as a response to a crisis in refugee numbers that does not exist by any reasonable measure. Playing the numbers game in this way contributes to the creation of an internal frontier as it makes protection a matter of politics rather than a matter of law. It seeks out its own space

---

61 Fitzpatrick, J, (2000), op cit.
62 Fitzpatrick, (2000) op cit, p 295.

between not explicitly breaking international law but not complying with international standards and accepted norms. It also refers to international law begrudgingly, belittling it as a buffer between the so-called illegal acts of refugees and state impotence whereby the state would prefer to simply turn refugees around and send them home. As such, the Temporary Protection Visa, even after the 2004 changes, creates the opportunity to discursively re-position and distort representations of the obligation not to *refoule*: an obligation that applies irrespective of whether Australia's Migration Laws have been broken.

The introduction of the TPV category secured the removal of rights from TPV holders, placing them into a techno-legal realm where the language of rights is subordinated to a bureaucratic 'restriction of services':

> The government considers it inappropriate to provide TPV holders with the more generous range of settlement services available to refugees and others resettled permanently in Australia under the humanitarian program.[63]

The discourse of deterrence contributes to a hegemonic representation of TPV holders as deviants and rationalises the removal of a series of human rights that are accessible to others with a more regularised migration status in Australia. Yet the TPV regulations demonstrate the deformation of the deterrence discourse as it is deployed in refugee policy debates. In domestic law and order debates, deterrence in part operates on the assumption that individuals are physically removed from society as a punishment for their crime, and as a broader message to other individuals that they risk the same fate if they choose to act in a similar fashion. In contrast, the discourse of deterrence within refugee policy requires the complicity of the community to enforce the act of deterrence as TPV holders move alongside us, yet, through force of government regulation and community policing, are removed from full engagement within the community. While the principle of deterrence within domestic law and order debates relies somewhat on the principle that once you have spent your allocated time in prison you should be released into the community, for TPV holders there is an expectation on the part of the government that they will return to

---

63 Question on Notice: Illegal Immigration: Detention Centres, 17 August 2000, Ruddock, House, p 19370.

their country of origin at the end of the three-year period. The action of deterrence in refugee policy is ongoing and conceivably unending in contrast to the fixed-term nature of deterrence in domestic law and order debates. The TPV was developed in the context that onshore asylum seekers subject to mandatory detention were positioned as illegal, yet over 90 per cent have been recognised as in need of protection under Australian and international law. It ensured their existence continues to be precarious and assists in their ongoing positioning as illegal and undeserving. The Temporary Protection Visa maintains that refugees on TPVs are still not legitimate and should not be treated as refugees despite meeting all the requirements the international and Australian system has placed in front of them.

Temporary protection has been resisted because it represents a shift away from the strict rule of law approach of the Convention refugee protection regime.[64] When causes of flight are likely to endure, then temporary protection is a dilution of refugee protection as we have known it.[65] Using Gibney's articulation, the Australian TPV policy has seen the aim of humanitarianism subsumed by the aim of control. The act of temporary protection cannot be understood as one of gratuitous humanity[66] (as it has been understood in other locations) but an act of gratuitous control. The politics of that control, in the guise of deterrence, has created an intra-territorial frontier. As those refugees who seek onshore protection move through the traditional frontier of the border and the first intra-territorial frontier of the immigration detention centre, it becomes necessary to create a further frontier within everyday life. The TPV has to be punitive if it is to be a deterrent.[67] And the enactment of the punishment, that is the TPV, has opened up a new space in the community, a new intra-territorial frontier where people neither belong nor are traditionally excluded.

---

64 Ibid.
65 Ibid.
66 Ibid, p 287.
67 Esmaeili, H, and Wells, B, (2000), 'The "Temporary" Refugees: Australia's Legal Response to the Arrival of Iraqi and Afghan Boat-People' 23(3) *UNSW Law Journal* 224. 'The arrangements penalise genuine individual refugees who seek protection in a 'non mass-influx' situation'.

Site 3 – The 'Pacific Solution': Creating the extra-territorial frontier

The refugee:

> We request from old men women and children of Manus Island to help us to get out from this jail.[68]

The Manus islander:

> Our people are mostly illiterate. They don't understand. They haven't been asked about any of this.[69]

The border riding politics of non-entrée are not new, but their contemporary manifestations and ramifications are far reaching and increasingly complex. There can be no doubt that the policies and politics of deterrence as they occur at the traditional territorial frontier – the border – are the most crude expressions of sovereignty and arguably the most dangerous and demeaning manifestations of the deterrence rationale.

In examining this third site of deterrence, I consider the Pacific Solution as the creation of the extra-territorial frontier. In concluding this argument the experience of interdiction, offshore processing and temporary protection that operated in and around Guantánamo Bay by the US is outlined. While Australia adopted a version of temporary protection at odds with mainstream European models, the use of extra-territorial sites to realise deterrent objectives sees Australia taking many lessons from the US/ Guantánamo Bay experience. The Pacific Solution, in particular, has made a significant contribution to what Green and Grewcock have referred to as the third major zone of global exclusion – the South East Asia/ Australasia rim.

> The Minister for Immigration and Multicultural and Indigenous Affairs, Philip Ruddock, today confirmed the Government's intention to continue sending a strong signal to people smugglers and their clients. The Minister has outlined ongoing funding for offshore processing of unauthorised boat arrivals in the 2002-03 budget ... 'We know that the smugglers' inability to deliver their clients to the

---

68 Sign hung over the fence of the refugee detention centre on Manus island. Reported in *Sydney Morning Herald*, 6 February 2002, 'A prison in paradise' by Greg Roberts, p 11.
69 Ibid.

Australian mainland has had a significant impact on their operations and it is important that we stand firm', Mr Ruddock said.[70]

The Pacific Solution has come to refer to the dramatic policy shift in refugee policy post-Tampa. The Norwegian freighter, the MV Tampa rescued 430 persons from sinking vessel that had been en route to Australia in August 2001. The Tampa had been sailing for Singapore but after taking onboard the asylum seekers it changed course for Christmas Island. With the number of people it was now carrying the ship became unseaworthy. The Australian government refused to allow the ship to dock, placing Australia in a precarious position vis-a-vis its refugee protection responsibilities as well as international maritime law. In declaring that 'those people will never set foot on Australian soil' the government hastily made arrangements with Nauru and then New Zealand and began developing a new raft of legislation that would prevent not only those onboard the Tampa from reaching Australian territory to seek protection, but all others who followed. The Tampa eventually transferred its passengers onto an Australian navy vessel and they were transported to Papua New Guinea and Nauru. At the end of January 2002, over 1550 refugees were detained in Nauru or Papua New Guinea with 130 refugees accepted by New Zealand for resettlement.

The thrust of the new legislation was the prevention of asylum seekers from reaching the Australian mainland or from engaging Australia's protection obligations on one of Australia's outlining islands or territories. The *Migration Amendment (Excision from Migration Zone) Act* 2001 (Cth) required the excision of a host of islands and territories, including Ashmore Reef, Christmas Island and the Cocos Islands. These are now considered not to be part of Australia for the purposes of migration. Therefore, if asylum seekers do reach these destinations they cannot engage Australia's protection obligations as they are defined an 'offshore entry person'. In turn, any 'offshore entry person' can be taken to declared countries (nominated in s 198A of the *Migration Act* 1958) where refugee determination is conducted. Those found to be refugees may indeed be resettled in Australia if protection is not available from other

---

70   Ruddock, P, (2002), Offshore Processing Developments and Related Savings, <www.minister.immi.gov.au/media_releases/media02/r02033. htm>, accessed 5 September 2002.

countries.[71] The *Migration Amendment (Excision from Migration Zone) (Consequential Provisions) Act* 2001 (Cth) introduced a new visa regime 'to deter people moving from or bypassing other safe countries where they could gain or seek effective protection' according to the Australian government.[72]

The two sites, Manus, an island of Papua New Guinea, and Nauru, are geographically located within the Pacific. Papua New Guinea was a former Australian colony and Nauru was formerly administered by Australia. Refugees were housed in detention run by ACM with their status determined and documented by a combination of IOM, UNHCR and Australian Immigration officers. While hundreds of the asylum seekers were granted status, many were not immediately resettled and were continued to be held in detention in Nauru and Papua New Guinea.[73] Children in detention on the islands did not fall under the remit of the HREOC inquiry into children in detention. For over 360 children held in camps there were no educational facilities and the harshness of the camps, physically and emotionally, has been noted. Despite this, we know little about the acts of self-harm and protests that took place within the detention camps and can only assume the exacerbated psychological impact on refugees.

The Pacific Solution depended upon the systematic disrespect for international law and standards as well as the laws of other nations, not to mention Australian laws. The detention of asylum seekers on Manus and Nauru has been considered by UNHCR as inconsistent with the provisions of the Refugee Convention.[74] Nauru has not signed the Refugee Convention and while Papua New Guinea has signed the Convention it has a reservation against Art 31(1) that requires refugees not be penalised for crossing borders unauthorised by the receiving state.

The lack of education facilities for children in detention on Manus and Nauru further places Australia, as well as Nauru and

---

71 Taylor, S, (2002), 'Exclusion from Protection of Persons of 'Bad Character': is Australia Fulfilling its Treaty-Based Non-Refoulement Obligations?' 8(1) *Australian Journal of Human Rights* 83.
72 US Committee for Refugees, (2002), *SeaChange: Australia's New Approach to Asylum Seekers*, Washington: US Committee for Refugees.
73 Oxfam Community Aid Abroad, (2002), Still Drifting, <www.caa.org.au/campaigns/refugees/still_drifting/summary.html>, accessed 20 August 2002.
74 'Pacific Solution inconsistent with convention: UN' *The Australian*, 2 August 2002.

Papua New Guinea, in breach of the Convention on the Rights of the Child. Moreover, the ad hoc and rushed establishment of the system occurred outside recognised regional organisations that have been established to promote good governance in the region. It is worth noting that while a recent Pacific leaders forum reached agreement on concerns regarding people smuggling, the broad (and previously vocal) unhappiness of the Pacific with Australia's cavalier approach to the environment was muted. This re-ordering of Pacific priorities now simply reflects Australia's agenda with blatant disregard for other nations. This was drawn out most starkly when it was revealed that Australia had also approached East Timor and Tuvalu to take asylum seekers. Both nations are confronted by large existing and potential refugee problems from the violence that ensued in East Timor's move to democracy, and from the threat of rising sea waters engulfing the entire nation of Tuvalu.

The Pacific Solution breaches the Constitution of Nauru as well as that of Papua New Guinea. In running counter to the Constitutions of the respective nations, Australia has now introduced the practice of privatised mandatory (and indeterminate) detention to the Pacific. While this raises a range of practical concerns (ie, access to lawyers and arbitrary detention) it also further complicates the slippery nature of sovereignty within the extra-territorial frontier. The relocation of Australian refugee determination to these islands has required the abdication of Australian sovereignty from its territorial base and required its disembodied expression in refugee processing in other territories. However, with the operation of the detention centres in the hands of privatised firms, PNG and Nauru not only ceded their territory for the expression of extra-territorial sovereign control by Australia but allowed this to be realised daily by a multi-national corporation that stands apart from inter-state arrangements. Most notably these Constitutional breaches have occurred in relation to access to lawyers and arbitrary detention.

Section 42.2 of the Papua New Guinea Constitution states:

> A person who is detained shall be given adequate opportunity to give instructions to a lawyer of his choice in the place which he is detained, and shall be informed immediate on his arrest or detention of his rights under this subsection.

Article 5.1 of the Constitution of Nauru states that: 'No person shall be deprived of his personal liberty, except as authorised by law in any of the following cases'. Article 5.1, Pt (h) provides for detention 'for the purpose of preventing his unlawful entry into Nauru, or for the purpose of effecting his expulsion, extradition or other lawful removal from Nauru'. However, those detained on the island are being detained primarily because Australia has requested their detention, not for any of the listed reasons outlined in the Constitution (including Pt (h)). Article 5.2 of the Constitution also provides that:

> A person who is arrested or detained shall be informed promptly of the reasons for the arrest and detention and shall be permitted to consult in the place in which he is detained a legal representative of his own choice.

However, in June 2002 and again in May 2004, the Nauruan government refused to grant visas for a group of Australian lawyers to travel to the island.

The stickiest legal manoeuvring in realising the 'Pacific Solution' has meant that the processing of refugee applications in Manus and PNG was largely carried out by Australian immigration officials and the IOM, it has not been done under Australian law.

Most worryingly, the tail end of the 'solution' depends upon the forcible repatriation of those found not be refugees. This is now allowed for in the *Migration Legislation Amendment (Transitional Movement) Act* 2002 (Cth). This legislation enables 'certain non-citizens' or a 'transitory person' to be moved through Australia and removes their ability to claim asylum in the process. It has been introduced to ensure the forcible repatriation of unsuccessful refugee applicants from Nauru and Manus back through Australia and onto a third country. This can be done using a range of forces – from restraining a person, removing the person or use of such force as is necessary and reasonable, and the power to 'place' a person on a vehicle or vessel. These measures introduce into the body of refugee law coercive measures that enable the forced removal of failed refugees with little or no independent legal oversight. The exertion of this sovereign control occurs across an extra-territorial space. The coercive enactment of sovereignty now happens on the soil of other countries or while in transit. This most potent form of coercive sovereignty occurs away from the sovereign territory and instead takes place within the extra-territorial frontier.

The Pacific Solution was sold to the Australian people and the governments of Nauru and Papua New Guinea as a short-term measure. However, for the period 2002-2004, the Australian government budgeted over $430 million for offshore processing locations such as Nauru and Papua New Guinea.[75] The extra-territorial frontier now has few temporal constraints with the government clearly not believing its own rhetoric that the Pacific Solution was only ever a temporary measure. Moreover, the establishment and ongoing viability of offshore processing depends upon the distortion of aid packages. 'Additional Aid' for Nauru and Papua New Guinea acted as inducements to realise Australia's policy of offshore processing. As Fry has noted:

> The vulnerable and small societies of the Pacific did not just *happen* to be approached by Australia: they were approached *because* they were vulnerable and depended on Australia.[76]

Australia positioned its own priorities of deterring onshore asylum seekers above the stability and good governance of island nations. The already unstable political conditions in Papua New Guinea were exacerbated by the issue adding to the reasons for the removal of the Foreign Minister of Papua New Guinea (for not agreeing to accept more asylum seekers and an extension of processing time) and the eventual electoral defeat of the Governor of Manus Province.[77] The Prime Minister of Nauru described the 'Pacific Solution' as the 'Pacific Nightmare'.[78] The Memorandum of Understanding between the countries leaves the period for offshore processing on Nauru open ended and has therefore caused significant public unease. In short, Australia has offered aid packages in return for the indeterminate incarceration of refugees.

In conducting refugee determination offshore, the Pacific Solution was also meant to control Australia's previous 'generosity' towards these 'queue jumpers' who were cast as not really refugees at all. Many Afghan refugees taken to Nauru were not recognised as refugees because of the changed circumstances in Afghanistan after the fall of the Taliban. The UNHCR has noted that had they been taken directly to Australia and not had their determination delayed, they would most likely have been found to be Convention refugees.

---

75 Oxfam Community Aid Abroad, (2002), Still Drifting, op cit.
76 Fry, G, (2002), 'The "Pacific Solution"?' in W Maley, A Dupont, J Fonteyne, G Fry, J Jupp, and T Do, *Refugees and the Myth of the Borderless World*, Canberra: Department of International Relations.
77 Oxfam Community Aid Abroad, (2002), Still Drifting, op cit.
78 Dodson, L, and Douez, S (2002), 'Pacific Solution a nightmare: Nauru', *The Age*, 31 July.

Over 40 per cent of those processed offshore were found to be refugees. Most notably, a large number of those were determined on appeal. Thirty-four of the 65 Iraqis rejected were overturned on appeal, as were ten of the 13 Palestinians and two of the five Sri Lankans.[79] The establishment of offshore processing is also sending important messages to internal decision-makers; their oversight of refugee determination has been too 'generous' and the processes too 'technical'.

The rationale for deterring refugees through offshore processing depends on an understanding that if refugees do land on the Australian mainland there is no way the land can then repudiate them – and repudiate them is the aim of deterrence. Therefore, this land must be protected from its own weakness, even if that means removing some of that land, and certainly the waters, from notions of the sovereign. The frontier is the zone in which interdiction and offshore processing must take place. While the rhetoric is of maintaining sovereign control the enactment of control is exterior to the sovereign territory. The deterrent force of offshore processing has depended on the creation of an extra territorial frontier. This frontier has been a space in which the legalities of international law and the compromise of national law do not hamper refugee determination. It is a space that can be bought through the exertion of regional power. Most notably the extra-territorial frontier is a site of deterrence which remains almost totally unseen.

In conclusion, the establishment of offshore refugee processing by the Australian government has obviously drawn a number of lessons from the US experience of offshore processing in Guantánamo Bay, Cuba, and Panama. In the 1990s the US government implemented a temporary protection policy in the form of safe havens on US military bases in Guantánamo Bay, and the Panama Canal Zone, all of which were outside the territorial boundaries of the US. Domestic political conditions, namely public fears of massive Cuban migration, was a driving force of the policy.

In moving from a policy which had welcomed those fleeing the communist Cuban regime in August 1994 President Clinton said:

> In recent weeks, the Castro regime has encouraged Cubans to take to the sea in unsafe vessels to escape their nation's internal problems …

---

79   Oxfam Community Aid Abroad, (2002), Still Drifting, op cit.

Let me be clear: The Cuban Government will not succeed in any attempt to dictate the American immigration policy.[80]

Today I have ordered that illegal refugees from Cuba will not be allowed to enter the United States. Refugees rescued at sea will be taken to our naval base at Guantánamo while we explore the possibility of other safe havens within the region ... The United States will detain and investigate and, if necessary, prosecute Americans who take to the sea to pick up Cubans. Vessels used in such activities will be seized.[81]

In short, the policy was one of interdiction at sea to ensure that no Cubans reached US shores and instead they would be taken to Guantánamo Bay (which already held over 15,000 Haitians). Short wave radio broadcasts were used to warn Cubans not to embark for the US, but despite theses efforts Cubans still attempted the journey. As a result, the US searched for co-operation from regional neighbours willing to take on some of the Cuban and Haitian migrants: Surinam, the Turks and Caicos Islands and several countries of the Eastern Caribbean agreed to accept migrants with the understanding that, in each case, the US would bear the cost and often the responsibility of running the operations.[82] None of these countries eventually took any of the refugees, instead the US signed a confidential agreement with Panama. The US then announced a policy to allow an annual minimum of 20,000 Cubans to legally migrate to the US though expanded visa and refugee processing and the use of the parole authority of the Attorney General. As Sartori notes:

The policy marked the first time that legal immigration was exchanged for efforts to deter illegal migration flows. It continues today and determines entry for all Cuban refugees, immigrants and parolees. However, to qualify for these opportunities Cubans in safe havens must apply from Cuba proper by registering with the United States' Interest Section in Havana for appropriate visas.[83]

The US further negotiated the 'voluntary return' of Cuban nationals who arrived in the US or in safe havens after August 1994.

---

80 Cited in Sartori, M, (2001), 'The Cuban Migration Dilemma: An Examination of the United States' Policy of Temporary Protection in Offshore Safe Havens' 156 *Georgetown Immigration Law Journal*, Vol 156, 319.
81 Ibid.
82 Ibid, p 329
83 Ibid, p 331.

Therefore, ordinary refugee determination was suspended with a form of temporary protection being granted within the offshore safe havens.

Both the US/Guatanamo Bay and the Australian/Pacific use of extra-territorial space developed amid heightened public debate and depended upon existing neo-colonial relations in their respective regions. Both cases point to the use of deterrence in building extra-territorial frontiers as a function of the increasingly punitive state. A punitive state seeks less and less engagement with international laws and standards, and increasingly more within bilateral agreements as a way to avert traditional recourse to notions of human rights. Most notably, the creation of extra-territorial frontiers occurred in a moment of perceived crisis, whether or not that crisis in numbers (the influx, the flood) was real. The Pacific Solution derogates from the belief that people in need of protection should be protected, and instead embodies a range of legal and extra legal arrangements whereby States impede refugees from gaining access to their territories.

Sites of deterrence as a site of state violence

Deterrence is a rationale that depends on a familiar and convincing rhetoric. It can be located within a law and order genre and is dependent upon the internal contradictions evident in narratives of the bordered state, individual choice and punishment. Deterrence continues to be conducted across three major sites – immigration detention, temporary protection and offshore processing. The use of deterrence narratives across these sites has developed intra- and extra-territorial frontiers in which the sovereign nation slips in and about its connection to the body politic and its connection to those fleeing other parts of the world. It is within these frontiers, frontiers that do not conform to traditional notions of borders (because they are spaces and lands), that the coercive state can act with unmitigated force the new and malleable versions of sovereignty.

Taken collectively, these narratives and sites of deterrence represent a moment of state violence. The intra- and extra-territorial frontiers deterrence has established provide the space for the state to act against the external other. Deterrence is a site of state violence as it depends on a host of illegalities or legal manoeuvrings that distance refugee determination and protection from the rule of law and locates refugee determination firmly outside the public gaze. The sites and narratives of deterrence create spaces where state violence goes largely undocumented and unknown. What is done in our name, deterrence, cannot (and we are told should not) be our concern. It goes to the heart of what we come to know as the (sovereign) nation and what can or cannot be conducted in its name.

Chapter 5

Policing the border

This chapter extends the analysis of the last to develop three themes that aid understandings of the refugee and state illegality. It does so by focusing on the most recent incarnation of what it is to be deterred: people smuggling. Where the last chapter was interested in what deterrence has come to mean, this chapter is interested in how deterrence, notably via the construction of people smuggling and concomitant law enforcement mechanisms, is completed. The first theme is the relationship between sovereignty and the attempt to regulate forced migration as a subset of irregular migration. The second theme is the construction of people smuggling and the transformation of law enforcement. These themes are informed by the growing international literature which shows that increases in human smuggling and the development of restrictive immigration policies, particularly border policing, are interlinked and reinforce each other. This chapter will examine the nature and consequences of the law enforcement effort that has become the material response of the Australian government and many other nations of the Global North to refugees. While the previous chapter argued that narratives of deterrence underpin sites of exclusion that may be read as sites of state violence, this chapter argues that the enforcement effort at the heart of border policing is based upon flawed understandings of irregular migration and sovereignty, and is transforming both refugee protection and the nature of law enforcement.

Sovereignty and regulating forced migration at the border

> The sovereignty of the state and border control, whether land borders or airports, lie at the heart of the regulatory effort.

Sovereignty led responses of the Global North to refugees, particularly those responses that cluster around the frontier are deficient. Arendt, writing on Western Europe in the interwar period, noted:

The nation-state, incapable of providing a law for those who had lost the protection of a national government, transferred the whole matter to the police. This was the first time the police in Western Europe had received authority to act on it sown, to rule directly over people; in one sphere of public life it was no longer an instrument to carry out and enforce the law, but had become a ruling authority independent of government and ministries. Its strength and its emancipation from law and government grew in direct proportion to the influx of refugees. The greater the ration of stateless and potentially stateless to the population at large – in prewar France it had reached 10 per cent of the total – the greater the danger of a gradual transformation into a police state.

The policing of the refugee frontier, those borders and borderlands that reach beyond the nation-state, depend upon understanding forced migration in terms of an influx of refugees to the Global North. However, irregular migration is not a 'free for all' but rather represents a management problem rather than a crisis. Sassen suggests that while there remain many differences in immigration policies of developed nations, there is a growing convergence in the rooting of immigration policies within a 'common set of conceptions about national borders and the role of the state'. Such convergence primarily takes place at the border and in a moment when traditional immigration policies are considered ineffective and pan national and regional approaches to immigration policy are taking shape, particularly in Europe. The key elements in this fundamental framework are:

> (1) the sovereignty of the state and border control as the heart of the regulatory effort (whether on land or at airports or consulates in sending countries); and (2) an understanding of immigration as the consequence of emigrants' individual actions (the receiving country is taken as a passive agent, one not implicated in the process. Refugee policy, in contrast recognizes additional factors as leading to outflows. The framework for immigration singles out the border and the individual as the sites for regulatory enforcement.

Devetak problematises the sovereign state in terms of four main elements relevant to the border policing function: violence, boundary inscription practices, deconstruction of identity as defined in security, and statecraft (foreign policy discourses).

First, the modern state is meant to protect citizens from violence but violence is what makes possible the modern state 'a shelter from violence'. Violence is therefore central to the ontological set up of states and is not simply deployed on a case-by-case basis for political or national security reasons. Notably, Devetak uses the work of Edkins in making this point. Edkins draws a continuum to illustrate the intimate relationship between the state and violence upon which she places Nazis, concentration camps, NATO and refugee camps. Edkin's examples are not divorced as separate and somehow historically and culturally distanced expressions of state violence but rather can and must be understood in relation to one another.

Secondly, the inscription of boundaries has been at the heart of the modern state. Devetak takes the position that the key question is not what sovereignty is but 'how it is spatially and temporally produced and how it is circulated'. Boundary inscription is therefore central to the differentiation of political space and renders the marking of boundaries a political and loaded act. How does boundary inscription simultaneously produce order and violence? As the last chapter argued, the border is no longer a line on a map, but a space and place for legitimate and illegitimate state behaviour.

Thirdly, Devetak raises the role of identity in sovereignty and how security is spatially conceived in relation to territory and how threats to that security are articulated. Attempts at coherent and homogenous political identities require the containment of threat or danger.

Finally, Devetak argues that sovereignty is fused to certain historically normalised interpretations of the state: they are neither natural nor neutral. The coupling of the state and sovereignty is inured by dynamic historical and cultural relations and representations which produce a political identity. In short, he argues that the state is made to appear to have an essence, a sovereign essence, through the performativity of the state ('statecraft'). Here Devetak and Sassen are as one: the state is not bounded before it takes up particular practices or relations but is rather constituted by the unending actions in the domestic and international realm. For the purposes of this chapter, this raises the possibility that the state is not just giving effect, but constituting its sovereign self by the enactment of border enforcement: violence, boundary inscription and identity.

Policing the border

The symbiotic relationship between refugees and the police is increasing around key zones of global exclusion: the US/Mexico border, the European Union and the South East Asian/Australasian rim. Examining these relationships uncovers the contradictory, yet stunted deployment of sovereignty-led responses of the Global North to refugees, particularly those responses that cluster around the frontier, marking and patrolling the border.

There are two main elements to border policing carried out on the Australasian rim. First, the border policing function undertaken by the military and the multi-agency approach that from 1998 to 2002 constituted 'border protection'. Such border protection has been the subject of numerous government inquiries that have raised serious concerns over the truthfulness of government accounts of the deaths of asylum seekers in the borderlands.

Subject to a developing body of literature, Tony Kevin has most recently argued that a range of government agencies have been co-opted into dubious border policing functions to deter and disrupt the flow of refugees to Australia. Dealing specifically with the sinking of the SIEV X and the deaths of 433 asylum seekers in October 2001, this work raises questions regarding how Australian government agencies had prior knowledge of the sinking and how that knowledge was 'systematically camouflaged, lied about, or withheld from Senate investigative committees ... '.[1] In short, border protection had manifested in overt and covert miscommunication on the part of border protection agencies and their bureaucratic counterparts. The second element of border policing has involved the development of the traditional law enforcement apparatus, namely the police, in the border policing function. It is this second element and its interaction with people smuggling that is the focus of this chapter.

A focus on policing efforts against refugees evidences the conflation of national security and refugee concerns. Such a conflation has significant consequences for the expansion of national security issues into traditionally internal policing domains, and the utilisation of external military apparatus for non-war functions

---

1   Kevin, T, (2004), *A Certain Maritime Incident: the sinking of SIEV X,* Melbourne: Scribe Publications.

involving international policing tasks.[2] While this approach has been commonplace for extended periods in conflict zones such as Northern Ireland, Israel-Palestine and South Africa, it is relatively novel in contemporary Anglo-American democracies. The reconfiguration of the coercive apparatus of the state disturbs the divisions made at the creation of the modern nation-state between policing and military functions that are usually held as a core tenet of democracy. The state monopoly on the use of force cannot be understood as an exception to the forces of globalisation and a bastion of the territorial sovereign state, but rather a complex example of the reinvention of the state itself and its performance to both internal and external audiences.

As Chapters 2 and 3 indicate, discourses of refugee criminality, and increasingly security, have informed the development of the border policing lexicon – commonly referred to in Australia as 'Border Protection'. Importantly, the border policing lexicon has facilitated discourses of deviancy from being a matter of individual refugee deviancy (as outlined in Chapters 2 and 3) to a matter of organised crime (particularly through people smugglers). No longer is 'refugee deviancy' simply a law and order issue but a matter of transnational organised crime. While border policing in Australia is carried out by a range of agencies (discussed below) this chapter will focus on the role of the federal policing (primarily carried out by the Australian Federal Police (AFP)). In routinely using the terms 'people smuggler', 'illegal entrant', 'illegal non-citizen' to refer to refugees, illegality has been ascribed to the presence of the refugee, a presence that remains legal under international law. Moreover, the border policing lexicon has historically relied on conflating issues of 'illegal immigration' with organised crime such as 'drug trafficking' and 'credit card fraud' which focus on the 'illegal' economies of people movement, and more contemporarily with national security issues that locate such 'illegal economies' as militarily concerns.

The AFP has identified its role in relation to these issues:

> Organised crime amasses significant reserves of undeclared and untaxed wealth to rival the economies of small countries and threatens not only the rule of law but the very primacy of the state. Thus traditional precepts as to what distinguishes or separates national security, military and law and order threats are themselves under

---

2   Andreas, P and Price, R (2001), 'From war fighting to crime fighting: transforming the American national security state', 3 *International Studies* 3, pp 31-52

challenge by global events. There is no greater imperative, therefore, in ensuring the security and integrity of Australia than to maintain law enforcement on the same plane of importance and relative capability as the nation's defence forces.[3]

In reaffirming the centrality of the state, law enforcement becomes interchangeable with reinforcing borders. However, law enforcement is seen as *responding* to the refugee as a security threat rather than the policing effort *actively contributing to its construction* as a security threat.

Such discourses have facilitated the transferral of border policing from what Andreas describes as 'low politics' to 'high politics', particularly as discourses of refugee deviancy have moved from that of a criminal threat to security threat. Burke has argued that security's claim to be a universal need and desire makes it compelling. Security, is a monological narrative, widely considered a predetermined and permanent constituent, disallowing the critique of policies except in narrow terms: 'Security claims to be universal, but lacks universal meaning. It claims to be a fundamental societal value, but draws up exclusive and violent divisions between society and its others'.[4]

The refugee, once made the focus of the border policing effort, is now to be dealt with as a matter of national security. No longer just a matter of the security of borders, or for an orderly immigration program, but for the security of all citizens.

As the previous chapter argued, discourses of deterrence render the law enforcement effort less interested in instrumental gains than symbolic messages. Border policing becomes an act of impression management:

> [P]olicing methods that are suboptimal from the perspective of a means-send calculus of deterrence can be optimal from the political perspective of constructing an image of state authority and communicating moral resolve ... For those state actors charged with the task of managing the border, the way their actions shape the perceptions of the audience ... ultimately matter more than whether or not the illegal border crossers are actually deterred. In fact, the feedback effects from some of the most popular parts of the law

---

3   Australian Federal Police, *Australian Federal Police Annual Report 1998-99*, Sydney: Australian Federal Police.

4   Anthony Burke, (2001) *In Fear of Security: Australia's Invasion Anxiety*, p xxx.

enforcement performance can actually create a more formidable control problem.[5]

Taken collectively, the discourses outlined above inform a border policing effort that is increasingly dislocated from either domestic or international expressions of the rule of law, and is invested in merged and open-ended policing jurisdiction and policing functions described in amorphous terms such as 'deterring' and 'disrupting' people smuggling activities. For example, in the case of Australia, the Australian Federal Police has redefined its remit to include policing out the refugee. The recent transformation of the AFP has been at least partially shaped through the construction of people smuggling as a matter of 'transnational crime' threatening 'national security'. The AFP, as the lead Commonwealth law enforcement agency, is now positioned as a key player in the prevention, deterrence and disruption of people smuggling. As recently as 1996-97, federal policing showed no interest in the area of people smuggling. The AFP now shares in the $353.3 million to be spent on border protection in the 2002 financial year (in contrast to the drastically reduced $7.3 million allocation to the work of UNHCR). The border policing effort further extends the role of the AFP into Indonesia. This chapter seeks to make two straightforward points in regard to the regulatory effort of law enforcement in relation to people smuggling. First, the greater the policing efforts to prevent people smuggling the greater the risk is to refugees of serious harm and death: 'target hardening'. Secondly, undertaking such activities federal policing distances policing from its territorial base. Additionally, once refugee policy is largely determined to be a matter of criminality, criminal investigation and law enforcement, the challenge to sovereignty that is apparent in the quasi-international realm of refugee policy dissipates. As federal policing overflows into neighbouring countries, so too does criminal policy overflow into other aspects government, including international humanitarian obligations.

In September 2000 the Minister for Justice issued a Ministerial Direction stating that the government now expects the AFP 'to give special emphasis to countering and otherwise investigating organised people smuggling' and that the 'AFP should also ensure that it provides an effective contribution to the implementation of the

---

5   Australian Federal Police, *Australian Federal Police Annual Report 1996-1997*, Sydney: Australian Federal Police.

government's whole-of-government approach to unauthorised arrivals'. This gave the AFP a clear remit in relation to refugees, as stated by the AFP:

> The AFP therefore has an interest in the enforcement of the criminal provisions of the Migration Act 1958. Its role is to investigate and prosecute offences against the Migration Act. This is done in accordance with the Australian Justice system and AFP investigations are undertaken with a focus on obtaining evidence for such prosecutions. In particular, the AFP engages in targeting the facilitators of people smuggling ventures.[6]

The police are 'protecting' Australia from conforming to international law as well as protecting malleable understandings of 'borders'. The AFP has also aided the collection of intelligence not only on 'people smugglers' but also those who seek to use their services to gain refugee protection. The manner in which this is done, free from territorial constraint, is at best vague, as they admitted to a Senate committee investigating this issue:

> The AFP does not have a border protection role in the same way that the Committee would understand the Australia Customs Service, DIMIA, Coastwatch and Australian Defence forces to have. Our role in protecting an Australian border lies in the provision of an investigatory function of offences that occur across the national barrier (eg, drug and firearm trafficking, environmental crimes, illegal immigration) ... The AFP maintains a very strong focus on fighting these crimes offshore, now commonly referred to as 'transnational' crime. The Committee would be aware that the AFP has no jurisdiction (police powers) beyond Australia's borders. As such, it does not have an operational role in other countries. The AFP makes up for this limitation by seeking the assistance of, and collaboration with, overseas law enforcement agencies.[7]

Gathering material for convictions extra-territorially means Australian police work is largely carried out by the Indonesian police and 'informants' such as those revealed in a Channel Nine television program. This program detailed a covert AFP operation inside Indonesia where statements were made alleging the AFP, at the very least, knew about the sabotaging of boats that were to sail to

---

6   Australia Federal Police Submission to the Australian Senate Legal and Constititional References Committee, Inquiry into the Migration Legislation Amendment (Further Border Protection Measures) Bill 2002, Canberra: Commonwealth of Australia, at 3.2.
7   AFP Submission at 4.1 and 4.2.

Australia. At worst, it was alleged that their informants were taking part in sabotage operations. The AFP responded to the allegations in the program by saying:

> The people who conduct the disruption – or the intervention – are the people with the power to conduct a disruption being the Indonesian National Police, the Indonesian defence and sometimes the Indonesia Immigration. We find we obtain information from informants, but informants do not disrupt. They have no power to disrupt.[8]

Despite locating the actual 'disruption/intervention' with the Indonesian authorities, the AFP works with these authorities. Indeed, it is their only 'base' in the 'investigation' of people smuggling in Indonesia. Importantly, under Indonesian law, people smuggling is not a crime. Presumably, anti-people smuggling policing by the INP occurs on the insistence of Australia where people smuggling is a crime. The questioning of Commissioner Keelty at a Parliamentary Inquiry made clear that the AFP does not operate within an identifiable human rights framework and that AFP disruption activities float free from international law and even domestic law:

> Senator Payne: The focus of the AFP's submission is about addressing transnational organised crime – understandably, I suspect. That is essentially because the AFP does not have a role in the observation of international obligations and things like that, isn't it? Your role is in the criminal aspects of this process?
>
> Commissioner Keelty: That is correct. [9]

Senator Payne's question first disassociates 'criminal aspects' from the framework of international law – the two separate functions cannot be simultaneously carried out. This places international law at odds with transnational border policing. Secondly, the question accepts the federal policing function in relation to transnational organised crime and locates it within 'criminal aspects'. Senator Payne's question, and Commissioner Keelty's response, affirms that when it comes to people smuggling, and possibly federal law enforcement more generally, the AFP is not fundamentally concerned

---

8   Ibid.
9   Australian Senate Legal and Constititional References Committee, Inquiry into the Migration Legislation Amendment (Further Border Protection Measures) Bill 2002, Canberra: Commonwealth of Australia, p 27.

with international obligations – including obligations under the Convention Relating to the Status of Refugees, the Universal Declaration of Human Rights, or the International Covenant on Civil and Political Rights. The reluctance of policing to engage with such traditional aspects of international law may be not be unusual, but when considering the proliferation of international law around traditionally criminal matters generally, and transnational crime and human trafficking specifically, the disassociation of the AFP role from international legal arrangements is surprising.

The lack of a clear accountability framework for the activities of federal policing inside Indonesia, let alone a human rights framework generally, raises grave concerns about the nature of the border policing effort. What kind of policing is being undertaken in pursuit of the amorphous notion of anti-people smuggling? The description of the AFP role in its evidence to the Committee seems disingenuous in its concerns for refugees as it contorts the legislation under question into a set of regulatory mechanisms that will bring the services of the AFP to the refugees. At one moment the Commissioner advocates the legislation as a way to deter refugees from coming and push them into 'mainstream activity' (one can only assume this means they need to join the alleged refugee 'queue' in Indonesia) or if they do come by boat, make them seek out the mainland of Australia as a landing point rather than the nearer Ashmore Reef or Christmas Island. If law enforcement bodies are committed to the wellbeing of the refugee then more details need to be made clear as to how their work in Indonesia facilitates refugees joining the alleged genuine 'queue' for refugee protection or how creating conditions under which substandard boats travel to the Australian mainland does not further jeopardise refugee lives:

> Chair: If people smugglers get more creative, that would make the job almost impossible for you, wouldn't it? You have a fairly extensive mainland to protect.

> Commissioner Keelty: That is right – and when I say that I mean you are right about the mainland of Australia – but, as pointed out in the figures I gave in the previous answer, it is more difficult for us to send resources to remote areas, because of the lack of infrastructure. At least if they come to the Australian mainland there is the potential for us to do something about them. The idea is to force them into the mainstream activity, and this is a deterrent to leaving passengers to their own fate on remote islands, where we have had people die.

> Chair: It is good to see that someone cares.

Commissioner Keelty: We do care, and it does not matter whether they are the people smugglers themselves or whether they are the passengers. This is a far preferable way for us to go, instead of having them left on a remote island.

Chair: So, basically, you are saying you would prefer them on the mainland, that you think this legislation will bring them there and that they will then be more manageable for you.

Commissioner Keelty: Yes. In a nutshell, and I think you touched upon it, as we advance any policy in law enforcement, whether that be Immigration policy or otherwise, the flexibility of the people smugglers is the flexibility of most transnational criminals, which is the ability to work around current legislation. We see this legislation as being a useful deterrent. The whole object is to force people to come to Australia through the correct procedures but, if they are going to commit a crime in the way they are sending people to Australia, we can at least try to get them sent to where there is some infrastructure support for them'.[10]

The outcome of the excision legislation 'target hardens' Australia as a refugee 'destination'. The AFP put it in the following terms when questioned by the Committee:

[B]ased on previous experience the AFP has already anticipated that the current successes in preventing, deterring and arresting those involved in seaborne people-smuggling will drive the people smugglers to either evolve new methodologies to evade detection or return to more covert means of illegal arrival in Australia. It is not foreseen that changes accompanying the introduction of the pro-posed amendments will affect the ability of the AFP to fulfill its role. In fact, the AFP views the proposed changes as potentially beneficial in the wider context as they are designed to send a deterrence message to potential smugglers and traffickers. Resultant changes should be understood to be, in effect, target hardening in terms of the ability of smugglers to get illegal immigrants to Australia and into the immigration process and a deflection of illegal immigrants to regional centres with better infrastructure.[11]

Various government, military and law enforcement bodies have collaborative stakes in the border policing effort in the same way that nations increasingly invest in bilateral and transnational agreements on people smuggling. The 'securitisation' of cross-border movement

---

10 Ibid, p 30.
11 Ibid, p 25.

of people depends upon such collaboration.[12] The pan-national approach to people smuggling has emerged through various regional and international forums. This has been particularly the case in Europe where border policing and people smuggling have found expression in the Schengen Agreement, the Dublin Convention, and the Tampere conclusions. The European Union, OSCE, the G8 Group, the UNHCR, UNICEF, IOM and other international non-government organisations have developed positions and programs on the issue. Morrison and Crosland estimate that there are over 30 intergovernmental bodies in Europe focusing on human trafficking and smuggling.[13] The majority of the European initiatives focus on border control. For example, Schengen provides for covert police operations and significant cross-border police collaboration.[14] Coupled with the extensive anti-people smuggling initiatives that rest within the framework of transnational organised crime, the provisions for surveillance and regulation of large population groups becomes not only possible but normalised through the Schengen Information System, EURODAC and Europol. Studies have shown that the use of such integrated systems of surveillance potentially impinges not only on the rights of generalised populations but specifically brings such surveillance to bear on refugees – those escaping the persecutory behaviour and human rights violations of home countries.[15] In relation to Australia, this has largely come in the form of regional agreements on people smuggling such as the Regional Ministerial Conference on people Smuggling, Trafficking in persons and Related Transnational Crime. Australia has also created an Ambassador for People Smuggling Issues from the office of the Minister of Foreign Affairs and Trade and included closer methods of co-operation between Australian and Indonesian police forces. Such co-operation has been conceptualised as:

---

12 Bigo, D, 'The Möbius Ribbon of Internal and External Security(ies)', in M Albert, D Jackson and Y Lapid (eds), *Identities, Borders, Orders: Rethinking International Relations Theory*, Minneapolis: University of Minnesota Press.

13 Morison, R and Crosland, J, (2001), *The Trafficking and Smuggling of Refugees: The Endgame in European Asylum Policy?* Working Paper No 39, UNHCR.

14 Green, P and Grewock, M, (2002) 'The War Against Illegal Immigration: State Crime & the Construction of European Identity', 14(1) *Current Issues in Criminal Justice* 87.

15 Andreas, P, (2000) *Border Games: Policing the US-Mexico divide*, Ithaca: Cornell University Press.

Should prevention strategies fail to remove the requirement or incentive to leave countries of origin or first asylum, disruption of secondary movement through the detection and interception of the people smuggler's route becomes the priority.[16]

The relationship between the AFP and the Indonesian National Police (INP) was formalised in a Memorandum of Understanding on transnational crime between the two bodies on the 15 September 2000. The AFP has given evidence that the MOU allows for 'the AFP and INP to provide advice regarding target selection, technical and management support of operations, informant management, information facilitation and assistance in financial reporting'.[17]

The great lengths to which the multi-agency approach to anti-people smuggling initiatives and policing the border are being pursued also signals a cross-jurisdictional merging of policing and military functions. It sees the merging of internal and external security concerns – not only where the criminal meets refugee policy, but also where the border is the point of convergence and security is not only a state affair but a boundary function. The borderland then becomes the vast space into which Zedner has described government 'casting about' for spheres of activity in which they can assert their sovereignty.[18] The police beat is militarised, becomes global and hones in on the most vulnerable for the unmitigated use of force and practices of exclusion. The moralising tone of interdiction policies resuscitates law and order and brings it to the high seas and border zones. Such tones can only be heard as state sovereignty territorially crumbles in other ways and the stakes in legitimating the use of force against the unprotected are raised. Such efforts cannot in any rational terms be considered a response to forced migration, but as a response to the condition of the state in late modernity. As social theorists have argued, a new form of sovereignty is emerging, with flexible and expanding frontiers. Rather than being tied to the traditional territorial nation-state, sovereignty is now a 'deterritorialising regime' with constant flows of movement and exchange.

---

16 The Hon Philip Ruddock, *Border Protection: People Smuggling – Australia's Experience and Police Responses – A Background Paper*, <www.minister.immi.gov.au/borders/detention/peoplesmugg_2.htm>, accessed 26 July 2002.

17 Select Committee On A Certain Maritime Incident, Report, *Senate Inquiry Report*, Ch 1, p 10.

18 Zedner, L, (2000), 'The Pursuit of Security' in T Hope and R Sparks (eds), *Crime, Risk and Insecurity* London: Routledge.

From the above discussion we can see how easily refugee protection is morphed into security. Border policing breaks free from standard measures of public accountability in a liberal democracy. Moreover, when refugee protection is usurped by the emerging lexicon of people smuggling and the focus becomes the response of the 'whole of government' to policing the border (whether by the military, the bureaucracy or traditional policing agencies), the state itself is transformed. While I agree with Crawford that '[a]s crime and insecurity have become unbounded so too policing is becoming cut free from its association with the modern state to incorporate a diversity of actors',[19] I also suggest that the state itself is cutting loose from territorial boundaries. As policing floats free from territorial bases, so too does state force and the state itself. Border policing that rests upon the transformation of a humanitarian issue into matters of criminogenic potential occurs in an environment free of criminal justice checks and balances but with all the coercive power of the meshed military and civil policing bodies. A more powerful expression of the coercive state would be difficult to find. Moreover, with the absence of checks and balances upon the bureaucratic structures that drive the military/civil policing of the border, the spectre of institutional deviance emerges without name or recognition, a deviance with the potential to harness unbounded coercive powers.

However, there has been state ambivalence about the merging of refugee, criminal and national security policies. Crawford has described such ambivalence in relation to the criminal as the 'residual capacity of the nation state to assert it sovereign authority, thus producing a volatile mix of criminal justice policies which are at one moment assured, expressive and morally toned, and at the next moment, hesitant, rationalistic and instrumental'.[20] When the criminal moment is transferred (geographically, politically and militarily) to the border, the state confronts the 'technocratic urge' to manage crime and insecurity while expressing fears and anxieties. The crisis in 'migration management' manifests itself in unaccountable and shifting policing forms that have violent outcomes for the refugee and an information vacuum for the citizen. The consequences of this include serious problems for the expression of traditional sovereignty, the unchecked violence of unbounded sovereignty and the development of new (yet old) techniques of control and practices

---

19 Crawford, A, (2002) *Crime and Insecurity: the governance of safety in Europe*, Devon: Willan, p 1.
20 Ibid, pp 9-10.

of exclusion. It also signals a moment in which the border policing practice becomes transferable to other suspect populations. While this has consequences for new suspect populations, it has broader ramifications for understandings of the policing/security apparatus beyond the domestic realm.

Sovereignty and transversal policing

The discourses of sovereignty identified above have informed narrow, but far-reaching responses to both refugees and people smuggling. They are far-reaching as they have informed not only the construction of crises but also the recrafting of the federal policing apparatus. Moreover, that recrafting has contributed to unshackling the federal policing effort from its traditional domestic base and physically taken it into other countries to enforce Australian laws – laws that do not necessarily overlap with the laws of those countries. In order to do so, the law enforcement function has needed to become a matter of national security and the federal policing function elevated to military status capable of making potent political contributions. Paradoxically, the national boundaries such policing has sought to preserve have needed to be transgressed for their own protection. It is only through the decline in the border that its protection becomes symbolically possible. The reinvention of law enforcement in the border policing effort against first, refugees, and second, terrorism, signals a shift in traditional understandings of security and policing functions that speak to the changing relationships between states and performances of statecraft:

> The traditional paradigm of security and insistence upon its traditional requirements naturalizes a sharp boundary between external and internal security, as well as military and police matters, and in the process obscures the fact that such a demarcation was produced as part of the development of the modern warfighting state. Recognizing that the functional distinction between military and police was an artifact of the mergence of a particular kind of state at a particular period leaves us better placed to consider the kinds of contemporary developments that may be the harbingers of another kind of state in another historical epoch with other forms of organised violence.[21]

Such transversal policing moments as those identified in this chapter, and the new kinds of state and interstate violence that they inform,

---

21   Andreas and Price, op cit, p 34.

REFUGEES AND STATE CRIME

will reshape relations between states in the region. How do such expressions of statehood manifest inside the villages and coastlines of the Indonesian archipelago? Can such transversal policing, in casting off its territorial base, be absorbed by other states without recourse to post-colonial and neo-colonial legacies in the region? The high status of the border policing effort and its intrusion into neighbouring countries can potentially have one of two outcomes, first, overwhelming change to the policing function as traditionally conceptualised and understood by domestic audiences and hence, potential alienation from them, or second, the rejection of the deterritorialised federal border policing function from neighbouring countries or significant groups within neighbouring countries. Both outcomes have significant negative consequences for the policing apparatus, for Australia's relations in the region and for the plight of those populations rendered suspect.

Border policing, as outlined in this chapter, cannot be understood as a rational response to forced migration but as integral to the condition of the state in late modernity. The new forms of sovereignty that border policing depends upon fracture the ontology of the nation-state and move us beyond the nation-state model of power at the very moment the harshest forms of border policing keep the territorial state alive. In the border policing moment new and old sovereignties are invoked and kept alive. The challenge then is how we wish to counter border policing and find new ways to conceptualise the kinds of policing/non-policing that come to characterise the late modern engagement of the deterritorialised state and the refugee.

Chapter 6

Refugees and the renegade judiciary

JONES: Where are we as we stand today?

PRIME MINISTER: Well, as we stand we are ready and able to start transferring the people from the Tampa to the Manoora and take them to Papua New Guinea, through Port Moresby, where they will be put on aircraft and taken to New Zealand and Nauru. That can't happen while the Federal Court injunction remains in place. The Federal Court will commence, or return to its hearing, I understand, this morning. So it is all waiting on that.

JONES: Many people would, of course, say that the Prime Minister of Australia, whomever he or she is, should be the person determining our destiny and our foreign policy position not the Federal Court.

PRIME MINISTER: Well, I understand that feeling but we live under the rule of law and that applies to prime ministers as well as everybody else. I really don't want to say any more about that. The matter is before the court. What I will say, however, is that the solution we have worked out is fair and humane …

JONES: All right, just on the Federal Court, and I know you can't say too much, but Julian Burnside QC for the Council of Civil Liberties told the Court yesterday that the SAS troops on board the Tampa were acting as migration agents and were bound by law to bring the boat people ashore.

PRIME MINISTER: Well, that is not our advice and our position was put very strongly by David Bennett QC, the Commonwealth Solicitor General. We, of course, through David expressed our total opposition to the court action, that the argument has no standing and we, of course, are seeking the complete dismissal of that application. But Mr Bennett has put the Government's case in the Court. I don't want to repeat what he said to the Court, suffice to say to your listeners that we don't believe that application has any legal basis at all but while ever there is a court injunction I and everybody else in this country is bound by it because, in the end, what defines us as a democratic, open society is that we believe in the rule of law. That rule of law must apply to all of us including the Prime Minister.

JONES: It was the same, Mr Justice North, though, who as a barrister acted on for the waterfront workers in 1986. He advised a seamen union in relation to massive strike action in Robe River. He represented the unions in the Mudginberri dispute. He represented the pilots when they were fighting the Hawke Government.

PRIME MINISTER: Well, I don't know … I understand some of those things are true, the others I just don't know, I haven't followed it. But, Alan, it's before a court. I don't want to get started into some slanging match with the Court. It is a matter for them to resolve because an action has been brought. But we have the strongest possible view that that application does not have a sound legal basis.

JONES: Had your legislation been supported in the Parliament last week by the Labor Party this action couldn't have been brought.

PRIME MINISTER: No, no, that legislation sought to take right outside the scope of the court anything that we did in relation to this matter. The answer to that is undeniably it could not have been brought because the legislation would have said that once an instruction had been given by an authorised officer that instruction was not reviewable before the courts.[1]

From gratuitous humanity to gratuitous control

In the above media exchange, the Prime Minister claims a humane and just solution while simultaneously insisting its justness and humanity should not be subject to independent testing. The Prime Minister claims he does not only adhere to the rule of law but *believes* in the rule of law while simultaneously acting directly against the basic premise that the judiciary should be able to review the powers of the Executive. The symbiotic relationship between the Prime Minister and the interviewer crafts the issue, which at its core are the sovereign rights of a country and the human rights of an individual, without a single mention of sovereignty or rights. Their absence casts a long shadow over this carefully choreographed media performance that presents the issue as a struggle between the Executive and the court. The absence of sovereignty and rights is, in part, at odds with how both the parliament and the courts have considered the issue within their respective domains. The interview successfully communicates that the government's response to the Tampa is about humanity, government actions might be against the

---

1   Part of an interview carried out by Alan Jones on Radio 2UE with the Prime Minister on 3 September 2001, <http://www.pm.gov.au/news/interviews/2001/interview1209.htm>, accessed 3 March 2002.

law, but *that law is already being changed by the government.* Legality is in a state of flux. The Tampa, as a matter of humanity, no longer needs the law, nor does it need rights, the rule of law or an explication of how popular, legal and political conceptions of sovereignty are at work. The exchange markets a refugee policy explained as gratuitous humanity but grounded in gratuitous control, and casts adrift the confines of law and rights.

The nature of democracy in Australia is changing and this is evident in the ways the demeanour of government has drifted away from legality when refugees are the subject. In the past, refugee policy had been underscored by a series of battles between the Executive (and largely the parliament) and the judiciary. The rule of law, even in its most diluted incarnation, has become a thorn in the side of the 'punitive populism' that characterises refugee policy. 'Judicial activism' has become a derogatory label for the work of judges, lawyers and human rights advocates. In the midst of this series of very public judicial/Executive tussles is a struggle over the language and ideas of legality/illegality of both refugees and government action. The sovereign right to determine legality and illegality is at the heart of this struggle and consequently this chapter.

It is the intent of this chapter to examine the conflict between the Executive and the judiciary on two interdependent levels: language use and substantive ideas. These battles have occurred across two main issues: unlawful detention (Constitutional) and the Convention definition of who is a refugee (notably in relation to gender). The operation of the rule of law, the doctrine of the separation of powers and the abrogation of international law, raise a series of inter-related questions: can sovereignty discourses underpin the containment of Executive excess or is sovereignty by default a byword for exclusion and indeed excess? Is there any regulatory and/or emancipatory power within sovereignty? What has been the negotiation of rights discourse in the refugee battles between the courts and the Executive? By exploring these questions I want to know whether these court cases promote a moment of acknowledging state criminality and hence censure. Does state action/inaction reach beyond the 'unlawful' or the 'discriminatory' and into the realm of criminality? Do these cases, as legal spectacles, debunk notions of the unlawful/illegal/criminal refugee? Examining these questions requires me to draw intermittently on the writings of Hannah Arendt, which recognise relations between the state, law and the refugee have always involved questions of state illegality and the compromise of the nation-state.

In this chapter I examine the 'joint authorship' of language between the courts and the parliament. The cases covered in this first section on unlawful detention are remarkable for the absence of the refugee – without a word spoken before the court they remain the primary victim. The absence of the victim is indeed critical to the difficulty the court has in conceiving of the state as criminal.

In examining the narratives of these cases I am offering a particular and partial account of the refugee in the hands of the judiciary. In utilising a frame of state criminality and the debunking of refugee criminality, this chapter is indeed itself a production of a counter-narrative. It is a counter-history that engages the 'official history' of unlawful refugee detention offered by the courts.[2] There is a contest within and between the narratives of each of the cases examined, all competing for legal recognition. How the refugee and the state are imagined is central to how the narratives unfold and the adequacy of legal and political terms deployed.[3] The narratives indicate the deficiency of legal terms and categories, the demarcation between victim and offender in 'administrative' matters. Choices in legal categories clearly delineate the competing narratives offered. The choices of legal categories and the choices of narratives used by each Justice across the cases are subject to both inter- and intra-conflict in judgments. As may well be expected, there is little closure in narratives that seek or manoeuvre around issues of sovereignty and rights. The socio-legal framework I have taken in this book prepares me to tell a story of state illegality with implications for ideas of state criminality.[4]

Unlawful detention

Over the past decade, a series of cases relating to the use of unlawful detention (for 'unlawful arrivals') during onshore refugee determination has highlighted the ways the judiciary has approached

2   I am indebted to the chapter by Bilsky, Leora, (2001),'Between Justice and Politics: the competition of Storytellers in the Eichmann Trial' in Aschheim, S, (ed), *Hannah Arendt in Jerusalem*, Berkeley: University of California Press.
3   Bilsky, op cit, p 240
4   Again I am indebted to the work of Leora Bilsky, op cit, writing on Arendt's depiction of the Eichmann trial.

notions of rights and sovereignty. I will stage a dialogue between the judiciary and the parliament in drawing on the court judgments and parliamentary Hansard across three cases: the *Lim* case, the *Tampa* cases, and the *Al Masri* case. The dialogue assists in tracing the potential of the judiciary in curbing the excesses of the administration and the potential of discourses of rights and sovereignty to recast government practices as deviant. Three major tensions run through the three cases examined: sovereignty/rights, legality/ illegality, and citizen/alien.

The Lim case

> In the present case, there is no suggestion that any of the plaintiffs is an enemy alien.[5]

Chu Kheng Lim v Minister for Immigration, Local Government and Ethnic Affairs (1992)[6] represented the first instance of judicial-Executive confrontation over refugee policy since the late 1980s. The action taken against the government by human rights advocates also reminds us that the role of civil society has been crucial in understanding what government actions are challenged and when. The case of *Lim* turned on the interpretation of the Constitution and whether the Executive had authority to detain an alien and whether that power was reviewable by a court. It also raised the issue of whether such detention placed Australia in breach of its international obligations.

The case was brought after 35 Cambodians, some of whom arrived in Australia in late 1989 and others in 1990, were detained. After two years their applications for refugee status were rejected. They applied for review of their case in the Federal Court which was scheduled to take place on 7 May 1992. They had also applied for release from detention while their claims were resolved. On the 5 May 1992 the Federal Parliament passed the *Migration Amendment Act* 1992 (Cth) which included provisions for 'designated persons' to be kept in custody. A 'designated person' was a person who had arrived by boat in Australia between 19 November 1989 and 1 December 1992 without an entry permit. The amendment to the Act introduced Division 4B under which s 54R stated that 'A court is not to order the release from custody of a designated person'. The

---

5   Mason CJ (at 9).
6   (1992) 176 CLR 1.

Lim case was brought to challenge the Constitutionality of s 54R. Chapter III of the Australian Constitution concerns the doctrine of the separation of powers. However, the aliens power in the Constitution also provides for the Executive to expel and deport aliens.[7]

Notably, if I return to Green and Ward's definition of state crime introduced in Chapter 1, we find the constituent parts of that definition correspond to the specific questions brought to the court in the case of Lim.

Green and Ward's definition says:[8]

> State deviance + human rights violation = state crime

The potential application in the case of Lim:

> Unlawful detention + breach of HR obligations (ie, ICCPR+CAT) = state crime

However, the *Lim* case resolved:

> Detention only invalid prior to legislation + (therefore) no question of HR violation considered = no state crime

Utilising the above definition in this instance draws on one of the censuring audiences that Green and Ward nominate: the courts. *Lim* had the potential to act as a significant moment of acknowledgement of state crime by the courts. The courts are an important site for such recognition, after which, it would be anticipated, the deviant state action would not only be acknowledged but would cease.

It is to the judgment of the High Court that I now turn with less of an eye on the outcome than on the narratives relied upon in the judgment, that is, the turning points where the similarities and differences in the legal narratives of the courts and the Executive become clear. In particular I am interested in the discourses that veer the narrative away from the state as criminal. I contend elements of this judgment kept the decision from engaging the criminality of state action.

First, acknowledging the shifting nature of illegal and legal state practice is avoided. Mason CJ argued that s 54R could be read in such a way that it could be assumed that the parliament never intended to go beyond Constitutional bounds in preventing judicial

---

7   Section 51(xix).
8   Green, P, and Ward, T, (2000), 'State Crime, Human Rights and the Limits of Criminology', 27 *Social Justice* 110.

review of those held in custody. In short, s 54R does not prevent a court from ordering the release of a person held in *unlawful* custody. Mason CJ said (at 9):

> [I]t would be quite extraordinary to ascribe to Parliament an intention to require a court not to release a person held in unlawful custody. Unless a clear and unambiguous intention to do so appears from a statute, it should not be construed so to infringe the liberty of the subject.

This is a somewhat decontextualised statement considering the Parliament had almost simultaneously manoeuvred to ensure the kind of detention at stake in this case could no longer be considered illegal. The parliament was transferring the illegal to the legal, the unlawful to the lawful. At the very moment the Chief Justice sought to pin the intention of the parliament on the assumed state/place of legality, that very legality was shifting.

Brennan, Deane and Dawson JJ formed their judgment around the re-establishment of the sovereignty of the courts. Consequently, the struggle between the judiciary and the Executive was most fully played out in their reasoning. The power of the courts to define legality was firmly re-established in relation to the protections of adjudging and punishing criminal guilt, Brennan, Deane and Dawson JJ said (at 23):

> It would, for example, be beyond the legislative power of the Parliament to invest the Executive with an arbitrary power to detain citizens in custody notwithstanding that the power was conferred in terms which sought to divorce such detention in custody from both punishment and criminal guilt. The reason why that is so is that, putting to one side the exceptional cases to which reference is made below, the involuntary detention of a citizen in custody by the State is penal or punitive in character and, under our system of government, exists only as an incident of the exclusively judicial function of adjudging and punishing criminal guilt. Every citizen is 'ruled by the law and by the law alone' and 'may with us be punished for a breach of law, but he can be punished for nothing else' …

Secondly, clearly locating the power to detain within the judicial realm and in relation to the penal and punitive, the Justices discursively separate themselves from the use of administrative detention and that detention which claims to be non-penal and non-punitive. As such they locate their court apart from, and not a part of, the process that detains asylum seekers.

Thirdly, to keep state actions from being considered illegal, the non-citizen must be repeatedly invented and asserted. Most notably, Brennan, Deane and Dawson JJ are at pains to use this separation as the marker of legality and illegality – not of the non-citizen but of the state. State actions of the sort questioned would certainly be repugnant if carried out against ordinary citizens, but arguably acceptable if carried out against non-citizens:

> If the first element – ie, 'non-citizen' – of the definition of 'designated person' for the purposes of Div 4B had been omitted with the consequence that those provisions purported to apply to Australian citizens, Div 4B would be plainly beyond the legislative competence of the Parliament and invalid … It would also be that Div 4B, if not confined to non-citizens, would purport both to authorize involuntary imprisonment of citizens by Executive designation and to deprive the courts of jurisdiction to order that a citizen, who had been so designated by the Executive, be released from custody if his or her detention in custody was found to be unlawful. Such a conferral upon the Executive of an essentially unexaminable power to imprison a citizen would, for the reasons given above, be inconsistent with the Constitution's doctrine of the separation of judicial from Executive and legislative power and its exclusive vesting of judicial power in the courts. Ultimately, the critical question in the present case is whether the effect of the confinement of the application of the provisions of Div 4B to non-citizens or aliens is to avoid such conflict between the provisions of Div 4B and Ch III of the Constitution (at 25).

The question before the court is how the citizen must be clearly demarcated from the non-citizen and hence differentially treated in terms of the lawfulness of state actions.

Fourthly, democracy must remain imprecise. McHugh J said:

> The line between judicial and Executive power in particular is very blurred. Prescriptively separating the three powers has proved impossible. The classification of the exercise of a power as legislative, Executive or judicial frequently depends upon a value judgment as to whether the particular power, having regard to the circumstances which call for its exercise, falls into one category or another. The application of analytical tests and descriptions does not always determine the correct classification (at 30).

By remaining imprecise, the separation of powers between the judiciary, the Executive and the parliament are always in contest and are, within certain parameters, always shifting. While democracy remains malleable at these borders it is a difficult task indeed to invoke the criminal to describe the actions or inactions of the state.

Fifthly, circumscribing the issue as one of Executive inter-ference in the judiciary hermetically seals the issue from a broader 'state-as-criminal' reading. Interference implies meddling, intrusion, prying, nosiness or intervention. Intervention is the most serious of the synonyms for mounting a case of the criminal state, but it is hardly compelling. However, there were two moments within the judgments of the *Lim* case that hint at a deviant state narrative.

First, language became an important point of departure in the grounding of the issues raised above. It is in the dispute over language that I will suggest the judiciary has most significantly contested the refugee-related powers of the Executive. Responding to discourses of deviancy has been central to courts asserting the importance of judicial review in containing Executive powers. The question remains whether the contest over language facilitates the transformative use of language generally and the transformation of deviancy discourses specifically. For example, Gaudron J began her judgment considering the concept of citizenship:

> It is no doubt correct to say that 'alien' has become synonymous with 'non-Citizen' and that was accepted by this Court in *Nolan v Minister for Immigration and Ethnic Affairs* (1998) 165 CLR 178). But that conceals a number of questions: when did it become synonymous? With what effect in relation to persons, if any, who were not aliens but did not become citizens? Must it remain so? (at 3)

Questioning language, in this instance, helps probe whether the Executive, legislature and court have authored a shared language that underpins the creation of crises and responses to these crises. It also raises the question of whether such language underpins the designation of legality and illegality associated with the collapsing of some words into others, that is, alien = non-citizen. The conflict between the courts and the Executive has often been a dispute over in the use and meaning of language and in particular the signifiers that represent the refugee. Gaudron J continues:

> It may never be that the occasion to answer these questions that I have formulated will ever arise. However, membership of the com-munity constituting the Australian body politic, for which the criterion is now, but was not always, citizenship ... is a matter of such fundamental importance that, in my view it is necessary that the questions be acknowledged even if they are not answered. (at 4)

Notably, Gaudron J asserts that the concept of citizenship is entirely statutory and most importantly:

> [I]t is not a concept which is constitutionally necessary, which is immutable or which has some immutable core element ensuring its lasting relevance for constitutional purposes. Because citizenship is a concept of the kind indicated, it cannot control the meaning of 'alien' in s 51(xix) of the Constitution'. (at 5-6).

This may be read as indicating that the alien cannot be constructed simply in relation to the fixed state of citizenship, which indeed is not fixed at all. Most notably this means that the alien cannot be simply cast as the binary opposite of the citizen and hence the signification of the other. Concomitantly, this leaves open the possibility of reconfiguring the lawfulness of state action that was rooted in this binary form.

The intent is to restrict parliament from giving its own meaning to the term 'alien' in order to expand its powers under s 51(xix) of the Constitution, and further 'it certainly does not authorise the transformation of a non-alien into an alien by statutory redefinition of citizenship or by repeal or amendment of legislative provisions dealing with citizenship' (at 6). Gaudron J concludes that it is only in the clear and unforced point of overlap: where 'non-citizen' remains synonymous with the meaning of 'alien' then ss 54L and 54N of the *Migration Act* remain valid.

Gaudron J (at 9) argues that designation as an 'alien' does not in and of itself justify administrative detention:

> Detention in custody in circumstances not involving some breach of the criminal law and not coming within well-accepted categories of the kind to which Brennan, Deane and Dawson JJ refer is offensive to ordinary notions of what is involved in a just society. But I am not presently persuaded that legislation authorising detention in circumstances involving no breach of the criminal law and travelling beyond presently accepted categories is necessarily and inevitably offensive to Ch III. That does not mean that the power conferred by s 51(xix) permits of laws for the detention of aliens merely because they are aliens.

In essence this argues against the inherent illegality routinely ascribed to the status of alien. Moreover, it considers such action as 'offensive to ordinary notions of what is involved in a just society'. However, the gap, between offending a just society and state crime remains as difficult to ascertain as ever.

Despite the sophisticated analysis of language at the heart of Gaudron's J reasons, the unnamed spectre of sovereignty re-emerges, and the complexities of language representation raised above are usurped:

> Aliens, not being members of the community that constitutes the body politic of Australia, have no right to enter or remain in Australia unless such right is expressly granted. Laws regulating their entry to and providing for their departure from Australia (including deportation, if necessary) are directly connected with their alien status. And laws specifying the conditions on and subject to which they may enter and remain in Australia are also connected with their status as aliens to the extent that they are capable of being seen as appropriate or adapted to regulating entry or facilitating departure if and when departure is required ...

Sovereignty is returned to trump any nuanced reading of the alien. Sovereignty re-assigns the stasis of 'alien' and hence returns it to its position as the subordinate and other of citizen. Sovereignty, even in its absence, is a point of convergence – where the most complex categorisations become reducible to a one dimensional reading of sovereignty. Sovereignty reaffirms the difference that was previously problematised.

The second moment that suggested the development of a deviant state narrative was that prior to the hastily-introduced legislation, the plaintiffs' detention was considered illegal. McHugh J said:

> The source of the power to detain the plaintiffs in custody before the Amendment Act passed is unclear. Absent a statutory power of detention no public official has any power to detain an alien who has entered the country whether or not that person's entry constituted an illegal entry ... (at 17)

McHugh J further said that the burning of the plaintiffs' boats prevented their departure as provided for under s 88 of the *Migration Act*.[9] Therefore s 88 could not 'justify the detention of the plaintiffs when the boats upon which they arrived had been destroyed'.[10] Nor was s 92 relied upon. Section 92 required the government to arrest a person and bring them before a prescribed

---

9   Section 88 was concerned with the custody of prohibited entrants during stay of vessel in ports.
10 McHugh, J (at 19).

authority within 48 hours of the arrest or as soon as practicable after that period. However, McHugh J concludes:

> Consequently, the plaintiffs may have been detained unlawfully before Div 4B was enacted. But that circumstance, if it is true, does not mean that Div 4B is invalid in its application to the plaintiffs. That Division does not seek to make lawful what was previously unlawful. It operates prospectively. Any rights that the plaintiffs may have in relation to their earlier detention are unaffected by Div 4B. (at 21)

Finally, a discourse of human rights is not significantly addressed in the decision of the court. As a result of the first issue before the court being decided in the negative, the second question regarding Australia's international human rights obligations was not addressed. The High Court did note, however, that there was provision in the amended Act for it to prevail over all other legislation, including the *Human Rights and Equal Opportunity Commission Act* 1986. In essence, the domestic expression of international human rights, contained in the *Human Rights and Equal Opportunity Commission Act*, cannot trump the amended legislation in question. It was further noted that the entry into a treaty by Australia does not necessitate a change in domestic law. This removes any direct engagement by the court with international human rights discourse in the *Lim* case. The status of the alien is embedded on the wrong side of expressions of sovereignty, be that in language, in legislation, or in judgment – regardless of how close government practice came to illegality.

I now turn to the pre-emptive strike by the parliament in passing legislation directly relating to this case two days prior to the court decision. Parliamentary debate on the introduced amendments to the *Migration Act* indicates the intention of the legislation was to criminalise asylum seekers in an effort to deter their arrival:

> [T]he *Migration Act* creates a number of criminal offences dealing with such matters as illegal entry to Australia, obstruction of officers and escaping from custody. In line with the Government's determination to reduce the number of illegal entrants in Australia, the penalties provided in the Act have recently been reviewed.[11]

---

11 Hand, The Hon GL, Migration Amendment Bill (1992), Second Reading, 5 May 1992.

In order to do so the Minister was at pains to introduce into the lexicon new words to signify old practices:

> References to powers of arrest will be removed from sections 92 and 93 and from a number of related sections to ensure that no confusion arises between the powers under the Act to take persons into what might be termed 'migration custody' and the power to arrest persons for criminal offences ... Officers who exercise powers under the *Migration Act* related to migration processing and/or removal from Australia. Those powers are, therefore, not subject to the restrictions set out in the *Crimes Act* 1914 which apply to the power to arrest persons for criminal offences. However to make this distinction absolutely clear the term 'arrest' has been removed from a number of sections of the Act and replaced with the term 'detain in custody.[12]

A new lexicon is required for the processes of criminalisation to be set in place and popular discourses take up the designation of the refugee as criminal.

On the one hand, this new lexicon helps shift Executive practice away from the normal checks and balances associated with the operation of state power against the criminal, and, on the other hand, the Executive attempts to maintain a veneer of respectability in relation to international human rights obligations by not procedurally naming practices as criminalisation:

> The Government is conscious of the extraordinary nature of the measures which will be implemented by the amendment aimed at boat people ... Australia will, of course continue to honour its statutory and international obligations as it has always done.

The opposition equally noted:

> It is clear from the terms of the legislation that it in no way alters the obligations we have to offer protection to genuine refugees, as defined by the UN conventions and protocols. The legislation specifically notes that those rights are not affected.[13]

However, restriction of judicial review was always the clear intention of the legislation:

---

12 Ibid.
13 Ruddock, The Hon, Migration Amendment Bill (1992), Second Reading, 5 May 1992.

The most important aspect of this legislation is that it provides that a court cannot interfere with the period of custody. No law other than the Constitution will have any impact on it.[14]

The significance of moving detention away from judicial review was justified as an interim measure, one still in place over a decade later:

> [T]his legislation is only intended to be an interim measure. The present proposal refers principally to a detention regime for a specific class of persons. As such it is designed to address only the pressing requirements of the current situation. However, I acknowledge that it is necessary for wider consideration to be given to such basic issues as entry, detention and removal of certain non-citizens.[15]

The opposition was more sanguine. Indeed, opposition statements resolutely asserted the sovereignty of the parliament to make decisions in relation to administrative detention. In so doing, the decisions of the courts were considered 'contrary to the law', and the court itself was considered to operate upon the basis of 'discretion':

> It is our view that no court should have the authority to undertake the release of people into the community contrary to the express wish of the Parliament, expressed in the *Migration Act*, as to the basis upon which entry permits will be granted. In other words, having eliminated any discretion from Ministers and ourselves, subject to only two specific sections in the Act, I and my colleagues do not believe that any other body should operate under its discretion or inherent powers to release people into the community contrary to the law.[16]

The opposition therefore raised the 'interference' of to simultaneously belittle the role of the courts ('discretion') and highlight the dangerousness of the courts to government policy and the community at large ('contrary to the law'). Naming illegality now included the parliament nominating the illegality of the courts. Notably, the law stays somehow immutable, and material, something in possession of either the parliament or the courts. In the absence of rights, such law was certainly never in the possession of the refugee.

---

14   Hand, The Hon GL, op cit.
15   Hand, The Hon GL, op cit.
16   Ruddock, The Hon, op cit.

The Tampa cases[17]

The Tampa cases refer to the *Victorian Council for Civil Liberties v Minister for Immigration and Multicultural Affairs*[18] and, on appeal, *Ruddock v Vadarlis*[19] brought in response to the rescuing of asylum seekers by the MV Tampa. The distinction between law and justice was central in the Tampa case. In short, where the Federal Court ruled in relation to justice, the Full Court of the Federal Court ruled in relation to law. The dissonance reveals a great deal about how the illegality of the state is created through language and through the narratives developed in the judgments.[20]

North J in *Victorian Council for Civil Liberties v Minister for Immigration and Multicultural Affairs*[21] handed down his decision on the fate of the MV Tampa on the 11 September 2001. The central claim of the applicants was for a writ of habeas corpus that would bring the rescuees to Australia. That is, the applicants claimed the respondents were unlawfully holding 433 asylum seekers aboard the MV Tampa off Christmas Island. Secondly, the applicants contended that the Executive had no independent power to detain non-citizens for the purpose of expulsion considering the extensive provisions for the detention of non-citizens contained in the *Migration Act*. In essence, the statutory provisions of the *Migration Act* replace any Executive power to detain non-citizens. North J granted habeas corpus and ordered the rescuees be brought to Australia. Their detention on board the MV Tampa amounted to false imprisonment. North J held that the Executive had no independent surviving prerogative power to detain non-citizens for the purpose of expulsion considering the extensive powers contained in the *Migration Act*.

As the case unfolded, the federal government made arrangements for those onboard the MV Tampa to be taken to Nauru and Papua New Guinea for processing in what was dubbed 'The Pacific Solution'. Most importantly, the government introduced the Border Protection Bill 2001 into the House of Representatives. It was passed in the House but defeated in the Senate. The purpose of the Bill was

---

17 *Victorian Council for Civil Liberties Incorporated v Minister for Immigration and Multicultural Affairs (& Summary)* [2001] FCA 1297; *Ruddock v Vadarlis* [2001] FCA 1329.
18 [2001] FCA 1297.
19 [2001] FCA 1329.
20 The background to the MV Tampa was covered in Chapters 3 and 4.
21 [2001] FCA 1297.

to make legal directions to use force to remove a ship from Australian territorial waters; to prevent court proceedings from being initiated against such directions and to remove the capacity of individuals on such a ship from applying for protection visas. A raft of legislation was passed through both houses of parliament in the following months, part of which validated government actions in relation to the Tampa.[22]

In relation to the first issue challenged in the court, that of whether those on board the MV Tampa were being detained, and whether the Executive had the power to operate such detention, the government contended that those on board were not detained as they were free to go anywhere, other than Australia. In the findings of North J we see a shift away from dominant understandings of sovereignty and a counterpoint to the absence of rights discourses in the Australian courts. If you like, it is a significant moment in what Sassen has called the 'unbundling' of sovereignty. My intention here is to trace the use of language and ideas in this judgment that points to an expanded application the concept of sovereignty in relation to the refugee. Is there a chance that sovereignty can be transformative for our understanding of the state and the refugee? Is it possible that the courts could be a site for such transformation and in turn provide a moment for the acknowledgement of state crime?

North J found:

> In my view the evidence of the respondents' actions in the week following 26 August demonstrate they were committed to retaining control of the fate of the rescuees in all respects. The respondents directed whether the MV Tampa was allowed to go and not to go. They procured the closing of the harbour so that the rescuees would be isolated. They did not allow communication with the rescuees. They did not consult with them about the arrangements being made for their physical relocation or future plans. After the arrangements were made the fact was announced to them, apparently not in their native language, but no effort was made to determine whether the rescuees desired to accept the arrangements. The respondents took to themselves the complete control over the bodies and destinies of the

22 See the *Migration Amendment (Excision from Migration Zone) Act* 2001 (Cth); *Migration Amendment (Exsicion from Migration Zone) (Consequential Provisions) Act* 2001 (Cth); *Migration Legislation Amendment Act (No 6)* 2001 (Cth); *Border Protection (Validation and Enforcement Powers) Act* 2001 (Cth); *Migration Legislation Amendment (Judicial Review) Act* 1998 (Cth); *Migration Legislation Amendment Act (No 1)* 2001 (Cth); *Migration Legislation Amendment Act (No 5)* 2001 (Cth)

rescuees. The extent of the control is underscored by the fact that when the arrangements were made with Nauru, there had been no decision as to who was to process the asylum applications there or under what legal regime they were to be processed. Where complete control over people and their destiny is exercised by others it cannot be said that the opportunity offered by those others is a reasonable escape from custody in which they were held. The custody simply continues in the form chosen by those detaining the people restrained'. (at [81])

The judgment positions the government as an active agent in the creation of the situation onboard the MV Tampa. The respondents are not cast as simply reacting to a pre-existing situation. Control was designated in the hands of the government. A discourse which locates the government in control is of course at odds with wider discourses regarding refugee policy as being 'out of control' and the necessity of various enforcement strategies required to bring it under control. Once the government is located as having control then their actions cannot be cast as simply responsive. Their actions can be considered pre-emptive, provocative, and indeed unlawful. The alleged neutrality of the exercise of sovereignty (as posited in *Lim*) is no longer a bounded closed event.[23]

The 'unbundling of sovereignty'[24] evident in this decision was, however, conducted within a carefully delimited role for the Court. North J said:

> The question of Australia's policy towards refugees is a matter of great current debate in our community. It is important for me to stress that the role of the Court is to determine questions of law which are brought to it. That is what I have done in this case. The written reasons explain how I have come to my conclusions. It is not part of the function of the Court to interfere in the policy decisions made by government. But it is part of the function of the Court to determine if the government respondents have acted within the law. (Summary at [7])

The strict interpretation of the role of the court is, on the one hand, clear – it is interested in law and not policy nor public debate. The court cannot invest in the individual opinion of judges. In seeking to plainly apply the law in this instance, North J, marks out (1) the significance and power of the court; and (2), the treatment of the -

---

23 Sassen, S, (1996), *Sovereignty in an Age of Globalization*, New York: Columbia University Press, p 91
24 I am indebted to the writing of Saskia Sassen for this term.

refugee which is the broader context in which the judicial application of law takes place. There are many similar such 'context'
statements that North J may have made. For example, in relation to
government response to border control, illegal immigration or
response to ships at sea. He chose the refugee as the object and the
government as the acting subject. In particular, he most clearly
demarcated the relationship between the government and the
refugee in terms of Executive power and the individual rights of the
refugee. North J said:

> The *Migration Act* gives the government very wide powers to detain
> and remove unlawful non-citizens who are about to enter or who are
> in Australia. These powers, however, also confer certain rights on the
> detainees. (Summary at [8])

The judgment recognises government power to 'police' immigration
and control admission to (and exclusion from sovereign) territory
while simultaneously recognising the claims of individuals (including 'non-citizens') upon the (sovereign) state. The judgment also
acknowledges that bearing rights and being in detention are not
mutually exclusive states. Notably, the power of the government is
not free-flowing but contained in statute. While in essence this
stressed the independence of the judiciary it placed the judgment at
odds with popular and Executive understanding. This is not to
suggest that by stealth the judgment did indeed pronounce a policy
position, but rather the judgment refuted the framework of the
Executive as being the only, or even the most appropriate, framework to locate this judgment within.

   The court further noted that it was not simply interested in
law but justice: 'Ultimately, the consideration which must guide me
is the interests of justice in all the circumstances' (at 34). While,
generally, the law and justice maybe synonymous, they are distin-
guishable concepts. In relation to refugees, they have arguably
drifted further and further apart over the past decade. From the
outset, the applicants are located within an interest for justice. They
are not a nuisance or a delay but motivated by conscience. The
judgment contrasts refugees with the moves set in train by the
government (the 'Pacific Solution') to undermine any finding of the
court. In explaining attempts to have parties mediate, North J notes:

> It is probably best I think for the parties to have a short time to
> consider whether they are prepared to engage in the process of
> mediation. That should be seen against the background that there

has been evidence given this afternoon, particularly evidence relating to the intentions of the government consequent upon the
arrangement that has been reached ... It seems to be undoubted that
the applicants have moved the Court out of strong feelings based on
conscience and justice and there may be room for those concerns to
be addressed in some sort of procedures in consultations with the
respondents. (at [41])

Central to the judicial narrative was debunking the notion that those
onboard the MV Tampa had made a series of decisions that brought
them to their detained state. In essence, their detention was not self-
inflicted. In rejecting the position that their detention was 'self-
inflicted', North disrupts the prevalent discourses of choice that
surround those that seek asylum in Australia. To dispute the dominant discourse of choice is also to disrupt popular concepts of the
deviancy of refugees and the victim status of the sovereign state.
North J brings into the narrative the agency of the Executive (via the
SAS) and implicitly the laws of the sea (via Captain Rinnan) as well
as grounding the circumstances of those on board in experiences of
persecution. The judgment understands the situation beyond the
individual refugee which narratives of choice rely upon for their
affect. Instead choice becomes the frame for Executive action.
Combat between the court and the Executive sharpened when the
legal arguments and the role of the court came into focus:

First Mr Bennett argued that the detention was only a technical
detention because the respondents had power to expel the rescuees
without statutory authority. Thus the detention was in aid of the
exercise of a valid power. Even if there is such a power its existence
is not sufficient to negative the right of the rescuees to be released.
This flows from the high value placed in our society on personal
liberty. ... (at [99])

Then the respondents contended that the Court should not stand in
the way of the exercise by the Executive of its attempt to protect the
borders of Australia. There is a legitimate place for the deference of
the Court to the action of the Executive. However, the power of the
Executive must be exercised within the law. The Act has provisions
enabling the protection of Australian borders against illegal entry.
The Executive chose not to use those powers. The choice by the
Executive to use an unlawful process to detain and expel the
rescuees cannot exclude the rescuees from the benefit of an order for
release. (at [102])

Finally, it was submitted that the existence of the Nauru/NZ arrangements should persuade the Court not to order the release of the rescuees ... Prima facie, the rescuees have the right to their liberty and to their own choice as to their future course of action. They should not be forced by the exercise of discretion by the Court to accept a plan which they did not formulate or approve. ... (at [103])

The open combat between the court and the respondent reaches its peak at 102. The court locates any policy of government as needing to operate within the law and so long as it does the court will pay 'deference'. This makes clear the terms upon which combat between the courts and the Executive is unnecessary – when the Executive acts within its own law. It requires narratives of choice to be supplanted by discourses of rights. The judgment rejects the techno-legal rationality that belittles detention to 'technical detention'. The narrative is then woven in such a way that every (sovereign) power of the state is countered by the claims of the refugees. The individual rights of refugees to make claims on the state are not narrowly configured but rooted in broader notions of liberty. Rights were not just a matter of seeking access to refugee determination but access to a form of freedom. This was then coupled with the argument that the government was not acting within the confines of a valid law and hence their acts were illegal. In finding the unlawfulness of state action, the court simultaneously dismissed the imputed deviancy of the refugees in their attempts to claim asylum. In staying close to the application of law, the judgment makes clear that access to further rights of asylum will follow in accordance with international and domestic law. Preventing access to process rights is not a valid defence for the unlawful detention. The passage locates refugees not only as bearers of rights but as able to decide whether they exercise those rights. Individual rights claims upon the state cannot be resisted by the state in this way, nor the refugee's agency be dissolved. The judgment rejects statements based on unmediated notions of the sovereign territorial state (ie, border control) and through the legitimate rights claims of those onboard the Tampa offers a more conditional reading of sovereignty. Consequently, a discourse of rights is instituted into the judgment.

The discourse of rights deployed, however, is not a basic application of international treaty obligations in the domestic realm. The passage compels a connection between the citizen and the refugee. Not just any connection between citizen and refugee, but one based on a notion of shared dignity: 'any citizen has standing to vindicate the fundamental right of the rescuees not to be expelled'. This is about the connection, across a border, of ordinary people and the role of the court in recognising (and promoting) that act of solidarity. The importance of this connection is heightened by the fact that the member of the Executive charged with legal rights and responsibilities in relation to Commonwealth legality and illegality is a respondent (the Attorney General). In short, where the government fails to provide for an act of shared dignity (between the state and the non-citizen) then the ordinary citizen is even more compelled to step forward – not as an act of humanity but as an act of shared and fundamental rights:

> The applicants' claims that they have standing to seek an injunction to restrain the respondents from removing the rescuees from Australia are simple and compelling. They say that the acts of removal are unlawful. The unlawful actions of the respondents transgress the fundamental liberties of the rescuees. The rescuees are unable to bring proceedings themselves. The Attorney-General, who might otherwise act in the enforcement of law in the public interest, is himself a respondent. (at [123])

> Were the matter free from authority I would hold that in the unusual circumstances of this case, any citizen has standing to vindicate the fundamental right of the rescuees not to be expelled from Australia in the absence of a power to do so. However, the question is not free from authority. (at [124])

The decision in the Federal Court was immediately appealed. Black CJ, Beaumont and French JJ heard the appeal which overturned the original decision. The dissenting judgment by Black CJ extended the rights-based narratives developed in the original judgment and more directly engaged the issue of sovereignty upon which his colleagues would base their majority decision endorsing the validity of Executive action in relation to the MV Tampa.

Black CJ found:

> It cannot be doubted that a nation-state has a sovereign power to exclude illegally entering aliens from its borders, and to legislate for this purpose ... It is said that, in this case, the people rescued by the MV Tampa may be lawfully prevented from entering Australia in the exercise of this sovereign power, but not in exercise of power derived from legislation. (at [4])

There is also no doubt that as a general principle of law there is no Executive authority, apart from that conferred by statute, to subject anyone in Australia, citizen or non-citizen, to detention. (at [5])

It may be accepted that ancillary powers of detention and expulsion must travel with a power to exclude ... But on the view I take, the undoubted power of the Executive to protect Australia's borders against the entry of unlawful non-citizens in times of peace derives only from statute. (at [7])

First, the dissenting judgment decouples sovereignty from detention. Sovereignty is primarily expressed in the power to exclude aliens. Black CJ does not identify those on board as aliens, but people rescued. In short, it is legal for the government to exclude those onboard as an operation of sovereign power that does not need legislative base. This is at odds with the power to detain which is legislatively based and therefore cannot be exercised by the Executive in the pursuit of sovereign rights. The coupling of exclusion and detention is considered a misreading of what is an acceptable exercise of sovereign power.

Secondly, the dissenting judgment decouples sovereignty from the national interest. Not only does sovereignty become mediated and changing but so does the 'national interest'. The national interest is not fixed nor solely determined by the Executive. Importantly, standards of international human rights are positioned as having some stake in the determination of the national interest. This offers a serious challenge to the coupling of sovereignty and national interest in a way that traditionally makes the two conceptually inseparable and state action unchallengeable:

The reference in the stated object to 'the national interest' is important and is suggestive of a recognition by the parliament of its unquestioned power to determine comprehensively what the national interest shall be in this respect. An object so defined tends to point against an intention that there should be some residual Executive power to determine, outside the statute, and in relation to the removal and deportation of persons whose presence in Australia is not permitted by the Act, what the national interest requires in any particular case. (at [44])

Thirdly, the dissenting judgment disputes the development of parallel powers of the Executive with those already in existence in statute regardless of the many and heated calls for the recognition of parliamentary and territorial sovereignty. In short, this confirms that sovereignty (in the guise of border protection) cannot justify any and all choices of the Executive which in fact have a foundation in law, such as the act of detention:

> As I have endeavoured to show, once a particular statutory regime is in place their can be no parallel Executive right in the area expressly covered ... It would be a strange intention to impute to the Parliament that a parallel system of unregulated Executive discretion should be available, or not available, according to whether an officer for the purposes of s 189(2) happened to be on board, for example, a Commonwealth vessel tasked for border protection. (at [61]).

By contrast, the majority decision relied on the indiscernible meshing of sovereignty with all aspects of the issues before the court. Beaumont J for the majority was primarily concerned as to whether the court was actually invested with the power to issue a writ for habeas corpus. His judgment stayed close to jurisdictional concerns. Beaumont J said:

> Finally, it should be added that this is a municipal, and not an inter-, national, court. Even if it were, whilst customary international law imposes an obligation upon a coastal state to provide *humanitarian assistance* to vessels in distress, international law imposes no obligation upon the coastal state to resettle those rescued in the coastal state's territory. This accords with the principles of the Refugee Convention. By Article 33, a person who has established refugee status may not be expelled *to a territory where his life and freedom would be threatened for a Convention reason.* Again, there is no obligation on the coastal state to resettle in its own territory. Any extra-judicial assessment of Executive policy in the present circumstances should be seen in this context. (at [126]) (his emphasis).

Humanitarianism is countenanced in relation to a ship but dismissed in relation to people onboard the ship. The judgment positions the court as offering 'extra-judicial assessment of Executive policy'. This is at odds with a notion of application of law or examination of justice offered in North's J earlier judgment. It also redirects our focus to arrangements for the 'Pacific Solution' rather than the specific act of detention aboard the MV Tampa.

The judgment of French J, for the majority, relied on the need of detention to enact exclusion in the operation of (warranted and valid) sovereign power of the Executive. In this sense, exclusion and detention remain coupled and, taken together, are indisputable powers of the sovereign. French J said:

In my opinion, the Executive power of the Commonwealth, absent statutory extinguishment or abridgement, would extend to a power to prevent the entry of non-citizens and to do such things as are necessary to effect such exclusion ... The power to determine who may come into Australia is so central to its sovereignty that it is not to be supposed that the Government of the nation would lack under the power conferred upon it directly by the Constitution, the ability to prevent people not part of the Australian community, from entering. (at [193])

Detention becomes a matter of 'arranging for their departure from Australian territorial waters'. Detention is a detail of enacting sovereignty. Sovereignty becomes lived on the bodies of those detained, although it is not actually understood as detention but a method of enabling exclusion. Detention is not a matter of rights or liberty. Notably, the judgment distances such findings from any approval or understanding of Executive policy. Indeed, the judgment returns the responsibility for checking the legality of policy to parliament. Notably, however, the judgment ends with two 'backhanders'. First, the judgment, by default, questions whether the exercise of the sovereign power has been made 'wisely and well' and, second, that those bringing the action should be commended for their commitment to the rule of law. Both comments sit uncomfortably with the developed judgment which has a firm eye on the 'arrangements' made by the Executive for those on board the MV Tampa as the appeal progressed. It is as if the response of the Executive to the MV Tampa created a momentum that the court was impotent to counter. The court was left to note the (absence of) wise implementation of power and commend the exercise of conscience on the part of the plaintiffs. It acknowledges the absence of those onboard the MV Tampa and the difficulty of those seeking protection to make claims against a state seeking to exclude them (let alone hear their claims). The majority judgment considered challenging the actions of the Executive as commendable, but holding the Executive accountable within the court impossible.

As the opening interview in this chapter indicated, the response of the Executive to the initial decision by North J was unrelenting. Every aspect of the legislative response can be read in the comments of the Prime Minister: 'Every nation has the right to effectively control its borders and to decide who comes here and under what circumstances, and Australia has no intention of surrendering or compromising that right'.[25] Even the introduction of the *Migration Amendment (Excision from Migration Zone) Act* 2001 (Cth) used the exact timing of this statement to determine the moment from which the islands were no longer part of Australia for the purposes of migration. From 2pm on 8 September the islands became excised from Australia. The MV Tampa revealed the renegade potential of the judiciary in relation to refugees particularly and the rise of unfettered Executive power generally. The result was, however, patchy. The outcome for refugees was disastrous. But the parameters for the unbundling of sovereignty in the judgments of North J and Black CJ were seen, and the tracings of state illegality in relation to state crime are perhaps coming into view.

The Al Masri case

Sovereignty was implicit and unspoken in the case of Al Masri. *Al Masri v Minister for Immigration and Multicultural and Indigenous Affairs*[26] involved the use of indefinite detention for the purposes of removing from Australia a failed applicant for asylum. Mr Al Masri's application for refugee status was rejected by a delegate of the Minister and was unsuccessfully appealed on one occasion to the Refugee Review Tribunal. Mr Al Masri then determined he would return to the Gaza Strip. However, the Australian authorities had not been able to secure his return. The *Migration Act* provides that an unlawful non-citizen who asks to be removed should be removed 'as soon as reasonably practicable'.[27] Mr Al Masri was still in detention eight months after he requested to be removed. His application to the Federal Court was for a writ of habeas corpus.

Mr Al Masri claimed that s 196(1)[28] of the *Migration Act* provided that an unlawful non-citizen be kept in detention until

---

25 Howard, The Hon J, *Illegal Immigration*, House of Representatives, 29 August 2001.
26 [2002] FCA 1009
27 Section 198(1).
28 Section 196:
    (1) An unlawful non-citizen detained under section 189 must be kept in immigration detention until he or she is: removed from Australia under section 198 or 199; or deported under section 200; or granted a visa.
    (2) To avoid doubt, subsection (1) prevents the release from immigration detention of a citizen or a lawful non-citizen.
    (3) To avoid doubt, subsection (1) prevents the release, even by a court, of an unlawful non-citizen from detention (otherwise than for removal or deportation) unless the non-citizen has been granted a visa.

removal, but the power to detain is limited to a reasonable time and terminates when there is no reasonable likelihood of removal. In short, the section does not provide for indefinite detention. The respondent, the Minister, argued that the length of detention is unrelated to its lawfulness. In essence, it was an argument that all immigration detention ought to be considered lawful.

In her influential essay, *Decline of the Nation-State; The End of the Rights of Man*, Arendt characterised the inter-war state response to the stateless person as 'how can the refugee be made deportable again?'[29] Mr Al Masri was indeed stateless, neither Israel nor surrounding states would accept him. The response of nation-states to refugees has been to intern the 'undeportable': 'the only practical substitute for a nonexistent homeland was an internment camp. Indeed, as early as the thirties this was the only 'country' the world had to offer the stateless'.[30]

The *Al Masri* case shifts from focusing on the use of unlawful detention through the Executive to the control specifically exercised by the Minister over the practice of unlawful detention. The distinction between the Executive and the Minister may be superfluous, however, it does indicate the close identification between the regime of immigration detention and the Minister. While the Minister remained central to the government's approach to the MV Tampa, the court regarded the Executive in totality and denoted them as 'respondents'. In *Al Masri*, it was the actions of the Minister alone that was charged as being unlawful and hence the judgment repeatedly denoted the respondent as the 'Minister'.

The judgment begins with a clear and unchallenged statement regarding the physical and mental impacts of indefinite detention upon Mr Al Masri. In so doing, the judgment locates itself within a frame that prioritises the narrative of the detained over the narrative of a detention regime. While Mr Al Masri was described as having been harmed by the regime, the court proceedings are a result of the action and agency of Mr Al Masri and the inaction of the Minister.

Both the applicant and the respondent argued that two sections of the *Migration Act* needed to be read together (ss 196(1)(a) and 198)[31] to determine whether the lawful detention permitted

---

29   Arendt, H, (1966), *The Origins of Totalitarianism*, Florida: Harcourt, p 284.
30   Ibid.
31   Section 198:
      An officer must remove as soon as reasonably practicable an unlawful non-citizen who asks the Minister, in writing, to be so removed.

under the Act had indeed become unlawful for going outside the bounds of the legislation. The applicant argued that indefinite detention goes beyond the terms and provisions of the Act. The Minister claimed that as long as detention serves the (eventual) purposes of deportation then it remained within the terms of the Act. The Minister sought from the court a suspension of ordinary understanding of reasonableness.

> The Minister accepts that under s 196(1)(a) he is only entitled to detain the applicant pending the applicant's removal but contends:
>
> *'In the circumstances of the applicant the obligation is to detain until it is reasonably practicable to remove as requested. The scheme of the provisions in sections 189, 196, and 198 of the Act does not admit of the possibility that the applicant can be released otherwise. The reference to reasonable practicability in section 198 denies any implication that the length of detention must be 'reasonable' assessed independently of considerations of whether it is practicable to remove'. ...*(at [15])
>
> If a court is satisfied that the Minister is not taking 'all reasonable steps' or that removal is 'not reasonably practicable' the implicit limitations on the detention power will not have been complied with or met and continued detention of the removee will no longer be authorised by the Act. (at [40])
>
> For the above reasons I do not accept the Minister's submission that the only implicit limitation on the power is purposive. (at [41])

The judgment regarded with suspicion the Minister's refusal to table evidence as to the prospects of Mr Al Masri's removal. The court granted the Minister the option of 'something less than the "full details"' and when not done the Minister further drew disdain from the court.

> I regard the failure of the Minister to place the most recently available information before the Court to enable a view to be formed as to the prospects for the applicant's removal in the foreseeable future, as significant. It is some eight months since the Minister was first obliged to procure the applicant's removal from Australia as soon as reasonably practicable. The final affidavit of the solicitor acting for the Minister suggested that revealing to the Court the 'full details' of factual information as to the prospects for the applicant's removal would be likely to prejudice his removal to Gaza. No basis was put forward for that view. In any event, something less than the 'full details' of the relevant communications may well have sufficed. Accordingly, I do not regard the Minister as having provided a sufficient explanation for the absence of evidence as to the present prospects of the applicant's removal. (at [51])

The Minister's case rested on the assumption that a privative clause existed which prevented judicial review of the detention of Mr Al Masri. The judgment took some time to rebut this argument using the submissions of the respondent's lawyers. Consequently, the power to review the use of unlawful detention remained unshaken in the judgment. It concluded:

> Accordingly I have concluded that the Minister has failed to discharge the burden imposed upon him to prove that the continued detention of the applicant is lawful. Consequently, the applicant's continued detention is unlawful. (at [53])

The judgment may well have ended there. However, it went on to locate the narrative of the detainee within a discourse of rights. This engagement was made possible primarily through a critique of language and the discursive construction of the refugee within legal texts. Initially this is achieved by distinguishing between unlawful entry and the right not to be unlawfully detained. In essence, while being found to have acted outside the law (unlawful entry) one does not lose the right to be treated according to the law. The judgment discursively problematises the notion of unlawful entry through the use of quotation marks and similarly questions the deployment of the position no 'right' to remain:

> I would add that even if there was a discretion to refuse habeas corpus or an order for release there is no proper basis for exercising that discretion in the present case. The legislature has defined the applicant as an 'unlawful non-citizen'. However, although the applicant may have entered Australia unlawfully and does not have any 'right' to remain in Australia that is not relevant as to whether he can be lawfully detained … . (at [58])

While the point at issue may have been whether Mr Al Masri's 'unlawful non-citizen' status gave a discretionary reason to refuse his release, Merkel J was developing an alternative narrative. From the above preliminary critique, the judgment launches an assault on the ways language underpins false interpretations of both basic principles of common law as well as specific rights guaranteed under the Refugee Convention:

> In any event, while it is literally correct to describe the applicant as an 'unlawful' entrant and an 'unlawful non-citizen' that is not a complete description of his position. The nomenclature adopted under the Act provides for the description of persons as 'unlawful non-citizens' because they arrived in Australia without a visa. This

does not fully explain their status in Australian law as such persons are on-shore applicants for protection visas on the basis that they are refugees under the Refugee Convention. (at [60])

The Refugees Convention is a part of conventional international law that has been given legislative effect in Australia: see ss 36 and 65 of the Act. It has always been fundamental to the operation of the Refugees Convention that many applicants for refugee status, will, of necessity, have left their countries of nationality unlawfully and that therefore, of necessity, will have entered the country in which they seek asylum unlawfully. Jews seeking refugee from war-torn Europe. Tutsis seeking refuge from Rwanda, Kurds seeking refuge from Iraq, Hazaras seeking refuge from the Taliban in Afghanistan and many others, may also be called 'unlawful non-citizens' in the countries in which they seek asylum. Such a description, however, conceals, rather than reveals, their lawful entitlement under conventional international law since the early 1950s (which has been enacted into Australian law) to claim refugee status as persons who are 'unlawfully' in the country in which the asylum application is made ... (at [61])

Notwithstanding that the applicant is an 'unlawful non-citizen' under the Act who entered Australia unlawfully and had his application for a protection visa refused, in making that application he was exercising a 'right': conferred upon him under Australian law. As he is entitled to do under the Act, the applicant has now requested his removal and the Minister is obliged to remove him but, in the circumstances of the present case, the Minister is no longer entitled to detain the applicant pending his removal'. (at [63])

The judge begins by rejecting the commonplace and legislative definition of Mr Al Masri ('unlawful non-citizen') and then replaces it (with 'onshore applicant for protection visa'). He then substitutes the power of the Executive with that of the Refugees Convention. It is the Convention that is positioned as having the definitional moment as mediated through domestic legislation. He draws on well-accepted examples of refugeehood to underpin the importance of the definitional moment residing with the Refugees Convention. For it to be otherwise would remove any legal force from the international concept of refugee protection. Mr Al Masri is no longer constituted as being an illegal outsider but as a person exercising a valid and important right with a basis in both international and domestic law. The Minister's arguments to justify unlawful detention carry no weight as they fall outside a framework of international and domestic rights.

In finding the ongoing detention of Mr Al Masri unlawful and ordering his release, the combat between the courts and the Executive heightened. A little over a week after his court ordered release Mr Al Masri was arrested and taken to a police lockup in Port Augusta on Friday 31 August even though Mr Al Masri had reported to authorities everyday.[32] The Federal Court again ordered his release and again the government sought his arrest. The spokesperson for the Minister insisted: 'The *Migration Act* says he must be detained because he doesn't have a visa, he's unlawfully in the community'.[33] The court ordered that the Minister must not detain Mr Al Masri without giving the court 24 hours prior notice. The Minister maintained: 'There is an obligation ... that if people are here without a visa and are available for removal, they should be detained'.[34] Using the police, the Minister defied the intent of the court decision. The work of the court in establishing Mr Al Masri as neither refugee nor criminal did not prevent the questionable policing of Mr Al Masri by the Minister. This was not at all dissimilar to Arendt's description of the situation in the 20th century:

> [I]t would seem that the very undeportability of the stateless person should have prevented a government's expelling him; but since the man without a state was 'an anomaly for whom there is no appropriate niche in the framework of the general law' – an outlaw by definition – he was completely at the mercy of the police ... In other words, the state, insisting on its sovereign right of expulsion, was forced by the illegal nature of statelessness into admittedly illegal acts.[35]

Soon after, Mr Al Masri was deported.

These three cases increasingly demonstrate the use of alternative regulatory regimes by Executive (sovereignty) and the courts (rights). Both regimes fundamentally reconstitute the refugee and the state. Sovereignty has been the explanatory force behind Executive action. Court-deployed discourses of rights have increasingly sought to challenge discourses of sovereignty, but has still not reached any comprehensive rights-based approach to the refugee. The absence of the refugee potentially inhibits the courts ability to

---

32 Cynthia Banham (2002), 'Asylum Seekers Stays Free, Court Rules', *Sydney Morning Herald*, 3 September.
33 Ibid.
34 Lauren Ahwan, 'Court does "deal" for Palestinian', *The Age*, 3 September.
35 Arendt (1966) op cit, pp 283-84.

categorically render the state criminal. The lack of voice silences the refugee and the removal of the refugee as a reliable witness in state illegality. The dehumanisation of unlawful detention continues into the legal narrative. As Bilsky has argued in her writings on Arendt's reporting of the Eichmann trial, although the moral obligation to bear witness is a strong one, whether the courtroom is the appropriate forum is disputable. The court case, Bilsky resolves, 'has the function of authorising the movement from private to public by weaving the private story into the web of communal stories that are authorised by the judgment of the court'.[36]

The rights-based approach may be read as an attempt, usually through international law, to recognise the refugee as having inalienable rights, and challenges the designation of the refugee as an outlaw or criminal. This ensures that the 'normal' (ie, applicable to the citizen) institutions and principles of law applied to the refugee. As Arendt noted:

> The stateless person, without right to residence and without the right to work, had of course constantly to transgress the law. He was liable to jail sentences without ever committing a crime. More than that, the entire hierarchy of values which pertain in civilized countries was reversed in his case. Since he was the anomaly for whom the general law did not provide it was better for him to become an anomaly for which it did provide, that of the criminal.[37]

Convention definition

Increasingly, the courts and the Executive have also come into conflict over the application of the Refugee Convention. As a result of their reviews of the decisions of the Refugee Review Tribunal (RRT), the Federal Court in particular, but also the High Court, have been the subject of stinging criticisms from the Executive, particularly the Minister for Immigration. The Minister has accused the courts of over-reaching their powers and bypassing legislative intent. In short, the courts have been viewed as applying the Convention too widely. The Chief Justice of the Federal Court issued an unprecedented public statement defending the independence of the courts.[38] The judicial application of the Convention definition has

---

36 Bilsky, op cit, p 250.
37 Arendt, op cit, p 286.
38 Irving, H, (2002), 'The Buck Stops Elsewhere', *Sydney Morning Herald*, 23-24 November, Spectrum, p 8.

been a particularly troubling site of combat for the government. The application of the definition, as embodied in the *Migration Act*, requires a more direct engagement with international law (ie, the Refugee Convention) and is also a direct statement on the effective decision-making of both Departmental officers and members of the RRT. Not only do the courts apply international law to domestic law, their decisions also act as a commentary on the legal functionality of the two decision-making tiers that go before judicial review. An examination of the application of the Convention definition has been a potential site for the curtailment of unlawful government action, such as unjust rejections of valid claims. In short, wrong decisions in refugee determination put at grave risk the lives of refugees. Consequently, the content of refugee determinations, similar to the use of detention or interdiction at sea, seriously compromises the rights and lives of the refugee as well as providing a site for the censuring of unlawful state action.

The Convention definition of who is a refugee has always been highly complex and contested terrain. As the previous chapter showed, the application of the Convention definition has arguably been most contentious in relation to the ground of particular social groups and gender. By additionally utilising gender and particular social groups as a case study in this chapter, I seek to locate the judicial application of the Convention definition in relation to gender at the heart of debates over notions of sovereignty, state protection and state delinquency. In short, I contend gender is at the heart of the court/Executive battle for multiple forms of sovereignty. Amid the 'unbundling of sovereignty' my question is whether the courts, in the application of the Refugees Convention, are a site for what Sassen has called the 'strategic instantiation of gendering'[39] as well as the strategic censure of the state.

The Khawar case

Naima Khawar and her children arrived in Australia on a tourist visa from Pakistan in 1997. Ms Khawar lodged an application for a protection visa in September 1997 which was rejected in February 1998. The applicant appealed the decision to the Refugee Review Tribunal which also rejected her claim. She appealed successfully to the Federal Court which remitted the case back to the RRT. The

---

39   Sassen, S, (1998), *Globalisation and Its Discontents: Essays on the New Mobility of People and Money*, New York: The New Press, p 83.

Minister appealed the decision in both the Full Court of the Federal Court and the High Court. On both occasions the appeal was rejected.

Ms Khawar suffered persecution at the hands of her husband and her husband's family. The violence she suffered was never disputed by the various decision-makers, indeed they all noted it as persecutory. Ms Khawar had sought protection from the police in Pakistan on four occasions. The Tribunal did not however take into account the failure of state protection in Ms Khawar's case.

Federal Court

In *Khawar v Minister for Immigration and Multicultural Affairs*,[40] Branson J set aside the decision of the RRT noting that the tribunal had made no finding on Ms Khawar's claim that she could not receive protection from the police (at 11). Branson J specifically noted the tribunal did not give any:

> [C]onsideration to information touching generally on the status of women in Pakistan or on the prevalence of domestic violence against women in that country, and without reference to the applicant's evidence that her husband had said words to the effect that the police could do nothing about his violence towards her' (at [12])

Instead, the tribunal characterised her problems as being 'peculiar to their relationship' and that the 'Convention was not intended to provide protection to people involved in personal disputes' (at [12]).

The appeal was based on the omission of the tribunal member to consider the failure of the state to act to prevent such violence (at [15]). In so doing Branson J drew on the reasoning of Lord Hoffman in *Islam*[41] who made a corollary between gender and race persecution, asking whether a Jewish man attacked in Nazi Germany experiences racial persecution because '[h]e was attacked by a competitor who knew that he could receive no protection because he was a Jew' (at [24]). In making this comparison, Lord Hoffman (and by extension Branson J) is raising gender to an equal status with race in informing persecutory behaviour. Utilising such a culturally and politically powerful example, recognising gender related persecution and the failure of state protection, is a straightforward example of the purpose of the Convention.

---

40   [1999] FCA 1529.
41   *Islam v Secretary of State for Home Department* [1999] 2 WLR 1015.

In remitting the decision back to the RRT on the basis of an error of law, Branson J made extensive guiding remarks which read as a 'how to' lesson in applying the Refugee Convention to cases of gender-based persecution. In doing so, her judgment rests on the utilisation of the *Department of Immigration and Multicultural Affairs Guidelines on Gender Issues for Decision-makers*. The Guidelines draw significantly on international human rights law and literature spawned by 'women's rights are human rights' scholarship and campaigns. The decision was remitted back to the RRT with the intention that the decision be located within a human rights paradigm generally and a women's human rights framework specifically:

> As to the appropriate approach to be adopted by a decision-maker assessing a gender-based claim for a protection visa, reference may usefully be made to a document published by the Department entitled 'Guidelines on Gender Issues for Decision-makers' dated July 1996 ('the Guidelines Document'). The Guidelines Document was developed to help officers in the Department in assessing gender-based claims by, amongst others, applicants for protection visas. The Guidelines Document identifies international instruments in which obligations to protect the human rights of women may be found. (emphasis of Branson J) (at [38])

The international instruments are then listed and the exact relevant passages of the guidelines noted and offer a step-by-step decision-making checklist for the tribunal member. Branson J positions this alternative reading as requiring the tribunal to apply the Guidelines and a rights framework, rather than re-reading, stretching or reconstituting Ms Khawar's experiences to fit the existing decision-making framework. It is the legal narrative that is in need of altering, not the narrative of the claimant.

Full Federal Court

The Minister appealed the decision in *Khawar v Minister for Immigration and Multicultural Affairs*. In *Minister for Immigration and Multicultural Affairs v Khawar*[42] Mathews and Lindgren JJ dismissed the appeal with Hill J dissenting.

Hill J begins with the tension between the Executive and the courts in the contemporary application of the Convention. That tension is characterised as the equally valid concern of states to restrict immigration on the one hand, and on the other hand the

---

42   [2000] FCA 1130.

valid extension of the Convention to those genuinely in need of protection. Hill J places the Executive as operating a restriction over the courts in the application of the Convention and duly notes the role of civil society in compelling a wider application of the Convention. Working within this tension he outlines the dilemma as follows:

> Although it might be said that there have always been refugees, it was not until the 1951 Convention relating to the Status of Refugees that any general attempt was made by international consensus to provide international protection for a person who was a refugee and for that purpose to define who a refugee was ... The Convention and the events which led up to it were, as Hathaway in his *The Law of Refugee Status* Butterworths 1991 notes, a compromise between the reality of a seemingly unstoppable flow of involuntary migration across European borders and the increasing attempts of nation-states to restrict immigration. That is not to say that the meaning of the Convention today must be confined to the problems that presented themselves to the international community in the early 1950's (cf *Chen v Minister for Immigration and Multicultural Affairs* (2000) 170 ALR 553 at 568 per Kirby J) and it is clear enough that there has been a widening over the years of the persons who are genuinely in need of international protection. Nevertheless, the tension between the humanitarian purpose of international intervention to protect those in need of assistance and the legitimate domestic desire of states to limit migration must, to some extent, operate as a restriction on the ability of Courts to widen unduly the scope of the definition. Particularly, there is a danger of extrapolating, from the fact of ill-treatment or discrimination and the sympathy or indeed indignation which such ill-treatment or discrimination engenders in those who would wish to promote a civil society, a conclusion that in international law the person who is ill-treated or discriminated against is, just for that reason, a refugee. (at [3])

In what at first seems quite a banal reading of contemporary responses of the Global North to irregular migration and the impact of a globalised civil society, the narrative offers some less than banal rationales. First, in acknowledging that the Convention has now been widened to persons who are genuinely in need of protection it implicitly locates women and gender related persecution as one of the latter beneficiaries. Protection is then reduced to 'humanitarian' purpose which is more easily usurped by the needs of 'legitimate domestic desire(s)' to limit immigration. Secondly, the final section of the paragraph creates a dichotomy between sympathy and indignation, raised within civil society regarding the 'ill treatment or discrimination' (no longer persecution), and the valid (read legal) application of the refugee definition. There is a 'danger' associated with equating sympathy and indignation with protection. While in many ways I agree that sympathy can utilise problematic understandings of the other, taken in this judgment, it can only be assumed that while some applicants duly deserve sympathy, they can not legitimately also expect this special kind of international protection. Taking these two observations together, there is a great privileging at work: on the one hand, there remains the spectre of the unarticulated but authentic and original refugee and on the other hand the contemporary applicant who stretches and strains the definition to fit present day sympathies. Within this framework, the privileging of sovereignty renders the Convention distorted when applied to the 'new' (woman) refugee.

Deliberating about whether inaction or failure of state protection may constitute persecution, Hill J pre-empts the outcome of his discussion by framing Ms Khawar's experience as one of 'ill-treatment' – 'horrendous' but not persecution. Persecution can only be applied in its legalistic sense, persecution cannot be applied as one person describing the experiences of another. Moreover, persecution cannot be applied to the failure of state protection because it is well known that there are serious defects in the operation of state protection for women surviving domestic violence in Australia. It seems difficult to grant refugee status to one who is suffering the kinds of persecution women can and do suffer in Australia. At the very moment a bridge in global understandings of violence against women may be built, at the very moment an articulation and examination of the operation of power in society may make some link between women in the Global South and the Global North, the Refugee Convention is designated no such bridge:

> Mrs Khawar has undoubtedly been ill-treated. The harm which the Tribunal found to have been perpetrated against her by her husband was horrendous by any standard. Except so far as the context requires that the harm inflicted arise by reason of membership of a particular social group there could be little doubt that the harm inflicted upon her could aptly be described as persecution. A different question arises if it is suggested that the persecution she suffered was not, as such, the ill-treatment from her husband, but the inactivity or inability of the police to prevent a repetition of the conduct. It would, in my mind, be an incorrect use of the word *persecution* to apply it to a failure or lack of interest by the police to come to the aid of a person who has been beaten at least where the law provides, if enforced, adequate

protection and there is no government policy that police ignore calls for help. There is, and it is not a matter of which we can be proud, a lack of enthusiasm in the authorities in Australia to come to the aid of women who are victims of domestic violence, but it would not be suggested that the State is, or for that matter the police are, persecuting those women in Australia. Persecution involves the doing of a deliberate act, rather than inaction. (Hill J, at [10])

As Hill J concludes, the layers of legalistic argument, within a framework of limiting irregular migration, fall away to reveal the heart of the reasoning. Ms Khawar's experiences of persecution were her responsibility. At last the judgment says outright what it has been hedging towards for 74 paragraphs: Ms Khawar was beaten because she 'aroused the ire' of her husband.

In summary, I am of the view that the present case does differ from *Islam*. On the narrower view the social group is *'women with alcoholically abusive husbands'*; on the wider view it is women as such. The persecution that is feared is being beaten. It may be possible to say that it is being beaten in circumstances where State assistance is ineffective. But the beating which is feared does not, as such, arise because the victim is a woman; it arises because the victim has aroused the ire of the drunken husband … not all women are subject to the potential of being beaten. Something more is involved. That something more is the association through marriage with an abusive and alcoholic husband. Further, it is not suggested that the State is complicit in the abuse that is suffered by a woman married to an alcoholically abusive husband. (His emphasis) (at [75])

The majority judgment by Mathews J (with whom Lindgren J agreed) again utilised a framework of international human rights and specifically drew on the work of non-government organisations working on women's human rights (potentially the kinds of bodies conjuring up sympathy and indignation in civil society noted by Hill J) Matthews J noted:

If it were found that the explanation for the discriminatory absence of protection was a pervasive view of the authorities, whatever its own explanation and genesis, that women deserved less fundamental rights and freedoms than others, it would be entirely in conformity with the purposes of the Convention that they should be protected as refugees. (at [126])

There remains, however, an assumption that the persecution Ms Khawar suffered was private and only became public when the state failed to protect her. There is a residual understanding that domestic violence is unconnected to the public realm (pre-state protection), not influenced by prevailing power arrangements in broader society. The causation of domestic violence begins and ends in the home, only the response to domestic violence can be understood as potentially occurring outside the home. This critique is equally valid of the *Islam* case in the House of Lords which was used extensively in the judgment.

The discriminatory application and enforcement of human rights is then considered central to the failure of state protection. However, this analysis is not then extended to disrupt the analysis that the harm suffered remained primarily of a private nature. The failure of state protection (as the discriminatory denial of human rights) turns the private harm into a public matter, but the rights-based discourse does not transform the violence Ms Khawar suffered into a public issue in and of itself:

> [I]t is an error of law to insist upon the presence of any particular adverse attitude, emotion or state of mind on the part of the persecutor. But clearly the motivation for the persecutory conduct must be something perceived about the particular social group. If it is necessary to say so, I would hold that a state perception of a particular social group as 'inferior', 'less deserving' or 'second class' by reference to the rest of society, and, in particular, a view of members of the group as not possessing the same human rights as the rest of society or, if possessing them, as not entitled to have them enforced and protected to the same extent as the rest of society, would constitute a motivation that would be entirely consonant with the Convention's definition and preamble ... (at [141])

> Finally, it seems right to say that the fact that the police have failed to protect a woman from her husband's violence will not necessarily provide the bridge between the state and privately motivated harassment. Firstly, the failure may be atypical. Secondly, it may be due to the attitude or ineptitude of a particular police officer. Thirdly, it may be due to systemic inefficiency. Fourthly, the police may be reluctant, for good or bad reason, to become involved in a particular domestic dispute. Unfortunate as the woman's position would be, these various explanations (and perhaps others) would serve to displace any suggestion that she was a refugee as defined. Something more is required. In my view, that 'something more' would be satisfied at least by a sustained or systemic absence of state protection for members of a particular social group attributable to a perception of them by the state as not deserving equal protection under the law with other members of the society, whatever the origin or explanation of that discriminatory perception might be. (at 160)

Utilising a rights-based discourse does not always enable progressive or holistic understandings of the refugee's experiences. Simply because this case eventuated in the positive for Ms Khawar does not mean that problematic assumptions regarding the nature of violence against women are challenged. When this judgment also drew on the example of two shopkeepers in Nazi Germany made by Lord Hoffman in *Islam*, there was no sense of contradiction that the example was deployed without any countenance of the 'private' realm informing the analysis. There was no sense that the example used by Lord Hoffman raised a 'private' dispute between shopkeepers (one Jew, one non-Jew) that became a public matter through the failure of state protection in the same way in *Khawar*. In the case of *Khawar*, the 'private' dispute between husband and wife (one male and one female) became public through a failure of state protection but remained in essence private. The non-discriminatory application of the Convention utilising a human rights discourse did not shake the firm assumption that domestic violence, however repugnant, will remain a private matter.

The High Court

In *Minister for Immigration and Multicultural Affairs v Khawar*[43] the battle over the definition of refugee status vis-a-vis sovereignty was continued in the High Court. McHugh and Gummow JJ set up a precise framework for judicial review by utilising domestic law expressions of protection that do not seek to 'over stretch' the Convention:

> [T]he Act is not concerned to enact in Australian municipal law the various protection obligations of Contracting States found in Chs II, III and IV of the Convention. The scope of the Act is much narrower. In providing for protection visas whereby persons may wither or both travel to and enter Australia, or remain in this country, the Act focuses upon the definition of Art 1 of the Convention as the criterion of operation of the protection visa system. (at 45)

They continue: 'the Convention is not to be approached with any preconceptions as to the preference of a 'broad' or a 'narrow' construction or vice versa' (at [47]) and further 'the Convention was deliberately confined' (at [48]).

---

43   [2002] HCA 14.

In a detailed discussion of protection, McHugh and Gummow JJ note the legitimate limitations upon sovereignty regarding the application of the Convention definition. In dismissing the appeal, Gummow and McHugh JJ again raised the spectre of credibility, within which notions of rights, sovereignty or convention definitions never need to be countenanced:

> [I]t should also be emphasised that nothing said here forecloses the Tribunal from making a finding upon what, in a sense, is a threshold issue. This is the question whether Mrs Khawar's case has been fabricated and whether she is on good terms with her husband who is alleged also to be in Australia. (at [89])

In the reasons of Kirby J the conflict again shifts from being between the Executive and the courts to between the Executive and the Tribunal. Kirby J takes a more confrontational tone to the approach of the Tribunal. Indeed, his reasoning begins with the sub-headings, 'The neglected material before the Tribunal' and the 'defect in the Tribunal's approach'. Kirby J begins with: 'In order to appreciate the significance of the omission in fact-finding committed by the Tribunal in approaching the application made by Mrs Naima Khawar … ' (at [94]). Kirby J (at [97]) noted that there was substantial material tended to the Tribunal in the form of Human rights briefs regarding the position of women in Pakistan and their access to the legal system which was not duly considered.

Outlining the tribunal's flawed approach to the case (positioning Ms Khawar's persecution as a personal matter, not because she was a member of a particular social group) Kirby J suggested that to come to a conclusion without engaging with the specifics of fact that Ms Khawar outlined was 'scarcely lawful'. In essence this is about ensuring a clear case-by-case approach that does not draw upon assumptions regarding the nature of domestic violence as falling outside the Convention. It also demands the voice of the refugee in the full telling of their story as being worthy of full consideration. Kirby J said:

> Taken in isolation such a finding might seem to be one of fact – assigning harm that was accepted to have been proved to a cause based on a particular family's domestic disputes. If that were all, the decision would have to be affirmed by the courts, confined as they are in this respect to correcting errors of law on the part of administrative decision-makers. But when the significant factual material tendered by the respondent is taken into account, the material before the Tribunal arguably takes on a different character. It is then

possible, indeed essential, to consider the family dispute concerning the respondent in the light of the material about the serious legal, social and practical disadvantages suffered by the respondent and women in her position which she presented to the Tribunal. *The Tribunal might still conclude that the respondent did not fall within the Convention definition. But I could scarcely do so lawfully without considering, and making essential findings of fact about, the case that the respondent had propounded to bring herself within the convention definition.* In short, it was open to the tribunal to reject the respondent's application. But in light of the substantial, apparently reliable and consistent material that she had produced concerning the situation in Pakistan affecting her and persons like herself, it was not open to the Tribunal to ignore the respondent's claim that her case was a paradigm instance of the discrimination of Pakistani law and official practice against women in her position, which amounted to persecution. (at [100]) (my emphasis)

Understanding where persecution exists in Mrs Khawar's claims, Kirby J interprets the specific application of the Convention historically (at [110]). It is the Convention that holds the definitional moment, and domestic law grants it expression. The 'broad humanitarian object of the Convention' is preserved. Again the framework in which the decision is taken must be historically grounded within a legitimate application to contemporary conditions to resist popular understandings of the judiciary 'over reaching' the intention of the Convention and its domestic expression:

[I]t is the purpose and content of the Convention that will illuminate the boundaries of the idea of persecution in the Convention. That purpose and content can, in turn, only be understood by reference to the history and broad humanitarian object of the Convention ... It, and the municipal law giving it effect, were designed to ensure that the unredressed affront to humanity that occurred in the middle of the twentieth century and before would not be repeated.

The Convention is then positioned in need of non-discriminatory application, true to its intended and proper purpose as it emerged post World War II. Such non-discriminatory application would seem to uphold the notion of women's equality before the law, in this case international law:

It is the recognition of the failure of state protection, so often repeated in the history of the past hundred years, that led to the exceptional involvement of international law in matters concerning individual human rights. In that context, the International Covenant on Civil and Political Rights ... and the Convention on the Elimination of All Forms of Discrimination against Women ... (to both of which Australia is a party) are obviously important in expressing the concept of women's equality before the law and the unacceptability of the state and its agencies discriminating unjustly against women solely by reason of their sex. (at [111])

Once the proper and non-discriminatory application of the Convention is established, Kirby J is then at ease to rebuke any temptation of cultural relativism in dismissing Mrs Khawar's claims. Cultural explanations for violence against women are usurped by a focus on whether protection of the law is discriminately withdrawn. The agency returns to the state that withdrew protection (not simply failed to protect), rather than any recourse to any and all cultural conditions that fostered the violence. Kirby J said:

> Many countries (including, at least until quite recently, Australia) have afforded imperfect protection to women who suffer domestic violence. It does not follow that it is impossible to distinguish those countries that, however imperfectly, provide agencies of the law and non-discriminatory legal rules to address the problem from those countries that, for supposed religious, cultural, political or other reasons, consciously withdraw the protection of the law from a particularly vulnerable group within their society. (at [130])

While some commentators have noted the trouble with cultural relativism comes from an unresolved theoretical standoff,[44] the causes are far more ordinary and everyday. Some women do gain asylum from simplistic cultural explanations of gender persecution devoid of any developed understanding of violence against women. However, both sexist and cultural stereotypes rely on essentialist understandings of both gender and the Global South.

In *Khawar*, the judgment used cultural relativism to dismiss the claims of Ms Khawar with diffuse comments regarding the policing priorities in Pakistan and the difficulty of understanding between North and South. Callinan J in dissent:

> The first basis upon which the appeal succeeds is that there is no finding of fact by the Tribunal that the government of Pakistan was complicit in violence to women in abusive relationships. The evidence fell short of that: inactivity or inertia of itself does not constitute persecution. It is very difficult, indeed impossible for an

---

44 Anker, D, (2001) 'Refugee status and violence against women in the "domestic" sphere: the non-state actor question', 15 *Georgetown Immigration Law Journal* 391.

Australian court to assess according to our own standards or the standards of other countries the policing priorities of those countries. There needs to be, for persecution to have occurred, elements of deliberation and intention on the part of the State, which involve, at the very least a decision not to intervene or act. (at [155])

There is now a growing body of research that points to how refugee decision-makers depend on linking gender based persecution to practices attributable to 'non-Western 'foreign' cultures'[45]. In short, without the clear 'foreignness' of cultural practice, gender persecution has often been dismissed or overlooked by decision-makers. The search by decision-makers for what Sinha has called 'cultural culpability' in cases of gender persecution has marked key US cases.[46] Such 'cultural culpability' is rooted in stereotypes about the helpless Third World woman, the wickedness of the Third World man, and the backwardness of state protection. This produces refugee discourses notable by positioning the cultural, political and legal superiority of Western life.[47] Some commentators have noted, for example, that writings on refugee law leave one with the impression that social mores only exist in third world countries generally and Muslim countries specifically.[48] In *Khawar*, to keep domestic violence an issue for Pakistani policing priorities, and to maintain the distance between the public and private realms Callinan J concluded the violence suffered was from the 'personal characteristics of her relationship with her husband' (at [152]) and located the failure of state protection back with Ms Khawar. In the clause 'albeit that her vulnerability as a woman in an abusive relationship may have contributed to the reluctance of the police to assist her' (at [152]) the problem is located with the abusive relationship and not with the policing priorities noted earlier. The moment of persecutory truth resides with lawyers and the Tribunal, who see the violence suffered in the homes of their clients and the applicants before them but are never positioned as being close to the violence themselves or

---

45 Sinha, A, (2001), 'Domestic Violence and US Asylum Law: Eliminating the 'Cultural Hook' for Claims Involving Gender-Related Persecution', 76 *New York University Law Review* 1562.
46 See Musalo, K, (1999) "matter of R-A: An analysis of the decision and its implications', 76 *Interpreter Releases* 117 (9 August).
47 Crawley, H, (2001), *Refugees and Gender: Law and Process*, London: Jordans, p 10
48 Spijkerboer, T, (1994), *Women and Refugee Law: Beyond the Public/Private Domain*, The Hague: The Emancipation Council.

positioned to understand the violence beyond the physical space it takes place within. Callinan J noted:

> What there is here is what sadly occurs from time to time every-where, as any experienced lawyer knows: violent family discord of which the unfortunate first respondent is the victim and in respect of which the police are reluctant interveners. (at [154])

Parliamentary response

The Migration Legislation Amendment Bill (No 6) 2001 had the purpose to 'define certain key terms used by the Federal Court and the Refugee Review Tribunal (RRT) in determining refugee status so as to narrow the interpretation given to the definition of 'refugee' (in particular the elements of 'persecution', 'membership of a particular social group' and 'particularly serious crime'). It also made provision for adverse inferences to be drawn from an absence of documen-tation or from a person's refusal to give sworn statements verifying the truth of information provided. While this legislation was not a direct response to the decision in *Khawar*, the case, and others like it, certainly informed the development of the legislation.

The legislation sought to target the 'effectiveness of Aust-ralia's tribunal and court system in assessing claims for refugee protection' in the context that Australia 'is not free to choose those to whom it will offer protection once they arrive in Australia'. Once the refugee arrives in Australia the breach of territorial sovereignty overflows into the determination process, and in particular in the judicial review of protection decisions which go beyond an 'accep-table' breach of sovereignty. The 'over reaching' of the Convention in cases of judicial review, notably those utilising particular social group and those involving gender-based persecution, have been a notable breach of sovereignty for the Executive.

This legislation emerged amid a raft of legislation limiting judicial review including granting jurisdiction to the Federal Magistrates Court concurrent with the Federal Court on migration matters – the Migration Legislation Amendment Bill (No 1) 2001 restricting access to the courts for judicial review and preventing class actions in migration matters. The Digest notes that while these other pieces of legislation deal with limiting judicial review, No 6 deals with the content of the decision-making process.

In the absence of clear legislative guidance, the domestic inter-pretation of Australia's international obligations to refugees has broadened under cumulative court decisions. The argument of the government was that Australia now provides protection visas in cases lying well beyond the bounds originally envisaged by the Convention. These 'generous' interpretations of the Convention allegedly encourage people who are not refugees to test their claims in Australia, adding to perceptions that Australia is a soft touch.[49] The substance of judicial decisions is considered to act as a 'pull factor' for refugees and undermine the deterrence policy of the government:

> Migration Legislation Amendment Bill (No 6) 2001 addresses two very important issues: the integrity of our immigration program as it relates to illegal immigrants who manipulate our system; and the Federal Court, which aids them with its out of control interpretations as to what is a refugee. ... We hear a lot about rights in the illegals debate. Here is one more: it is Australia's sovereign right to ensure that the United Nations convention is implemented, as the minister said, both responsibly and consistently ... federal judges have been making decisions about refugees which are well beyond what Australia signed up to in the convention and well beyond what the community accepts as fair.[50]

The refugee is returned to 'illegal' status, the Federal Court is again aiding and abetting the deviant refugee and Australia's sovereign rights (the courts being somehow outside this construction of Australia) are usurped. The Minister similarly equates the application of the Convention as not only usurping sovereignty but as contributing to the practice of people smuggling. Refugee protection is a form of 'generosity' that is 'appropriate' but the Minister does not raise the role of the courts in the errant application of the Convention that this legislation aims to curtail.

This was a detailed reading of the *Khawar* case. The case could easily be read as a 'win' for women and domestic violence and as another buffer to reduce refugee protection to the narrow confines of refugee policy rooted in notions of deterrence. However, I have sought to point out the more troubling aspects of the decisions across the three courts. The decisions offered a strategic but flawed instantiation of gender upon which sovereignty yet again was played out. The narratives, in part, recover women from their

---

49 Minister for Immigration and Multicultural Affairs, the Hon Philip Ruddock, MP, Second Reading Speech on the Migration legislation Amendment Bill (No 6) 2001, House of Representatives, Hansard.
50 Prosser, LP, Migration Legislation Amendment Bill (No 6) 2001: Second Reading, 20 September 2001, p 31119.

exclusion under the Convention but are yet to take principles of non-discrimination and equality before the law to the initial moment of violence against women. They only precariously contribute to women emerging as a gendered subject of international law. The woman refugee remains doubly confronting in relation to notions of sovereignty, and in a more limited way rights. Increasingly clear is that a rights-based framework does not always represent a serious extension of the judicial unbundling of sovereignty or an indictment of unlawful decision-making. However, it does provide a window for understanding legality and illegality when not only the refugee, but the woman refugee, threatens the substance and process of refugee determination and challenges the lawfulness of state interpretation.

Conclusion

> Limiting Executive power, dividing the totality of government power between branches and levels of government, insisting on checks and balances – these do not imperil Australia's sovereignty or status as a fully independent nation. Rather they reaffirm that sovereignty is exercised under the law and in accordance with the norms of constitutionalism.[51]

The spectre of the Executive losing control of sovereignty in the courts has been about the definitional moment regarding legality and illegality. In the above cases the courts have not been renegade, however, there have been challenges to frameworks of control, deterrence and gratuitous humanity. While frameworks of rights have played a significant part in the unbundling of sovereignty in this respect they have not always provided a predictable or consistent narrative frame.

The judgments examined across these four cases evidence, in an uneven way, resistance to what Arendt has called the nation conquering the state, where the national interest conquers the protection of the law, where only citizens enjoy the full protection of the law. While examining pre-war Germany, her words are equally valid for the contemporary responses of many nations of the Global

---

51 Evans, S, (2001), 'Constitutionalism, The Rule of Law and the MV Tampa, paper presented at the seminar, Boundless Plains to Share: Australia's Response to the MV Tampa Asylum Seekers, Centre for Comparative Constitutional Studies and the Institute for Comparative and International Law, 11 October, 2001, p 5.

North to refugees: 'the transformation of the state from an instrument of the law into an instrument of the nation had been completed; the nation had conquered the state, national interest had priority over law ...'.[52]

The deterioration in the legal language of the refugee, similar to what Arendt noted from the inter-war period, was crucial to the development of legal narratives in the above cases. So quickly the refugee moved from asylum seeker, to non-citizen, to unlawful non-citizen, to detainee, to people smuggled, to rescuee. It is certain that the narrative of the courts is as uncertain to the appropriate categorisation as is most of society. In the case of the court, however, such categories are legal as well as social and political, and consequently effect the legal placement of notions such as legality and illegality. Despite all of the most transformative moments in the legal narratives, and particularly in the language deployed, sovereignty remained nowhere more absolute than in relation to the control of immigration and exclusion of refugees. While the legal narratives offered moments of (partial) transformation, the sovereign power to exclude the alien other is robust and resilient. Nonetheless, what is most heartening from the legal narratives, taken collectively above, is that equality before the law, expressed in rights based frames demand another reading of sovereignty, one that is crucial to the very nature of the nation-state:

> For the nation-state cannot exist once its principle of equality before the law has broken down. Without this legal equality, which originally was destined to replace the older laws and orders of the feudal society, the nation dissolves into an anarchic mass of over- and underprivileged individuals. Laws that are not equal for all revert to rights and privileges, something contradictory to the very nature of nation-states. The clearer the proof of their inability to treat stateless peoples as legal persons and the greater the extension of arbitrary rule by police decree the more difficult it is for states to resist the temptation to deprive all citizens of legal status and rule them with an omnipotent police.[53]

---

52 Arendt (1966), p 275.
53 Ibid, p 290.

Chapter 7

Refugees, sovereignty
and state crime

This book began with a critique of law and order refugee politics and by mapping the potential of a state crime framework. Refugee-hood and refugee policy were the objects and the social sciences and the humanities were the lens. I now turn to examine social science and humanities as the object and refugeehood and refugee policy as the lens. While the following analysis can be applied across the social sciences and humanities, it specifically focuses on the field of criminology as it is the field of social sciences and the humanities that speaks directly to the collision of the refugee and criminal justice. However, a number of disciplines under the broad umbrella of social science would make an equally insightful examination (women's studies, sociology, law, public policy, political science, international relations). The refugee and the politics of refugee policy may be considered an example of the 'rapidly changing character of criminology's subject matter'[1] that speaks to the broader transformation of the social sciences and humanities. The refugee is not just another new area of interest, but may become a significant area in the redefinition of criminology's subject matter and centrally implicated in some of the foremost contemporary transformations of social life and social control. Consequently, this chapter turns first to the subject of criminology and secondly to the subject of sovereignty and then returns to the issue of state crime raised at various points throughout the book.

Refugee state crime

Forced migration is increasingly central to intellectual changes within the field of criminology. For example, with my emphasis:

---

1   Garland, D, and Sparks, R, (2000), 'Criminology, Social Theory, and the Challenge of Our Times', 40 *British Journal of Criminology* 189.

Criminologists – particularly those who draw upon a sociological tradition – have always sought to ground their analyses in a nuanced sense of the world as it is, and it is becoming, not least because the phenomena of crime and disorder have so regularly been traced to the *effects of social upheaval and dislocation*'.[2] And further 'The mobile and insecure world of late modernity has given rise to new practices of control and exclusion that seek to *make society less open and less mobile*: to fix identities, immobilize individuals, *quarantine whole sections of the population, erect boundaries, close off access*.[3]

When cast in a condition of enforced unfamiliarity guarded and cultivated by the *closely supervised space boundaries*, held at a distance and barred regular or sporadic communicative access – the *Other turns into an Alien* and is permanently locked and sealed in that condition, having been effectively 'effaced' – stripped of the individual and personal uniqueness which alone could prevent stereotyping and so outweigh or mitigate the reductionist impact of the law – also the criminal law.[4]

As some forms of mobility and dislocation become signifiers and responses to criminality, the other is transformed into the alien. In turn, as Bauman outlines in relation to high security prisons, the alien (refugee) is furthered transformed into the criminal. The cycle is completed. This cycle increasingly occurs against the backdrop of sovereignty altering traditional criminological terrain. For example:

There is more than a happy coincidence between the tendency to conflate the troubles of the intrinsic insecurity and uncertainty of the late modern/postmodern being in a single overwhelming concern about personal safety – and the new realities of nation-state politics, particularly of the cut-down version of state sovereignty characteristic of the 'gobalization' era.[5]

Conditions of late modernity and globalisation have prompted a renegotiation and even realignment of the social sciences generally and criminology specifically. As the discipline re-examines its traditional terrain as well as the vast spaces it has moved into, the intellectual questions that come to be posed redefine the focus, if not the craft, of doing criminology. It is my intention here to look at the changing order of the social world the criminologist studies through

---

2   Ibid, p 189.
3   Ibid, p 200.
4   Bauman, Z, (2000), 'Social Issues of Law and Order', 40 *British Journal of Criminology* 209.
5   Ibid, p 215.

a criminological craft that has political commitment and a strategic social justice focus. The conditions of refugeehood and state responses to the refugee are the navigational method through the theoretical terrain now engaging criminology. Therefore my coverage is at best cursory but nonetheless illustrative of the point that the issues raised in this book evidence the interlocking condition of the refugee and the condition of criminology. One does not contain the other (or ever could), but increasingly a consideration of one implicates the other.

Garland and Sparks posed the following question in relation to criminology and the refugee: 'if we are to develop modes of theorising and forms of empirical enquiry that respond to the social world in a *fully contemporary idiom* then on what kinds of theoretical resources can we draw and in what corners of contemporary thought might these be discovered?'[6] This chapter first considers relevant theoretical shifts *within criminology* relating to the inter-locking of the criminological and refugee conditions.

As was noted in Chapter 5, securitisation and crime control have decentred the study of criminal justice[7] (and even the criminal justice state[8]) and the study of regulation now extends well beyond the study of the state. The victim continues its rise and criminolo-gical research is increasingly redundant amid law and order rhetoric and a general mood of punitive populism. Most notably the condi-tions upon which the field of criminology developed across the middle period of the 20th century (narratives of inclusion, economic welfare commitment, etc) have radically altered. Individual choice is sold as the sole driver of criminality against a background of increasing and unending consumption.[9] Crime and social control have been taken out of the remit of welfare and placed within the context of control and security. Garland has labelled these social and political conditions the development of a 'crime complex' which depends on heightened crime consciousness by individuals and

---

6   Garland and Sparks, op cit, p 190.
7   See for example the edited collection by Crawford, A, (ed), (2002), *Crime and Insecurity: the governance of safety in Europe*, Devon: William. See, also Loader, I, and Sparks, R, (2002), 'Contemporary Landscapes of Crime' in M Maguire, R Morgan and R Reiner, (eds), *The Oxford Handbook of Criminology*, 3rd edn, Oxford: Oxford University Press.
8   Garland and Sparks, op cit, p 191.
9   See the work of Pat O'Malley for a discussion of interactions between individuals and the state regarding crime prevention, neo-liberalism and increasing risks. In particular O'Malley, P, (1998), *Crime and the Risk Society*, Aldershot: Ashgate.

heightened levels of fear and anxiety driving a constant state of being a potential victim of crime. The criminal is no longer the subject of treatment but the object of control. The criminal can no longer be transformed, therefore he or she must be contained, contained for the bad choices he or she routinely makes as designated by the increasingly anxious and frightened majority. Choice and order become the scaffolding for securitisation and crime control.

The shift to securitisation and crime control has occurred, particularly during the past decade, amid the spectre of globalisation. Therefore the concepts of choice and order can be read against this broader backdrop within which the refugee emerges as criminal subject/object. As Bauman reminds us, the kind of order (or norm) imposed in a society is itself a choice. Therefore when we consider securitisation and crime control framed by notions of choice, the concept reaches beyond individual choices to the choices societies, or the powerful within societies, regarding what constitutes order. What I have attempted to evidence in this book is that the state has not simply responded to the 'choices' of refugees (however bogus such a line of argument remains) but has made choices regarding the order/norms imposed in refugee policy. These choices are born out of a notion that forced migration is an imperfection, an anomaly that must be rejected rather than rectified/ rehabilitated just as the criminal is no longer to be rehabilitated.[10] The consequences of this choice are endless:

> 'Order' and 'norm' are sharp knives pressed against the society as it is; they are first and foremost about separation, amputation, excision, expurgation, exclusion. They promote the 'proper' by sharpening the sights on the improper; they single out, circumscribe and stigmatise parts of reality denied the right to exist – destined for isolation, exile or extinction.[11]

The warehousing of prisoners and whole populations is routine enough in the US and increasingly in the UK and in some States of Australia. Considering this, the question is whether the condition of the refugee, subjected to relentless discourses and practices of crime control will be transported via order/choice from the current state of isolation and exile to that of extinction. For if there is an end point

---

10   An idea at odds with the writings of Sassen canvassed in Chapter 5 regarding the circularity of migration.
11   Bauman, op cit, p 206.

for the application of crime control to the condition of the refugee, then Bauman's writing suggests that end point is extinction – could this be the end of the condition of refugeehood?

The political extinction of the refugee is a possibility because securitisation and crime control are all consuming. The opportunity, let alone the ability, to resist is almost absent. Any resistance comes to constitute the acts of 'desperate criminals'. As I drafted this chapter there were reports of immigration detention centres around the country set on fire by refugees. Coupled with various acts of escape into vast and barren deserts, the sewing up of lips, hunger strikes and self-harm, the fires are glossed over by the government that no longer needs to make the case that those inside are simply the criminals they always thought they were – failed refugee applicants, people who made a series of erroneous choices that have now turned violent. The circle of control is completed by turning the refugee into criminal. From taking a person seeking protection, imprisoning them, rejecting their claims, finding them undeportable to their country of origin and seeing them charged with lighting fires while in indeterminate detention and then convicted and moved into prisons. The morality of the (state) choice to exclude is affirmed by an act of *individual* social suicide on the part of the refugee rather than execution, as Bauman articulated in relation to the criminal justice system:

> It is the fault of the excluded that they did nothing, or not enough to escape exclusion. Excluding them is an act of good sense and justice; those who do the exclusion might feel sensible and righteous, as becomes the defenders of law and order and guardians of values and standards of decency.[12]

However, such a depiction of individual choice in the absence of any effective chance of resistance, is no choice at all. The expectation of those seeking protection to regulate their behaviour in ways that may increase rather than decrease their chances of survival is no choice at all. Immigration detention centres, unlike a previous era of imprisonment in the US, UK or Australia, have never been about disciplining bodies but have included in their remit realising formal mechanisms of criminalisation and control completing the other-alien-criminal circuit. How this occurs across a situation where original detention is 'administrative' and outside the checks and balances of the criminal justice system returns us to one of Arendt's

---

12   Bauman, op cit, p 207.

central questions in *On Totalitarianism*: how is the undeportable made deportable again? Deportability is made possible through the conversion of refugee to criminal, physically from the immigration detention centre to the prison, from being held under migration legislation to being convicted under criminal legislation. The undeportable is made deportable but not only from one country to the next, but from a system of administrative criminalisation into a criminal justice system transformed into but another apparatus in a much broader operation of security and control. Operating within securitisation and crime control frames, both the immigration detention centre and the prison now serve as what Bauman has called the laboratories of globalised society where 'the techniques of space-confinement of the rejects and waste of globalisation are tested and their limits are explored'[13] and thus bringing to perfection the 'technique of immobilization'. The undeportable no longer need to be made deportable for they are immobilised and habituated to their own extinction. The 'anomaly' of forced migration upon the shores of the Global North is eradicated.

The Global North has increasingly raised fears and anxieties over the numbers and backgrounds of refugees arriving by boat even though the state has become increasingly less interested in dealing with refugee-producing conditions, and in fact has participated in many international engagements that have caused refugee flows (Kosovo and Afghanistan in most recent times). In short, as governments have become increasingly disinterested in conditions that promote offending behaviour, they have become increasingly disinterested in the reasons why boatloads of Afghans, Iraqis, Iranians and Sri Lankans risk their lives to seek protection in Australia. Locating both the ordinary criminal and the refugee within punitive control oriented politics (as opposed to problem-solving politics) is not simply a coincidence. Rehabilitating the offender and resettling the refugee have both dissipated amid the shrinking of the welfare state. As fears over the uncontrollability of crime and the uncontrollability of refugees are raised we see that the state participates in increasing anxieties over personal dominion at the same time that conditions of globalisation raise anxieties over the dominion of the sovereign state. Ordinary person or sovereign state – your home is no longer your castle. Decreased personal safety becomes a consequence of the decreased power of the sovereign

---

13   Ibid, p 212.

state – cause and effect. As the gap between deviance and the law widens[14] (with the concomitant decreasing commitment to procedural rights), the resonance and applicability of international human rights are also diminishing in Australia. As the sovereign state comes under increasing challenge, its force becomes less mitigated, less checked.

The territorial sovereign state, which has sustained various assaults on its power, grants dominion to those able to secure personal safety and mobility which comes with that secure (non-suspect) identity. To those unable to secure/afford their own personal safety their mobility becomes itself suspect. Their forced territoriality to home/prison is in contrast to what Bauman identifies as the mobility and safety of the extra-territorial elite. Those that seek territorial protection, through their suspicious mobility challenges the few territorially rooted functions of the state in an anxious condition and sees the refugee designated with the forced territorially of the unsafe and immobile.

But this again is to tempt an analysis that locates the deviant as actor and the state as merely responder (from misguided to malicious). However, deviance rarely precedes regulation and rather regulation often creates the conditions upon which the other is created and then censured, produced and then excluded. The drive to regulate, to control, to impose order/norms, to discipline the flow of forced migration creates and engages categories that upon application can only be failed and thus have regulatory subjects designated dangerous:

> In potential dangerousness postindustrial citizens find the ideal way of reconciling the contradictory demands between ignoring identifiable collective characteristics and assessing unknown individuals. They build their old lines of bias on the new legitimising basis of danger and by doing so they resolve the conundrum of non-discrimination. Far from objective condition, presumed dangerousness is the major postindustrial criteria for distinguishing between those who should be avoided and those who can approach.[15]

> Critical engagement with human rights must grasp the consequences of these new forms of nation-state existence, particularly the changing role of the courts and deployment of the law against judicial oversight of Executive action. Crime and human rights are not

---

14 See Lianos with Douglas, M, (2000), 'Dangerization and the End of Deviance', 40 *British Journal of Criminology* 261.
15 Ibid, p 268.

reducible to one another, nor simply a complimentary language of denunciation. While scholars of globalisation routinely and repeatedly cite human rights as one of the most fundamental challenges to the unbridled force of the nation-state and evidence of growing supra national forms of governance that grant individuals rights claims upon state and supra state bodies, criminologists continue to study the effects of discarding some of the most basic rights within the crime control complex. For example, the right to silence and the right to legal representation evaporate for the criminal justice and refugee systems alike. Such rights are increasingly redundant (first for the suspect population and then for larger sections of the citizenry) and the dangerous are placed beyond the citizen, beyond a relation to the punitive state, beyond territorial protection, beyond rights.

Utilising rights based frameworks and the multifarious and ambiguous deployments of sovereignty, returns me to theories of state crime as a way to commentate on the functions and practices of the state amid local and global forces and declining roles for rights discourses. First, whether strategies of criminalisation can add to the development of criminological understanding even when they are turned against the state. Secondly, whether the deployment of state crime makes any advance on a deployment of 'human rights violation'. And thirdly, whether the deployment of state crime can be effectively considered beyond the literal and purely legal realms and therefore be considered as having a wider potential for conceptions of the state and state harm.

Within conditions of late modernity and globalisation, and amid expanding theoretical terrain, conceptions of the state, the citizen and the crime mutate and multiply, many of which yield important new insights and ways of thinking about the enterprise of criminology. Wanting state actions against refugees to be accountable necessitates questions about the legitimacy of state action. That yearning to say enough, this is not right and what an unfair way to run the show is not sated, within the theoretical resources criminology draws upon outlined in these preceding pages. Those writings bring so much to a study of the interlocking conditions of criminology and refugeehood, but they do not comprehensively respond to the *desire* to add to the commentary on the changing nature of the state with clearly defined state practices that require the intellectual expertise of criminology and social control.

When the nation-state, in various ways, distances itself from the international realm, as the Australian government has increasingly done, then it is left to voices from within to censure government action upon those whose status is primarily external to the nation-state. Allegations of human rights violations do not go far enough when the domestic distances itself from the international discourse of human rights. Those whose job it has been to traditionally study the courts, policing and punishment need to not only question the validity of criminalising refugees but explore the resources of the discipline in examining the position and behaviours of the state. Potentially, explanations of state crime form the basis not only of a critique of state action/inaction but also challenge the construction and deployment of the sovereign state required in the criminalisation of the refugee. For it is within that construction and deployment of sovereignty that original deviance and processes of redress exist.

Throughout this book I have attempted to highlight some of the potential sites (and why they have failed) of acknowledgement of state criminality. However, two areas need to be addressed when using state crime to understand the condition of criminology and the condition of refugeehood. First, engagements of the global south and global north; and second, understanding state crime within shifting conceptions of sovereignty.

This chapter now turns to consider the issue of sovereignty in the examination of the interlocking of the criminological and refugee conditions.

Sovereignty

The first loss which the rightless suffered was the loss of their homes, and this meant the loss of the entire social texture into which they were born and in which they established for themselves a distinct place in the world. This calamity is far from unprecedented; in the long memory of history, forced migrations of individuals or whole groups of people for political or economic reasons look like everyday occurrences. What is unprecedented is not the loss of a home but the impossibility of finding a new one. Suddenly, there was no place on earth where migrants could go without the severest restrictions, no country where they would be assimilated, no territory where they could found a new community of their own. This, moreover, had next to nothing to do with any material problem of overpopulation; it was a problem not of space but of political organization. Nobody had been aware that mankind, for so long a time considered under the image of family of nations, had reached the stage where whoever was thrown out of one of these tightly organized closed communities found himself thrown out of the family of nations altogether'.[16]

Immigration can be seen as a strategic research site for the examination of the relation – the distance, the tension-between the idea of sovereignty as control over who enters and the constraints states encounter in making actual policy on the matter. Immigration is thus a sort of wrench one can throw into theories about sovereignty.[17]

The development of refugee law has been considered a pragmatic way to reconcile the commitment of states to sovereign control over immigration to the reality of forced migration.[18] In short, for governments to maintain even a modicum of immigration control they need to be responsive to the plight of those coercively displaced. Despite considerable development in immigration law and control over the past century the right of exclusion has been considered inherent to state sovereign power.[19] Refugee law has been considered underpinned by the existence of a multinational society where there exists a range of political-administrative systems in 'watertight national territories'.[20] The development of the definition of refugee status has often been constructed by Western governments as the 'protection of helpless sovereign states against the wicked refugee'.

Sovereignty forcefully marks the boundaries between inside and outside, hence debates around sovereignty have been at the heart of the refugee condition throughout the last century. Temporal and spatial dimensions of sovereignty have accounted for some of the competing claims to essentialised, universalised and stabilised definitions of sovereignty.[21] Sovereignty as a structural attribute used borders to demarcate internal and external political spaces based on developments in industrial capitalism, instruments of violence and militarisation.[22] The refugee has been defined as those

16 Arendt, op cit 294.
17 Sassen, S, (1996) *Losing Control? Sovereignty in an Age of Globalisation*, New York: Columbia University Press, p 67.
18 Hathaway, J, (1991) *The Law of Refugee Status*. Butterworths: Toronto, 1991.
19 Goodwin-Gill, G, (1978), *International Law and the Movement of Persons between States*, Oxford: Clarendon Press.
20 Vernant, J, (1953), *The Refugee in the Post War World*, London: Allen and Unwin.
21 Weber, C, (1995), *Simulating Sovereignty*, Cambridge: Cambridge University Press.
22 Devetak, R, (1995), 'Incomplete States: theories and practices of statecraft' in J Macmillan and A Linklater (eds), *Boundaries in Question*, London: Pinter Publishers.

who lack the citizen's unproblematic grounding within a territorial space and so lack effective representation and protection.[23] In a world composed of sovereign territorial states, the refugee is an aberration of the 'proper' subjectivity of citizenship and defined by her (lack of) relationship to the temporal and spatial limits of sovereignty.[24] A territorialised state is represented as the necessary coherence from which normality of life flows, a pre-existing and established state of normality.[25] In this section I will discuss the relation of sovereignty to legitimacy, the reconceptualisation of sovereignty, and the relation of sovereignty to criminology through the criminalisation of refugees and understandings of state crime. It is my intention to sketch this vast terrain for those spaces into which criminological theory and practice may engage a reconceptualised sovereignty.

Sovereignty has been a recurring theme throughout this book from media representations of the integrity of the nation-state to battles between the judiciary and the Executive over the operation of valid power in the treatment of refugees. When sovereignty has been represented as having an essence it is often expressed in terms of territorial sovereignty and the right to exclude non-citizens: 'sovereignty is nowhere more absolute than in matters of "emigration, naturalization, nationality and expulsion"'.[26] Sovereignty rests on the processing of inclusions and exclusion that cut across considerations of rights and justice.[27] Yet as Sassen notes, immigration is also a wrench in the system of sovereignty, a limiting force. The international refugee protection regime has traditionally acted as a specific limiting force on sovereignty. Often this limiting force has been read as the impact of the human rights regime (vis-a-vis refugees) curtailing the decisions of the sovereign state. Similarly, the refugee arriving at the borders of the Global North has represented an incursion of sovereignty, a criminal incursion and one that insists on the equality of rights that receiving countries are increasingly reluctant to realise. As Bhabha describes it: 'the fraught and adversarial insistence on a shared universe of rights and

---

23 Soguk, N, (1999), *States and Strangers: Refugees and Displacements of Statecraft*, Minneapolis: University of Minnesota Press.
24 Ibid.
25 Ibid.
26 Arendt, op cit, p 278.
27 Brown, C, (2002), *Sovereignty, Rights and Justice: International Political Theory Today*, Cambridge: Cambridge University Press.

resources that the disenfranchised and persecuted peoples of the developing world import through their physical presence on the territory of developed states and through their claims to asylum'.[28]

Sovereignty and legitimacy

Sovereignty can help us understand the parameters of legitimate state action. Sovereignty has routinely been considered a sort of shorthand for claims of autonomy within a system of co-existing nation-states and of the possession of certain capabilities exercised without the approval of others.[29] Sovereignty has been the basic unit of entry into international society and the basis of state legitimacy. Therefore, such studies of sovereignty can add to criminological understandings of criminalisation and state crime through extending the terrain upon which state legitimacy is viewed.

Reus-Smit argues that the organising principle of sovereignty has never been self-referential but always justified to particular conceptions of legitimate statehood and rightful state action. He notes that in the 20th century that reference has increasingly related to the state's role as guarantor of certain basic rights and freedoms.[30] He acknowledges that these norms have failed to prevent many states from systematic violations of the human rights of citizens but nonetheless considers it important in defining the post war international system and society. Similar to many human rights scholars, Reus-Smit argues that the protection of human rights is integral to the basic moral purpose of the modern state – the tension that exists between sovereignty and human rights stems from the inherently contradictory nature of modern discourse of *legitimate* statehood, a discourse that seeks to justify territorial sovereignty with reference to 'ethical universalism'. In such a reading sovereignty becomes realisable only as a result of rightful state action. Sovereignty becomes intermeshed with legitimacy.

States claim a monopoly on the legitimate use of force and it is this claim that states may *appear* sovereign. Hoffman makes an argument that under conditions of modernity problems arise in the concept of sovereignty as absolute and containing unrestrained

---

28 Bhabha, J, (2002), 'International Gatekeepers?: The tension between asylum advocacy and human rights', 15 *Harvard Human Rights Journal*180.

29 Brown, op cit.

30 Reus-Smit, C, (2001), 'Human Rights and the Social Construction of Sovereignty', 27 *Review of International Studies* 519.

power.[31] However, he notes that at the same time such power must be limited and from this arises a central paradox for sovereignty when linked to the state. Modernism focuses explicitly on the relationship between legitimacy and force because it attempts to limit the use of force through the notion of individual human rights. Hoffman admits that it is legitimacy itself that arises from these limits but suggests that the problem is that if sovereignty is expressed through the states' claims to exercise a monopoly of legitimate force, how can these limits be enforced? In developing a post-statist concept of sovereignty, Hoffman argues that the concept of sovereignty can be reworked so that it denotes for example, the capacity of women 'as others' to govern their own lives. He argues that sovereignty does not have to involve domination and oppression but can be empowered to embrace the power of individuals to relate to others in ways that strengthen rather than undermine self-esteem and self-determination and promote self-sovereignty. I would argue that criminological theories of state crime lend some clarity to the paradox that Hoffman identifies.

Tilly argues that states operated as protection rackets with the advantage of legitimacy – an example of organised crime. Nordstrom extends Tilly's analysis to suggest that the link between war making, banditry and extraction are necessary for the continued success of the state. Tilly's argument rested on the proposition that states first forged power and then the means to protect this power and then fashioned legitimacy.[32] Sovereignty was thus a product of this process and not a natural or pre-existing state. Therefore, a refashioning of legitimacy becomes the potential when sovereignty is reconceptualised. However, the added clarity I note above, and the refashioning of legitimacy depend heavily on what a reconceptualised sovereignty may look like.

Reconceptualising sovereignty

Dominant understandings of sovereignty have effectively silenced more dynamic understandings of statehood and have inhibited more creative reconceptualisations.[33] Weber argues that there is no *natural* sovereign state because there is no *natural* foundation of

---

31 Hoffman, J, (1998), *Sovereignty*, Buckingham: Open University Press.
32 Discussed in Nordstrom, C, (2000), 'Shadows and Sovereigns', 17(4) *Theory, Culture and Society* 35.
33 Weber, op cit.

sovereignty.[34] Weber argues that to effect the sovereign state requires not just the creation of a myth to justify authority, but control must be gained of how its people are 'written' (constituted) and how their meaning is fixed. States are written effects of attempts to exert effective control over representation, both political and symbolic. The state must maintain the ability to make credible claims to both political and symbolic representation of 'its people' to maintain its presumed ability of representation and, ultimately, sovereignty.

Competing claims to write or draw boundaries between that which is within the sovereign jurisdiction of the state and that which is beyond it become the focus of a process of how foundations and boundaries are drawn and how states are written with particular capacities and legitimacies in particular historical moments.[35] Criminology, particularly with refugees as the subject, could potentially make significant contributions to how such boundaries are renegotiated, done away with or reinvented.

Hoffman has argued that the controversy surrounding sovereignty has historically been side-stepped by maintaining a clear distinction between inside and outside and the separation of political theory and international relations. This separation has also prevented the scrutiny of the inherent contradictions in the concept of sovereignty, which is conceived as both a limit to power and legitimate right to exercise absolute power.[36] Definitions of state crime may be just one means of possible scrutiny.

The rapidly-expanding field that makes the reconceptualisation of sovereignty its focus has sought to critique the ways sovereignty has been made to appear as if it has an essence and its defence of rigid boundaries, most notably territorial boundaries.[37] Increasingly, however, scholars are arguing that sovereignty is contingent, as is the autonomy exercised in its name. It has always been an intersubjective property relying on the recognition by others that states exist as sovereign states.[38] Devetak has argued that there is no completed state; it is ceaselessly being constituted and

---

34   Ibid, p 27.
35   Ibid.
36   Hoffman, op cit.
37   Devetak, R, (2001), 'Postmodernism' in S Burchill, R Devetak, A Linklater, M Paterson, C Reus-Smit, J True, (eds), *Theories of International Relations*, New York: Palgrave.
38   Devetak (1995), op cit.

reconstituted, but never a unified totality.[39] Others have argued that the inside/outside boundary of the nation is a function of the state's discursive authority: its ability in the face of ambiguity and uncertainty to impose fixed and stable meanings about who belongs and who does not belong to the nation.[40] This approach suggests that sovereignty today rests on claims to represent the will of the nation and produce seemingly fixed and stable foundations – what Doty has called the 'sovereignty effect'. [41] Doty argues that considering sovereignty as an effect renders sovereignty less an ontological problem of what it 'is' and more a question of determining what issues and uncertainties elicit responses in discursive practices that attempt to fix meanings and identities.

When I suggest criminology can add to and draw from efforts, particularly by scholars of international relations, to particularise formulations of state legitimacy and hence new understandings of sovereignty I am also responding to Soguk's call for conceptual and practical departures when we theorise refugee issues in which the sovereign state is problematised. We should start with the problem of modern statecraft and its drive to inscribe and stabilise a particularised figure of the citizen that the modern state represents and upon which basis the state claims to affect sovereignty and its power to rule.[42] The refugee is thus not reducible to an aberration of the assumed 'proper' subjectivity of the citizen and recognises instead the difficulties of compartmentalising life into categories such as 'citizen' and 'refugee'.

Sovereignty and criminology

Sovereignty has been more visible and contested in the field of international relations than politics or sociology.[43] Not surprisingly, it has captured relatively little criminological attention.[44] I asked in Chapter 1 whether sovereignty could help reposition criminality and the nation-state because sovereignty is the traditional basis upon

---

39   Ibid.
40   Doty, R, (1996), 'Sovereignty and the nation: constructing the boundaries of national identity', in T Biersteker and C Weber (eds), *State Sovereignty as Social Construct*, Cambridge: Cambridge University Press.
41   Ibid.
42   Soguk, op cit.
43   Brown, op cit.
44   With some exceptions, including Loader and Sparks.

which state responsibility and state protection turns. The sovereign, whether acting within the criminal justice system or within refugee policy, stands largely unchallenged within frames of securitisation and crime control. It may operate via many institutions, individuals and in varying ways, but it continues to carry the full force of the 'nation' in its determinations and actions.

The concept of sovereignty has traditionally been conceived as having two sides – internal and external.[45] Internal sovereignty has been concerned with the supreme authority within borders: often criminal justice or crime control. As internal sovereign authority transforms extra territorially, so too does external expressions of sovereignty. As Weber argues, international/domestic boundaries have changed depending upon where the sovereign intervention discourse had inscribed foreign policy as domestic policy (and vice versa), for example, the war against drugs or the war against terrorism.[46] According to Mills there is an evolving 'new sovereignty', which is a recognition of increasing interdependencies whereby sovereignty is moving downwards, upwards, inwards and outwards from the state incorporating human rights as a legitimating factor in the emerging global order. Loader and Sparks have asked whether 'we are witnessing a steady erosion of the distinction between 'internal' and 'external' security and, with it, the demise of sovereign states as principle guarantors of social order'?[47] They ask questions about the state of democracy and citizenship and whether new forms of transnational co-operation between government and criminal justice elites are emerging in ways inimical to democratic rights and liberties. Consequently, this chapter concludes by exploring how new conceptions of sovereignty leave the two foci of this book: the criminalisation of the refugee and understandings of state crime. Developments in international relations that seek to reconceptualise sovereignty in many ways shadow developments in criminological theory, theorisations of state crime outlined in Chapter 1.

---

45 Mills, K, (1998), *Human Rights in the Emerging Global Order: A New Sovereignty?*, London: Macmillan Press.
46 Weber, op cit.
47 Loader and Sparks, op cit, p 101.

Criminalisation of the refugee

Biersteker and Weber have argued that the ideal of state sovereignty is the product of the actions of powerful agents and the resistance to those actions by those located at the margins of power.[48] Realist accounts of sovereignty have argued for the concept as 'the appearance of a centralised power that exercised its lawmaking and law enforcing authority within a certain territory'.[49] It has been argued that neo-realist accounts that conflate population, territory and recognition into a concept of sovereignty ignores problems in the domestic domain and leaves the assessment of such problems (of internal sovereignty) to others. With the invention of the criminal refugee such realist accounts are decreasingly useful starting points. Indeed, the interlocking condition of the refugee and criminology (read here as the criminal) means such distinctions between the sovereign inside and sovereign outside are unconvincing. The interlocking condition depends upon new readings of sovereignty.

States have increasingly sought to privatise and decentralise immigration control while taking credit for comprehensive control of their borders. As Chapter 4 outlined and as Bhabha has recently argued, in this process, border control becomes exported beyond the physical confines of developed states.[50] Bigo's Mobius ribbon returns to mind as does Devetak's four components of a postmodern understanding of sovereignty.[51]

As was outlined in Chapters 4 and 5, the sovereign state has relied on a series of (often violent) boundary inscription practices in the reconstitution of sovereignty against the refugee. Such boundary inscription practices are required for the continuing existence of sovereignty. A form of statecraft, in Devetak's formulation of the term,[52] is deployed. That is, a practice of differentiation that relentlessly strives to separate, enframe or totalise a political space in a 'boundary producing political performance'. Crucial to this study is

---

48 Biersteker, T, and Weber, C, (1996), 'The Social Construction of State Sovereignty' in T Biersteker and C Weber (eds), *State Sovereignty as Social Construct*, Cambridge: Cambridge University Press.

49 Ibid, p 4.

50 Bhabha, op cit.

51 See Chapter 5 for further discussion.

52 Statecraft according to Devetak's formulations includes the operation of power by state institutions, enacted by state representatives to enforce state boundaries. See Pickering, S and O'Kane, M, (2002), 'Policing, Exile and Gender in States' Borderlands', 14(1) *Current Issues in Criminal Justice* 106.

that such a performance of statecraft depends upon implementing policies and practices both domestic and foreign that mutually support one another that in effect produce the sovereign state.[53] Those mutually supporting policies and practices have increasingly revolved around criminalisation, securitisation and control. Drawing on Foucault, Devetak argues that the performance of internal surveillance and practices of governmentality seek to normalise and homogenise a population to give it a sense of unity. Exclusionary practices which seek to guarantee security to the domestic sphere then differentiate the inside from the outside by securing the 'domestic inside' against a threatening and dangerous outside:[54] 'The security discourse which is facilitated by statecraft depends on the simultaneous internal and external containment of threats the overall effect is that statecraft re-secures the state by remarking boundaries'.[55] Similarly, Weber argues that disciplinary power is involved in the production of sovereign foundations and is illustrative of Foucault's general point that:

> Sovereignty and disciplinary mechanisms are two absolutely integral constituents of the general mechanism of power in our [modern] society' (1980a: 108). Within a logic of representation discourses of truth (sovereignty) legitimate uses of power (disciplinary acts of intervention). However dispersed, power refers to truth.[56]

The refugee is resistant to such disciplinary powers, in so much as she transgresses political and cultural borders and undermines familiar meanings of 'democratic' life and its institutions from within the domain of the citizen.[57] However, as Soguk points out, the refugee also accommodates and recuperates some of the conventional practices of 'democracy' through their participation in exclusionary legal, cultural, political and economic practices that privilege the citizen as the proper entity and the sovereign territorial state as the facilitator of the democracy.

Refugees, as Soguk notes, challenge democratic practices as they call into question the legitimacy of exclusionary political and cultural practices that centre on the citizen. The refugee moves into

---

53   Devetak, (1995) op cit.
54   See Lianos, M and Douglas, M, (2000), 'Dangerization and the end of Deviance, 40 *British Journal of Criminology* 261.
55   Devetak (1995) op cit, 3.
56   Weber, op cit, p 124.
57   Soguk, op cit.

the space of the citizen and exposes the limits of conventional narratives of 'democracy' as the domain of the citizen.[58]

State crime

Green and Ward's definition of state crime does not rely on an inherent property of the act but on the relationship between the act, the actor and audience. Those audiences of censure can be internal, external, from above or below. Coupling questions of legitimacy and audience (those who censure) finds the common ground between understandings of state crime and sovereignty.

Biersteker and Weber have argued that realist and liberal accounts of sovereignty have not paid adequate attention to how the practices of states and non-state actors produce, reproduce and redefine sovereignty and its constituent elements: population, recognition, authority, territory. They focus on the social construction of state sovereignty and hence the constitutive relationship between the state and sovereignty. Particularly the ways the meaning of sovereignty is negotiated out of interactions within intersubjectively identifiable communities and the variety of ways in which practices construct, reproduce and reconstruct both the state and sovereignty. This process is intimately tied to the process of constructing and reconstructing boundaries. This approach mirrors in some respects Green and Ward when they locate a definition of state crime within a relation between the act, actor and multiple audiences. Increasingly, the issue of audiences and human rights also moves to the centre of reconceptualisations of sovereignty. As Sassen argues:

> The concept of nationality is being partly displaced from a principle that reinforces state sovereignty and self-determination (through the state's right/power to define its nations) to a concept emphasizing that the state is accountable to all its residents on the basis of international human rights law. The individual emerges as the object of international law and institutions. International law still protects sovereignty and has in the state its main object, but the state is no longer the only subject of international law.[59]

If sovereignty is traditionally understood as a final and absolute authority in the political authority,[60] then there is little scope for

---

58   Ibid.
59   Sassen, op cit, p 103.
60   See, eg, Biersteker and Weber's discussion of Hinsley.

serious discussion of state legitimacy let alone state criminality. Brown suggests that traditional rigid conceptions of sovereignty 'obscure certain political questions concerning rights and justice, which may be embarrassing for the strong whose interests are being protected by avoiding such questions'.[61] With the reconceptualisation of sovereignty now well underway, there is no longer any finality to the condition of sovereignty, and hence traditional power is contested. One of those areas of contestation is in formulations of state crime.

Concepts of state crime are not simply about a moment of denunciation (as important and powerful as this may be) – but assist in the reconceptulisation of state legitimacy and hence state sovereignty. State crime shifts from being the expression of an intellectual thirst to politically and strategically condemn contemporary government practice and instead contribute to the reconceptualisation of sovereignty. A cursory glance sees the overlapping of state crime and the reconceptualisation of sovereignty in three ways: political struggle, legitimacy, and audience.

First, sovereignty if reconceptualised as a site of political struggle[62] meets the need for formulations of state crime to be both political and strategic. Such study by criminologists could garner further insight from the work of Devetak and his notion of 'transversal groups'. Transversal groups not only transgress national boundaries but also call into question the territorial organisation of modern political life and the spatial logic through which boundaries come to frame and constitute the conduct of political life.[63] Moreover, transversal movements challenge, negotiate and often subvert the violent boundary inscription practices of the state. Transversal groups have what Devetak calls a deterritorialising function of escaping spatial codes and practices of the dominant actor that makes possible a critique of the sovereign states modes of reterritorialisation and exclusion. For example, in a study by myself and Mary O'Kane with women from Burma who had fled to the Thai-Burma border, we argued:

> Focussing on women's experiences of the borderlands reveals how nation-states depend on the continuous and violent enforcement of territorial boundaries. Women's continuous movement around the

---

61 Brown, op cit.
62 See for example Weber (1995) op cit.
63 Devetak (2001), op cit.

borderlands between Thailand and Burma demonstrate interstate boundaries to be abstract, legal constructs that are lived through the material effects of enforcement by state representatives (army, immigration, police, intelligence) on the bodies of migrant people.[64]

That study evidenced state practices that enforced territorial space boundaries by focusing on women's experiences of policing that contradicted states' meta narratives of discrete, (assumedly) demarcated, fixed boundaries between two countries. Their stories instead illustrated how states may intentionally rely on practising the maintenance of 'flexible' boundaries as a way to pursue various other perceived state interests and the spaces in which the legitimacy (and potential criminality) of the state may be discernible. Such transversal practices become sites for 'from below' accounts of state legitimacy and potentially state crime in the borderlands in which the excluded becomes a defining voice in the construction and maintenance of state sovereignty.

Secondly, Weber argues that sovereignty defines the domain of a states' legitimate authority and intervention marks the outer limit, as such, the sovereignty/intervention boundary is the location of the state. If sovereignty defines (but is not reducible to) the legitimate authority of the state then sovereignty can be understood as a broader set in which state crime becomes a subset in definitions of state legitimation. State crime therefore marks the operation of particular powers of the state and their legitimacy within the realm of a reconceptualised sovereignty. When examinations of sovereignty and state crime are coupled in such determinations of state legitimacy, the formation of state identity becomes an obvious focus. Returning to Devetak's discussion of identity in the four elements of sovereignty (violence, boundary inscription, identity and statecraft) he identifies, the geopolitical creation of the external other in terms of dangerousness sees the substitution of threat for difference in the constitution of political identity.[65] By coding such threat/ dangerousness in spatial terms that are then passed off in moral terms, it becomes easier to legitimise certain politico-military practices which advance 'national security' at the same time they reconstitute political identities[66]. For example, in the European context, Green and Grewcock argue that the war against illegal

---

64   Pickering and O'Kane, op cit, p 106.
65   Devetak (2001), op cit.
66   Ibid.

immigration and the construction of the new European state is being formed on the basis of state sanctioned criminal behaviour:

> The response to 'illegal immigration' is primarily an issue of state identity. It is about the cultivation of a hegemonic European character/identity and their demonisation through the largely ideological device of the 'trafficker' justifies increasingly punitive, covert and extra-legal measures of deterrence.[67]

Thirdly, rather than taking an absolute or unitary notion of sovereignty, Mills has argued that legitimate sovereign authority is recognised as emanating from individuals as well as groups. Mills suggests that sovereignty discourse has marginalised other ways of thinking about social arrangements and the locus of power and authority.[68] I would add that it has also marginalised other ways to consider state legitimacy. Weber's research also evidences the importance of casting meanings in particular ways to enable specific forms of practice to take place legitimately in the eyes of a supposed interpretive community.[69] Therefore, understanding sovereignty as being judged according to its legitimacy requires recourse to a range of defining (and indeed condemnatory) discourses. One of which is state crime.

Conclusion

This chapter has briefly surveyed the terrain in which the interlocked condition of criminology and the condition of the refugee may be further explored, a condition applicable beyond the field of criminology. It has argued for a critical account that includes the study of state crime and the burgeoning field that seeks to reconceptualisation of sovereignty.

Overall this book has argued that the intensive regulation of the new regulatory state through increasing securitisation and control (unbridled and deterritorialised law and order), in and of itself, undermines the rule of law whereby the law no longer operates in its ordinary sense but is an empowering agent for officials as regulators of citizens[70] and non-citizens. Such agencies

---

67 Green and Grewcock, op cit p 99.
68 Mills, K, (1998), op cit.
69 Weber (1995) op cit.
70 Hirst, P, (2000), 'Statism, Pluralism and Social Control', 40 *British Journal of Criminology* 189.

increasingly rely on punitive, non-accountable, covert and extra-territorial powers. The government is therefore not limited but is everywhere, there is no retreat of the state:

> The new regulatory state is in danger of creating a post-liberal society, in which government becomes ubiquitous and arbitrary and rule application an arcane process. One might call this a *nouveau ancien regime.*[71]

None of the matters of forced migration can be settled by law enforcement, or the kind of regulatory legislation it has been subject to. Forced migration has at its core sovereignty, the promotion and defence of human rights and critical understanding of difference. Targeting those that are forced to migrate settles next to nothing. Nothing, unless those forced to migrate are transformed into some-thing else – in this case transforming refugees into criminals. How criminology responds to this state of play will shape its theoretical and empirical endeavours to come.

This book has suggested the interlocking condition of crimi-nology and the condition of the refugee and the terrain that under-pins that study is but one site upon which critical encounters may occur and new theoretical terrain engaged. But it is never simply a matter of new theoretical engagements. As the writing of Arendt reminds us, our response will shape the dangers we face in the future, and the legal and political conditions we set for others are those we are left to live among ourselves.

> The danger in the existence of such people [refugees] is two-fold: first and most obviously, their ever-increasing numbers threaten our political life, our human artifice, the world which is the result of our common and co-ordinated effort in much the same, perhaps even more terrifying, way as the wild elements of nature once threatened the existence of man-made cities and countrysides. Deadly danger to any civilization is no longer likely to come from without. Nature has been mastered and no barbarians threaten to destroy what they cannot understand, as the Mongolians threatened Europe for centuries. Even the emergence of totalitarian governments is a phenomenon within, not outside, our civilization. The danger is that a global, universally interrelated civilization may produce barbarians from its own midst by forcing millions of people into conditions which, despite all appearances, are the conditions of savages.[72]

---

71   Ibid, p 283.
72   Arendt (1966) op cit, p 302.

Selected Bibliography

Ahmed, S (2000) *Strange Encounters: Embodied Others, in Post-Coloniality*, London: Routledge.

Alexander, M and Mohanty, C (eds) (1997) *Feminist Genealogies, Colonial Legacies, Democratic Futures*, New York: Routledge.

Allan, S (1999) *News Culture*, Open University Press: Buckingham.

Anderson, M (1996) *Frontiers: territory and state formation, in the modern world*, Cambridge: Polity.

Arboleda, E and I Hoy (1993) 'The Convention Refugee Definition in the West' 5 *International Journal of Refugee Law* 66.

Arendt, H (1966) *The Origins of Totalitarianism*, Florida: Harcourt.

Bauman, Z (2000) 'Social Issues of Law and Order', 40 *British Journal of Criminology* 205.

Beck, U (1992) *Risk Society*, London: Sage.

Bell, A (1999) 'The discourse structure of news stories', in A Bell and P Garrett (eds) *Approaches to Media Discourse*, Oxford: Blackwell.

Betts, K (1998) *Ideology and Immigration: Australia 1976-1987*, Melbourne: Melbourne University Press.

Bhabha, J (2002) 'International Gatekeepers?: The tension between asylum advocacy and human rights', 15 *Harvard Human Rights Journal* 155.

Biersteker, T and Weber, C (1996) 'The Social Construction of State Sovereignty', in T Biersteker and C Weber (eds) *State Sovereignty as Social Construct*, Cambridge: Cambridge University Press.

Bigo, D (2001) 'The Möbius Ribbon of Internal and External Security(ies)', in M Albert, D Jackson and Y Lapid (eds) *Identities, borders, orders: rethinking international relations theory*, Minneapolis: University of Minnesota Press

Billig, M (1995) *Banal Nationalisms*, London: Sage.

Bilsky, L (2001) Between Justice and Politics: the competition of Storytellers, in the Eichmann Trial', in S Aschheim (ed) *Hannah Arendt, in Jerusalem*, Berkeley: University of California Press.

Border Protection (2002) Unauthorised Arrivals and Detention – Information Paper, February <www.minister.immi.gov.au/borders/detention/2002paper_2.htm> accessed 5 September 2002.

Brake, M and Hale, C (1992) *Public order and Private Lives: The Politics of Law and Order*, London: Routledge.

Brown, C (2002) *Sovereignty, Rights and Justice: International Political Theory Today*, Cambridge: Cambridge University Press.

Cain, M (2000) 'Orientalism, Occidentalism and the Sociology of Crime', 40 *British Journal of Criminology* 239.

Cavallaro, D, 2001, *Critical and Cultural Theory*, London: The Athlone Press.

Charlesworth, H (2001) *Writing on rights: Australia and the Protection of Human Rights*, Sydney: University of New South Wales Press.

Charlesworth, H and Chinkin, C (2000) *The Boundaries of International Law: A Feminist Analysis*, Manchester: Manchester University Press.

Chomsky, N (2001) *Rogue States*, London: Pluto Press.

Christie, N (1993) *Crime Control As Industry*, London: Routledge.

Christie, N (1986) 'The Ideal Victim', in E Fattah (ed) *From Crime Policy to Victim Policy: Reorienting the Justice System*, London: Macmillan.

Coats, L (1997) 'Causal Attributions, in Sexual Assault Trial Judgments', 16 *Journal of Language and Social Psychology* 278.

Cohen, S (2001) *States of Denial: Knowing About Atrocities and Suffering*, London: Polity Press.

Cohen, S (1993) 'Human Rights and Crimes of the State: the Culture of Denial' 26 *Australian and New Zealand Journal of Criminology* 97.

Cook, R (ed) (1994) *Human Rights and Women: National and International Perspectives*, Philadelphia: University of Pennyslvania.

Crawley, H (2001) *Refugees and Gender: law and processes*, London: Jordan Publishing.

Crenshaw, K, 'Demarginalising the Intersection of Race and Sex: A Black Feminist Critique of Antidiscrimination Doctrine, Feminist Theory and Antiracist Politics', in D Kelly (ed) *Feminist Legal Theory: Foundations*, Wesiberg, Philadeplphia: Temple University Press.

Cuneen, C (2001) *Conflict, Politics and Crime: Aboriginal Communities and the Police*, Sydney: Allen and Unwin.

Daniel, EV and Knudsen, JC (eds) (1995) *Mistrusting Refugees*, Berkeley: University of California Press.

Dauvergne, C (2000) 'The Dilemma of Rights Discourse For Refugees', 23(3) *UNSW Law Journal* 56.

Deacon, D, Pickering, M, Golding, P and Murdoch, G (1999) *Researching Communications: A Practical Guide to Methods, in Media and Cultural Analysis*, London: Arnold.

Debord, G (1983) *Society of the Spectacle*, Detroit: Black and Red.

Debord, G (1990) *Comments on the Society of the Spectacle*, London: Verso

Devetak, R (2001) 'Postmodernism', in S Burchill, R Devetak, A Linklater, M Paterson, C Reus-Smit and J True, *Theories of International Relations*, New York: Palgrave

Devetak, R (1995) 'Incomplete States: theories and practices of statecraft', in J Macmillan and A Linklater (eds) *Boundaries, in Question*, London: Pinter Publishers.

Doty, R (1996) 'Sovereignty and the nation: constructing the boundaries of national identity', in T Biersteker and D Weber (eds) *State Sovereignty as Social Construct*, Cambridge: Cambridge University Press.

Downes, D and Morgan, R (1997) 'Dumping the 'Hostages to Fortune'? The Politics of Law and Order, in Post-War Britain', in M Maguire, R Morgan and R Reiner (eds) *The Oxford Handbook of Criminology*, 2nd edn, Oxford: Oxford University Press.

Drew, P (1992) 'Contested Evidence, in Courtroom Examination: The Case of a Trial For Rape', in P Drew and J Heritage (eds) *Talk at Work: Interaction, in Institutional Settings*, Cambridge: Cambridge University Press

Eckert, P and McConnell-Ginet, S (1992) 'Think Practically and Look Locally: Language and Gender as Community Based Practice', 21 *Annual Review of Anthropology* 461.

Edkins, J (2000) 'Sovereign Power, Zones of Indistinction and the Camp', 25(1) *Alternatives* 19.

Ehrlich, S (2001) *Representing Rape: Language and Sexual Consent*, London: Routledge.

Esmaelli, H and Wells, B (2000) 'The "Temporary" Refugees: Australia's Legal Response to the Arrival of Iraqi and Afghan Boat-people' 23(3) *UNSW Law Journal* 224.

Evans, S (2001) *Constitutionalism, The Rule of Law and the MV Tampa*, paper presented at the seminar, Boundless Plains to Share: Australia's Response to the MV Tampa Asylum Seekers, Centre for Comparative Constitutional Law, 11 October.

Fairclough, N (1998) 'Political discourse, in the media: an analytical framework', in A Bell and P Garrett (eds) *Approaches to Media Discourse*, Oxford: Blackwell.

Ferguson, R (1998) *Representing Race: Ideology, Identity and the Media*, London: Arnold.

Fitzpatrick, J (1999) 'The End of Protection: Legal Standards for Cessation of Refugee Status Withdrawal of Temporary Protection' 13 *Georgetown Immigration Law Journal* 343.

Fitzpatrick, J (2000) 'Temporary Protection of Refugees: Elements of a Formalized Regime', 94 *American Journal of International Law* 278.

Frieberg, A (2002) *Pathways to Justice: Sentencing Review 2002*, Victoria: Department of Justice

Friederichs, D (2000) 'State Crime or Governmental Crime: Making Sense of the Conceptual Confusion', in J Ross, *Controlling State Crime*, 2nd edn, New Brunswick: Transaction.

Fry, G (2002) 'The "Pacific Solution"?', in W Maley, A Dupont, J Fonteyne, G Fry, J Jupp and T Do, *Refugees and the Myth of the Borderless World*, Canberra: Department of International Relations.

Garland, D and Sparks, R (2000) 'Criminology, Social Theory and the Challenge of Our Times', 40 *British Journal of Criminology* 189.

Gelsthorpe, L and Morris, A (eds) (1990) *Feminist Perspectives, in Criminology*, Buckinghamshire: Open University Press.

Gibney, M (2000) 'Between Control and Humanitarianism: Temporary Protection, in Contemporary Europe' 14 *Georgetown Immigration Law Journal* 689.

Gilroy, P (2000) *Between Camps: Nations, Cultures and the Allure of Race*, London: Penguin

Goodwin-Gill, G (1978) *International Law and the Movement of Persons between States*, Oxford: Clarendon Press.

Graydon, C (1998) 'East Timorese Asylum Seekers: Close to Home but No Justice, in Sight', 36 (Aug-Sept) *Arena Magazine* 24.

Greatbatch, J (1989) 'The Gender Difference: feminist critiques if refugee discourse', 1 *International Journal of Refugee Law* 518.

Green, P and Grewcock, M (2002) 'The War Against Illegal Immigration: State Crime and the Construction of a European Identity', 14(1) *Current Issues, in Criminal Justice* 87.

Green, P and Ward, T (2000) 'State Crime, Human Rights and the Limits of Criminology', 27 *Social Justice* 101.

Hall, S (1990) 'The whites of their eyes: racist ideologies and the media', in M Alvarado and JO Thompson (eds) *The Media Reader*, London: British Film Institute.

Hall, S, Critcher, C, Jefferson, T, Clarke, J and Roberts, B (1978) *Policing the Crisis: mugging, the state and law and order*, London: Macmillan.

Hardy, C and Phillips, N (1998) *No Joking Matter: Discursive Struggle, in the Canadian Refugee System*, Department of Management Working Paper No 11, in Human Resource Management and Industrial Relations, Melbourne: University of Melbourne.

Hathaway, J (1991) *The Law of Refugee Status*, Toronto: Butterworths.

Herman, E and Chomsky, N (1988) *Manufacturing Consent: the political economy of the mass media*, New York: Vintage.

Hirst, P (2000) 'Statism, Pluralism and Social Control', 40 *British Journal of Criminology* 189.

Hoffman, J (1998) *Sovereignty*, Buckingham: Open University Press.

Holzer, T, Schneider, G and Widmer, T (2000) 'The impact of legislative deterrence measures on the number of asylum applications, in Switzerland (1986-1995)', 34(4) *IMR* 1182.

Indra, D (ed) *Engendering Forced Migration*, Oxford: Berghahn Books, 1999.

Indra, D (1987) 'Gender: a key dimension, in the refugee experience', *Refuge* 6.

Justice for Asylum Seekers (2002) *Alternative Approaches to asylum seekers: reception and transitional processing system*, Melbourne, JAS.

Kjaerum, M (1994) 'Temporary Protection, in Europe, in the 1990s', 6(3) *International Journal of Refugee Law* 444.

Koser, K, Walsh, M and Black, R (1998) 'Temporary Protection and the Assisted Return of Refugees from the European Union', 10(3) *International Journal of Refugee Law* 445.

Kristeva, J (1991) *Strangers to Ourselves*, Hemel Hempstead: Harvester/ Wheatsheaf.

Kyle, D and Koslowski, R (eds) (2001) *Global Human Smuggling: Comparative Perspectives*, Baltimore: Johns Hopkins.

Lambert, C, Pickering, S and Alder, C (forthcoming) *Critical Chatter*, Durham: Carolina Academic Press

Lee, A and Poynton, C (eds) (1999) *Culture and Text*, Sydney: Allen and Unwin.

Lees, S (1996) *Carnal Knowledge Rape on Trial*, London: Hamish Hamilton.

Lianos M with Douglas, M (2000) 'Dangerization and the End of Deviance', 40 *British Journal of Criminology* 261.

Loader, I and Sparks, R (2002) 'Contemporary Landscapes of Crime', in M Maguire, R Morgan and R Reiner, *The Oxford Handbook of Criminology*, 3rd edn, Oxford: Oxford University Press.

MacLeod, A (1995) 'Hegemonic Relations and Gender Resistance: the new veiling as accommodating protest, in Cairo', in B Laslett, J Brenner and Y Arat (eds) *Rethinking the Political: gender, resistance and the state*, Chicago: Chicago University Press

McCorquodale, R (2001) 'International law, boundaries and imagination', in D Miller and S Hashmi (eds) *Boundaries and Justice: Diverse ethical perspectives*, Princeton: Princeton University Press

McLaughlin, G (1993) 'Refugees, migrants and the fall of the Berlin Wall', in G Philo (ed) *Message Received: Glasgow Media Group Research, 1993-1998*, Harlow: Longman.

Millbank, A (2001) *The Detention of Boat People*, Department of the Parliamentary Library, Current Issues Brief 8, 200-01.

Miller, D and Hashmi, S (2001) 'Introduction', in D Miller and S Hashmi (eds) *Boundaries and Justice: Diverse ethical perspectives*, Princeton: Princeton University Press

Mills, K (1998) *Human Rights, in the Emerging Global Order: A New Sovereignty?*, London: Macmillan Press.

Minister for Foreign Affairs Alexander Downer, Attorney-General Daryl Williams, Minister for Immigration and Multicultural Affairs, Philip Ruddock, Australian Initiatives to Improve the Effectiveness of the UN Treaty Committees, MPS 042/2001, <www.minister.immi.gov.au/media_releases/media01/r01042.htm> accessed 13 March 2002.

Minister for Immigration and Multicultural and Indigenous Affairs (2002) Border protection: Temporary Protection Visas, <www.minister.immi.gov.au/borders/detention/fs_64_tpv.htm> accessed 27July 2002.

Minister, Press Release (2002) Minister Commends SA Police for Assistance, 30 June.

Ministerial Conference Between Indonesia and Australia on People Smuggling, Trafficking, in Persons and Related Transnational Crime (2002) Co-Chairs' Statement, <www.dfat.gov.au/illegal_immigration/cochair.htm> accessed 13 March 2002.

Nadig, A (2002) 'Human Smuggling, National Security and Refugee Protection', 15(1) *Journal of Refugee Studies* 1.

Naffine, N (1997) *Feminism and Criminology*, Cambridge: Polity Press.
Nordstrom, C (2000) 'Shadows and Sovereigns', 17(4) *Theory, Culture and Society* 35.
O'Malley, P (1998) *Crime and the Risk Society*, Aldershot: Ashgate.
Oxfam Community Aid Abroad (2002) Still Drifting, <www.caa.org.au/campaigns/refugees/still_drifting/summary.html> accessed 20/8/02
Panalangan, R (2002) 'Territorial Sovereignty: Command, Title and the Expanding claims of the Commons', in D Miller and S Hashmi (eds) *Boundaries and Justice: Diverse ethical perspectives*, Princeton: Princeton University Press.
Parenti, C (1999) *Lockdown America: Police and Prisons, in the Age of Crisis*, London: Verso.
Park, K (1993) 'Kimberly Bergalis, AIDS and the Plague Metaphor', in M Garber, J Matlock and R Walkowitz (eds) *Media Spectacles*, London: Routledge.
Pickering, S (2004) 'Narrating Women and Asylum: hostile administrative-legal justice', in S Pickering and C Lambert (eds) *Global Issues, Women and Justice*, Sydney: Institute of Criminology Monograph Series
Pickering, S and O'Kane, M (2002) 'Policing, Exile and Gender, in States' Borderlands', 14(1) *Current Issues, in Criminal Justice* 106.
Pickering, S, and Gard, M, (2004) 'Women, in Privatised Prisons', in S Pickering and C Lambert (eds) *Global Issues, Women and Justice*. Sydney: Institute of Criminology Monograph Series
Refugee and Immigration Casework Service (2001) Federal Government Attempts to Downgrade Australia's Commitment to Refugees, Press Release, Monday 13 August, Melbourne: Refugee and Immigration Casework Service.
Reus-Smit, C (2001) 'Human Rights and the Social Construction of Sovereignty', 27 *Review of International Studies* 519.
Ruddock, P (2002) Offshore Processing Developments and Related Savings, <www.minister.immi.gov.au/media_releases/media02/r02033.htm> accessed 5 September 2002
Rundle, G (2001) 'The Opportunist: John Howard and the Triumph of Reaction', 3 *Quarterly Essay* 1.
Saadawi, NE (1980) *The Hidden Face of Eve*, London: Zed Books.
Sassen, S (1999) *Guests and Aliens*, New York: The New Press.
Sassen, S (1998) *Globalization and Its Discontents: Essays on the New Mobility of People and Money*, New York: The New Press.
Sassen, S (1996) *Sovereignty, in an Age of Globalisation*, New York: Columbia University Press.
Sartori, M (2001) 'The Cuban Migration Dilemma: An Examination of the United States' Policy of Temporary Protection, in Offshore Safe Havens' 56 *Georgetown Immigration Law Journal* 319.

Schwendinger, H and Schwendinger, J (1975) 'Defenders of Order or Guardians of Human Rights', in U Taylor, I Walton and J Young (eds) *Critical Criminology*, London: Routledge Kegan Paul.

Shacknove, A (1985) 'Who is a Refugee?' (Jan) *Ethics* 274.

Sinha, A (2001) 'Domestic Violence and US Asylum Law: Eliminating the "Cultural Hook" for Claims Involving Gender-Related Persecution', 76 *New York University Review* 1562.

Smart, C (1989) *Feminism and the Power of Law*, London: Routledge.

Soguk, N,(1999) *States and Strangers: Refugees and Displacements of Statecraft*, Minneapolis: University of Minnesota Press.

Sontag, S (1996) *Illness as Metaphor and AIDS and Its Metaphors*, Harmondsworth: Penguin.

Spijkerboer, T (1994) *Women and Refugee Law: Beyond the Public/Private Domain*, The Hague: The Emancipation Council

Sullivan, D (1995) 'The Public/Private Distinction, in International Human Rights Law', in J Peters and A Wolper (eds) *Women's Rights, Human Rights: International Feminist Perspectives*, New York: Routledge.

Sutherland, E (1949) *White Collar Crime*, New York: Holt, Rinehart and Winston.

Taylor, S (2000) 'Protection or Prevention? A Close Look at the Temporary Safe Haven Visa Class', 23(3) *UNSW Law Journal* 75.

Taylor, S (2002) 'Exclusion from Protection of Persons of "Bad Character": is Australia Fulfilling its Treaty-Based non-Refoulement Obligations?' 8(1) *Australian Journal of Human Rights* 83.

Taylor, U, Walton, I and Young, J (eds) *Critical Criminology*, London: Routledge Kegan Paul.

US Committee for Refugees (2002) *SeaChange: Australia's New Approach to Asylum Seekers*, US Committee for Refugees, Washington.

Vernant, J (1953) *The Refugee, in the Post War World*, London: Allen and Unwin.

Weber, C (1995) *Simulating Sovereignty*, Cambridge: Cambridge University Press.

Weber, L (2002) 'The Detention of Asylum Seekers: 20 Reasons Why Criminologists Should Care', 14(1) *Current Issues, in Criminal Justice* 9.

Young, A (1996) *Imagining Crime*, London: Sage.

Young, A (1990) *Femininity, in Dissent*, Routledge: London.

Yuval-Davis, N (1997) *Gender and Nation*, Macmillan: Basingstoke.

Index

Prisoners as Citizens
Human rights in Australian prisons

Editors: David Brown & Meredith Wilkie

Should prisoners be deprived of rights to such things as voting, personal safety, health, family connection, information, and education? In a series of 17 essays, many of them research-based, writers look at aspects of the surprisingly varied Australian prison situation. Topics include the nature of prison systems and populations, and historical and international perspectives. Also considered are the situations of particular prisoners, such as women and Indigenous Australians, as well as those from non-English speaking backgrounds, and those with intellectual disabilities. The collection is a timely and thought-provoking source of information.

SCAN

One of the most poignant aspects of this collection is the contribution that prisoners themselves make ... Collectively, [their] testimonies depict a deep-seated sense of feeling 'forgotten', anonymous and utterly disenfranchised ...

Practical measures that will immediately improve the recognition of human rights for prisoners are usefully discussed ...The book possesses a certain clarity and common-sense tone ... With a wide variety of contributors, the book represents a rich sourcebook of opinions on prisoners' rights. ... it is an important publication

Howard Journal of Criminal Justice

a landmark collection on prisoners' citizenship rights in Australia ... disturbing reading for citizens concerned about the decency and social justice of our democracy ...

Professor John Braithwaite

Australia's leading academics, activists and prison experts ... highlight why it is critical that these rights [of prisoners] be recognized by the Australian community. This is a timely, well-researched and important book.

Educational Book Review

A valuable and well-informed contribution to the debate about prisons and prisoners.

UNSW Law Journal

This outstanding and comprehensive collection of essays ... This is thoughtful but disturbing reading.

Reform

[A] very valuable analysis into many, if not most, of the changes [of the past two decades]. ... a scholarly contribution to the history and contemporary views of punishment and corrections [which] is full of surprises.

Civil Liberty

2002 • ISBN 1 86287B424 7 • paperback • 396 pp • $49.50

Achieving Social Justice
Indigenous Rights and Australia's Future
Larissa Behrendt

Larissa Behrendt attacks the chasm which has grown between Indigenous lives and aspirations in Australia, and the psychological *terra nullius* which continues, despite *Mabo*, to pervade so much of Australia's mythology and policy.

Writing with great power and clarity, Behrendt proposes practical short-term reforms, as well as longer term aspirational initiatives leading to institutional change that will facilitate greater rights protection and the exercise of self-determination including:
- a preamble to the Constitution
- a treaty
- the national self-image
- economic redistribution
- alternative institutional forms
- regional framework agreements
- a more energised politics
- Constitutional protection

A magnificent synthesis of Indigenous history and insights ... based in profound scholarship yet highly readable and accessible, it deserves the widest possible readership

Dr William Jonas AM

[A] remarkably lucid and readable book

Professor Ann Curthoys

A clear and unambiguous statement of what is wrong with the status quo from an Aboriginal perspective. It helps to define the unfinished business of reconciliation.
Fred Chaney AO

Behrendt provides perhaps the clearest articulation we have of what Indigenous Australians want and need – and how it might be achieved. This book will be debated, dissected, applauded and disagreed with in the years to come, and certainly quoted ... compulsory reading for anyone working or interested in Indigenous law and policy. ...

Most of the critical contemporary issues in Indigenous law and policy in Australia are discussed in the book ... most of the significant contributions to the debate are interpreted and responded to.

Behrendt writes with an honesty and clarity that is sometimes lost in the Indigenous law and policy debate, and offers constructive proposals ...
QUT Law Journal

2003 · ISBN 1 86287 450 6 · paperback · 208pp · $29.95

Islam

Its law and society

Jamila Hussain

Recent events have brought Islam and Muslims to the centre of the West's attention, leading many to ask what it means to be Muslim, keen to know what is fact and what is misconception.

Jamila Hussain explains the basic principles of the religion of Islam and its law, the Shariah, and how the Shariah is lived in the context of many different cultures throughout the World. The discussion includes:

- A brief survey of Islamic history and civilisation
- The development of Islamic law and how it is applied in modern conditions
- The position of women in Islam and the growth of Islamic feminism
- Family law and inheritance
- Modern reproductive technology
- Criminal law and evidence
- Banking and commercial law
- The Australian Muslim community

A new chapter examines Islamic laws of war and peace, and contemporary rulings on the conduct of Muslims in times of war.

Now in its second edition, this book is ideal for those who wish to acquire an introductory knowledge of Islamic culture and law in general and within Australian society in particular.

Praise for the first edition:

This book makes a timely and significant contribution to Australians' knowledge of Islamic civilisation
Law Institute of Victoria Journal

Addresses a number of commonly held misconceptions of Islam
Alternative Law Journal

An interesting and thorough introduction to a way of life
Tasmanian Law Society Newsletter

2003 • ISBN 1 86287 499 9 • paperback • 260 pp • $39.95

The Work/Life Collision

Barbara Pocock

Longer working hours, insecure jobs, child care, declining birth rates, parental leave, the 'mummy track', the success or failure of feminism – *The Work/Life Collision*, grounded in thorough quantitative and qualitative research, analyses how these factors affect each other, in particular the collision of work and care and its implications for how we live. ...

The stand out chapter in the book is Chapter 3 which considers the impact of the 'collisions and changes upon our community fabric'. ... The concluding chapter is simply magnificent. ... [The book] is an essential starting point for anyone researching the spheres of work, family and gender in Australia ... a landmark
Journal of Industrial Relations

The book is so graphic there are parts of it I could hardly bear to read but it is important to read it because it illustrates all the lifeless and painless socio-economic statistics we as policy planners see continuously rolling under our noses; it helps explain why those painless statistics actually represent a policy imperative.

Pru Goward

it should be a topic for discussion in staffrooms, at workplace union meetings, and on the agenda as an industrial and political issue.

Newsmonth

original and valuable ... It offers a new vision of the real experiences of Australian households ... This book is highly recommended and should be influential ...

Traffic

Pocock writes with persuasive clarity ...

Hobart Saturday Mercury

2003 • ISBN 1 86287 475 1 • paperback • 304 pp • $39.95

Jessie Street

A revised autobiography

Edited by Lenore Coltheart

Jessie Street's energy, charm and practical humanitarianism made her a key figure in Australian life for 50 years.

Her autobiography is as much a guidebook to her times as an account of her own intertwined dedication to peace and justice. From growing up in the Australian Bush to Moscow under Stalin and the Anschluss and Sudetenland crises in Europe in 1938. And people: Eleanor Roosevelt, Nancy Astor, Margaret Sanger, Jawaharal Nehru and many others.

Readers join suffragette marches in London, hear civil rights singers in the jazz clubs of New York, visit occupied Egypt, imperial India and outback Australia, and see destroyed cities where people somehow survived in London, Berlin, Leningrad, and Hiroshima after the second world war.

Jessie Street courageously went where no woman had gone before ...There is a good selection of photographs to accompany this rejuvenated text.
Nina Valentine, Ballarat Courier

To describe this autobiography as inspiring is an understatement. It is an extraordinary record of a remarkable life.
Anne Pender, Australian Book Review

Jessie Street emerges as a forthright, funny and incredibly determined achiever.
Jen Alexander, The Weekly Times

Among all great Australian women, Jessie Street has got to be very close to the top of the pile. What a remarkable life
Bruce Elder, Sydney Morning Herald

The life of pioneering feminist / socialist / activist Jessie Street was a crowded and dramatic one. Her writing is fairly matter-of-fact but what shines through is her preparedness to rock convention, her passion for ideas and her resolution in adversity
Steve Carroll, The Age Review

Jessie Street was an extraordinary figure, an original thinker dedicated to bettering the lives of others. ... One wonders what Street, with her profound belief in social justice, would think of Australian society today.
Penelope Hanley, Canberra Times

a fascinating first-hand account of a world at war and a brain at work.
Peter Salmon, Australian Bookseller & Publisher

2004 • ISBN • 1 86287 502 2 • paperback • 256 pp, b&w illus • $30

Restorative Justice

The empowerment model

Charles Barton

Restorative Justice –The Empowerment Model presents a powerful challenge to many current accounts of the criminal justice system.

Charles Barton gives a clear and insightful analysis of current restorative justice philosophy and theory. He uses a unifying and overarching principle of *empowerment* to provide a distinct and sound conceptual framework for restorative justice theory and practice.

Barton's focus is evenly balanced between theory and practice. His defence of the concept of primary stakeholder empowerment is followed by a step-by-step implementation process for mediators, circle keepers and group conference facilitators, complete with handy hints and specific instructions, seating plans and scripted prompts. Barton's book will strengthen practitioners' comprehension and facilitate their application of the practical process.

Barton also provides practical suggestions for all participants in restorative justice meetings, tailored to their respective positions and roles within the criminal justice system. These are presented in separate chapters for victims, offenders, supporters, as well as for professionals such as police, social workers and legal advocates.

A separate chapter is addressed to program managers, referring agencies, policy advisers and legislators on how they can best facilitate the adoption and proper implementation of restorative justice programs.

With its powerful combination of theory and practical know-how, this book is a must read for anyone with an interest in criminal and restorative justice.

Hawkins Press
2002 • ISBN 1 87606 716 0 • paperback • 208 pp • $49.50